SKYLANDERS TRAP TEAM™

TABLE OF CONTENTS

Portal Mastery

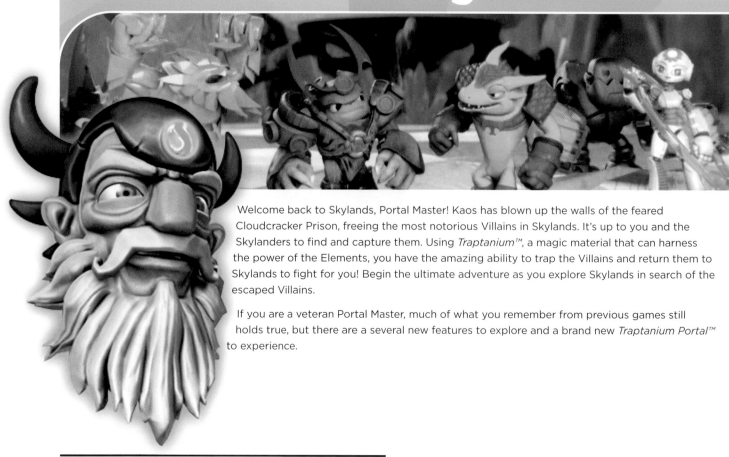

Welcome back to Skylands, Portal Master! Kaos has blown up the walls of the feared Cloudcracker Prison, freeing the most notorious Villains in Skylands. It's up to you and the Skylanders to find and capture them. Using *Traptanium*™, a magic material that can harness the power of the Elements, you have the amazing ability to trap the Villains and return them to Skylands to fight for you! Begin the ultimate adventure as you explore Skylands in search of the escaped Villains.

If you are a veteran Portal Master, much of what you remember from previous games still holds true, but there are a several new features to explore and a brand new *Traptanium Portal*™ to experience.

New Skylanders

Trap Team Skylanders

The newest type of Skylander is a Trap Master Skylander. For the most part, they work just like any other Skylander but these powerful Skylanders have legendary *Traptanium* weapons. Also, they are slightly larger than average Skylanders and are more powerful when fighting Villains. They can also open *Traptanium* Elemental gates. There are 16 new Trap Master Skylanders with which to adventure.

Meet the Minis

Mini Skylanders are pint-sized versions of their full sized counterparts. Previously, smaller Skylanders, called Sidekicks, were released but they were not playable characters. There are 16 Mini Skylanders and they have the same powers and upgrades as their full sized versions. These incredibly adorable figures represent some of the original Skylanders as well as several Giants.

Playable Villains

There are 46 Villains that escaped Cloudcracker Prison. Several of them appear in each chapter of Story Mode. Once you have defeated them, you can place a Trap of the same element into the *Traptanium Portal* to catch them in the *Traptanium* Crystal. When they are loaded into a Trap they can be released from the *Traptanium* Crystal, under your control, and their devastating powers will be used for good. A Villain can be played until their energy is used up and then they retreat back into the Trap. In a co-op game either player can use the active Villain currently placed in the Trap.

All captured Villains are stored in the Villain Vault at the Academy and can be placed in a Trap. Since only one Villain can be in each Trap at a time, The Villain Vault is used to manage which Villain you want to have in a Trap to take on your adventures.

To check on the status of Villains use the Wanted Poster in the pause menu or check the poster pinned to the tree at the start of the Academy. The Wanted Poster tracks which Villains have been defeated and if their quest has been completed. Each Villain has a unique Villain Quest they can complete in Story Mode. Doing so allows the Villain to evolve and sometimes earn a reward.

Traps

The Doom Raiders were imprisoned in Cloudcracker Prison until our old friend Kaos destroyed it. The shattered fragments of Cloudcracker Prison formed Traps for each type of element. The Traps can be used to capture the escaped Villains when they are defeated. After defeating a Villain, place a Trap of the same element into the *Traptanium Portal* to capture them in the Trap. There are six unique Trap Crystals for each of the eight original Elements plus a special one reserved for Kaos. Each Trap can only hold one Villain at a time but they can be swapped at the Villain Vault.

AIR

Breezy Bird

Tempest Timer

Storm Warning

Draft Decanter

Cloudy Cobra

Cyclone Saber

EARTH

Rock Hawk

Slag Hammer

Spinning Sandstorm

Banded Boulder

Dust of Time

Rubble Trouble

FIRE

Eternal Flame

Scorching Stopper

Spark Spear

Fire Flower

Searing Spinner

Blazing Belch

LIFE

Oak Eagle

Weed Whacker

Jade Blade

Emerald Energy

Seed Serpent

Shrub Shrieked

MAGIC

Biter's Bane

Axe of Illusion

Spell Slapper

Sorcerous Skull

Arcane Hourglass

Rune Rocket

TECH

Tech Totem

Factory Flower

Automatic Angle

Makers Mana

Grabbing Gadget

Topsy Techy

UNDEAD

Spirit Sphere

Haunted Hatchet

Spooky Snake

Spectral Skull

Grim Gripper

Dream Piercer

WATER

Tidal Tiki

Flood Flask

Aqua Axe

Wet Walter

Soaking Staff

Frost Helm

KAOS

New Traptanium Portal

A brand new *Traptanium Portal* comes with *Skylanders Trap Team*. The Portal has a Villain Vault that has a spot to insert the *Traptanium* Crystal to store capture Villains. The new Portal also has it's own speaker that allows the trapped Villains to talk while they are in the current Trap. Although the *Traptanium Portal* has been redesigned, it supports all previous released Skylanders and their current upgrades.

Portal Master Rank

Portal Masters can earn Stars to increase their rank and receive numerous types of rewards. The amount of Stars required to raise rank progressively increases. Each time a new rank is achieved a reward is given in a Star Box at the Main Hall of the Academy. There are several ways to earn Stars. These include playing through the chapters in Story Mode, completing Arenas, and overcoming Kaos Doom Challenges. The number of Stars required and their corresponding rewards are given in the following table.

Portal Master Rank	Stars Needed to Reach	Reward
1	N/A	None
2	2	Gem worth 1000
3	2	Instant Level Up
4	2	Batterson's Bubble (Trinket)
5	2	Wooden Hat
6	2	Instant Level Up
7	3	Teddy Clops (Trinket)
8	3	Gem worth 2000
9	3	Instant Level Up
10	3	Raver Hat
11	4	Instant Level Up
12	4	Ramses' Rune
13	4	Gem worth 3000
14	4	Shire Hat
15	4	Instant Level Up
16	4	Ramses' Dragon Horn (Trinket)
17	4	Gem worth 4000
18	4	Old Ruins Hat
19	5	Instant Level Up
20	5	Dark Water Daisy (Trinket)
21	5	Gem worth 6000
22	5	Medieval Bard Hat
23	5	Seadog Seashell (Trinket)
24	6	Instant Level Up
25	6	Mongol Hat
26	6	T-Bone's Lucky Tie (Trinket)
27	6	Gem worth 8000
28	6	Instant Level Up
29	6	Mabu's Medallion
30	6	Wilikin Hat
31	6	Kuckoo Kazoo (Trinket)
32	6	Instant Level Up
33	6	Elemental Radiant
34	6	Oracle Hat
35	6	Time Town Ticker
36	6	Instant Level Up
37	6	Sheepwrecked Hat
38	6	Cyclops' Spinner
39	6	Gem worth 10,000
40	6	Frostfest Hat

Earn Stars In Story Mode

Chapter Stars: 88
Complete Story Mode Bonus: 12

Each of the 18 Chapters initially has three Stars that can be earned upon completing the Story Goals, Dares, and Collections for that level. After clearing Story Mode, a fourth Star is available in a new category called Difficult Dares. Also, as a reward for completing Story Mode the Portal Master is awarded 12 additional bonus Stars. Note that the total of 88 Stars include four Adventure expansions that are sold separately.

Earn Stars in the Arena

Arena Stars: 30

Brock is back with a brand new Rumble Club that has six Arenas to test your mettle. There are four stages in each Arena and the first three award one Star each. The final stage rewards players with two Stars and a Hat if they can complete this last challenge, and thus finish the entire series.

Earn Stars In Kaos Doom Challenge

Kaos Mode Stars: 50

Kaos cursed the training simulator and each challenge gets progressively harder. There are 100 waves of enemies to survive and they are separated in to nine groups of Challenges. Each Challenge must be completed in order to unlock the next one. The number of Stars rewarded increases as the number of waves and level of difficulty increase.

What do I need to see everything in Story Mode?

In order to access everything found throughout the Story Mode, you need the following:

▶ **One Trap Master Skylander figure for each of the eight elements.**
▶ **One Trap of each of the eight elements.**

You could clear the main story of *Skylanders Trap Team* with only one Skylander figure, but Trap Master Skylanders are required to open *Traptanium* Gates. Also, a Trap of each element is needed to complete the Villain Quests.

Adventure Expansions

Previous Expansions

There were four Adventure Expansions for *Skylanders Spyro's Adventure™:* Dragon's Peak, Empire of Ice, Darklight Crypt, and Pirate Ship. *Skylanders SWAP Force™* introduced two as well, Tower of Time and Sheep Wreck Island. While playing *Skylanders Trap Team,* use the Adventure Expansions from those games during regular play to execute a special attack that damages every enemy on the screen.

Adventure Expansion Figure	Area of Effect Attack
Dragon's Peak	Fireballs
Empire of Ice	Ice Shards
Darklight Crypt	Shadowy Orbs
Pirate Ship	Cannonballs
Tower of Time	Gears
Sheep Wreck Island	Fireballs

New Trap Team Expansions

Four new toys will be released for *Skylanders Trap Team.* Each of these unlocks a new chapter in Story mode where you can earn Stars and capture new Villains. Mirror Of Mystery and Nightmare Express are the first two that will be released.

MIRROR OF MYSTERY

▶ Enter an alternate universe where good guys are bad and bad guys are good.

NIGHTMARE EXPRESS

▶ Take a wild trip through Flynn's imagination to "assist" him in recovering the Trolly Grail!

Magic Items

Adventure Packs usually include two Magic Items that aid your Skylander with a special attack or a beneficial effect. The Magic Items have a timer, but it resets whenever you start a new level.

ANVIL RAIN

▶ When you put this item on the Portal, anvils fall from the sky, randomly hitting enemies in the area. If an anvil hits your Skylander, it only knocks them back. It does not damage them.

GHOST PIRATE SWORDS

▶ This Adventure Item spawns in two swords that float around the screen, attacking the Skylander's foes.

HEALING ELIXIR

▶ This awesome item quickly heals your Skylanders while they wander around. Your Skylanders regain 30 health every second, but Healing Elixir has a short duration.

HIDDEN TREASURE

▶ When you use Hidden Treasure on a Story Level, a bonus treasure chest is randomly generated. Use the radar at the bottom of the screen to help locate the chest.

SKY-IRON SHIELD

▶ This Adventure Item causes two rotating shields to protect your Skylander for its duration. This item doesn't make your Skylander invulnerable, but it does make them tougher.

SPARX THE DRAGONFLY

▶ Sparx buzzes around, blasting enemies with his insect breath. He can only stay around for about a minute, but can really help in tough fights.

TIME TWIST HOURGLASS

▶ The Time Twist Hourglass slows down time, putting the game into slow motion for the duration of the spell. The catch is, your Skylander doesn't slow down!

VOLCANIC VAULT

▶ Using Volcanic Vault in *Skylanders SWAP Force* causes fire to rain down from the sky, damaging enemies for a short time.

WINGED BOOTS

▶ With this Adventure Item, your Skylander can run much faster than normal. This item is tremendously helpful during Time Attack.

Two special figures were made for *Skylanders Giants™*. They both can help clear out enemies and make for smoother travels.

DRAGONFIRE CANNON

▷ The Dragonfire Cannon blasts enemies every few seconds. It also follows Skylanders as they move through levels.

SCORPION STRIKER

▷ The Scorpion Striker Catapult lobs spiked balls at enemies. If the spiked ball doesn't hit an enemy in the air, it remains on the ground and explodes if an enemy gets close.

HOG HOARDER

▷ The Hog Hoarder increases the overall treasure you find.

HAND OF FATE

▷ The Hand of Fate stuns enemies so you can better manage a fight.

TIKI SPEAKY

▷ The Tiki Speaky talks to you and has a stun effect on enemies.

RAM ROCKET

▷ The Ram Rocket is a giant rocket-like ram that flies across the screen, damaging all enemies.

ARKEYAN CROSSBOW

▷ It generates an in-game crossbow with a lob attack. The bolt damages enemies it hits and also generates a watery wave that hits other nearby enemies.

BATTLE HAMMER

▷ A Battle Hammer appears over your Skylander's head. Whenever you press Attack 1 the hammer hits the ground in front of your Skylander (Skylanders still execute their normal attack, though). Nearby enemies take damage and are knocked back.

FIERY FORGE

▷ When placed on the Portal of Power, a cauldron floats over your Skylander's head. When enemies are near, the cauldron tips over and covers the ground with molten metal, producing an effect similar to Eruptor's attack, Eruption.

GROOVE MACHINE

▷ The Groove Machine follows Skylanders and plays music.

PLATINUM SHEEP

▷ The Platinum Sheep disguises your Skylander as a sheep and restores health over time. Enemies ignore the sheep and allow it to recover health in peace. While you can still move around, you can't perform any other actions (like attack) until the disguise is removed.

SKY DIAMOND

▷ When the Sky Diamond is active, every defeated enemy drops a diamond worth 25 gold. It's a great way to earn money quickly, to help pay for items and Skylander upgrades.

UFO HAT

▷ Placing this Magic Item on the Portal of Power unlocks the UFO Hat.

Meet The Skylanders

Skylander figures from different games have different colors on their bases. Skylander figures with a green base are from *Skylanders Spyro's Adventure™*. Skylander figures with an orange base are from *Skylanders Giants™*. Skylander figures for *Skylanders SWAP Force™* have a blue base. The newest Skylanders, those for *Skylanders Trap Team™*, have a red base.

Use the following pages to track your collections. The game also tracks your Skylanders under Collection found in the Pause menu.

Sidekicks are now Minis

Minis, once known as Sidekicks, are fully playable smaller versions of Skylander figures. In previous adventures, they tagged along with your full-sized Skylanders. These tiny powerhouses join the adventure for *Skylanders Trap Team!*

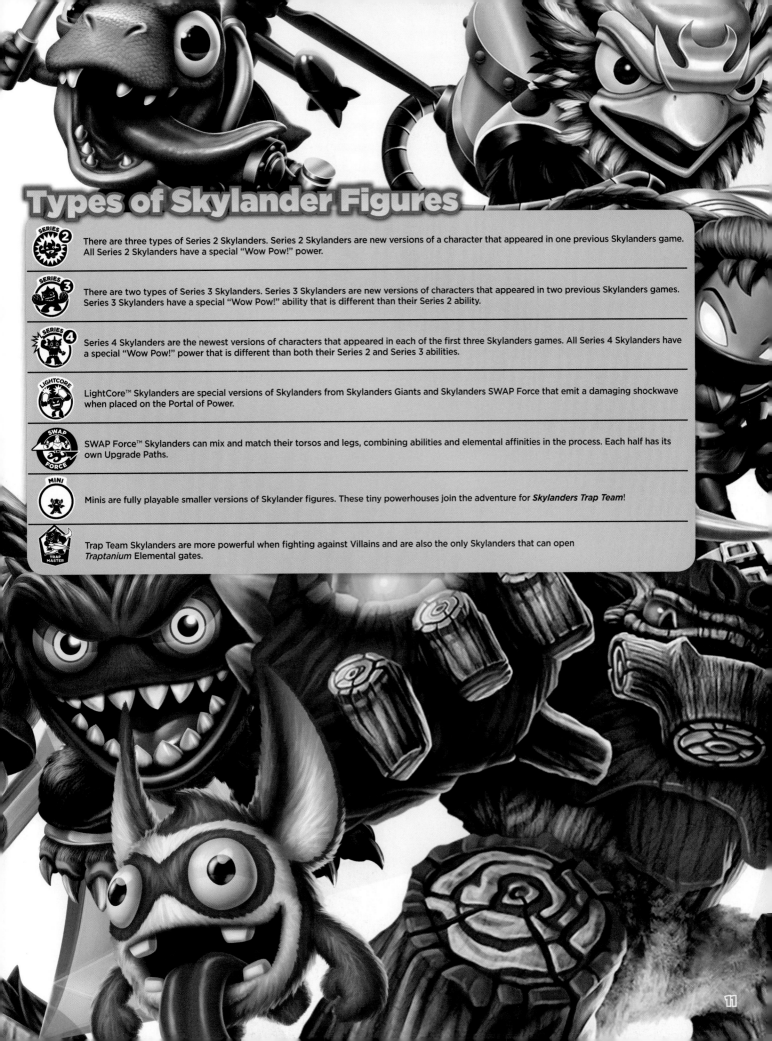

Types of Skylander Figures

SERIES 2 — There are three types of Series 2 Skylanders. Series 2 Skylanders are new versions of a character that appeared in one previous Skylanders game. All Series 2 Skylanders have a special "Wow Pow!" power.

SERIES 3 — There are two types of Series 3 Skylanders. Series 3 Skylanders are new versions of characters that appeared in two previous Skylanders games. Series 3 Skylanders have a special "Wow Pow!" ability that is different than their Series 2 ability.

SERIES 4 — Series 4 Skylanders are the newest versions of characters that appeared in each of the first three Skylanders games. All Series 4 Skylanders have a special "Wow Pow!" power that is different than both their Series 2 and Series 3 abilities.

LIGHTCORE — LightCore™ Skylanders are special versions of Skylanders from Skylanders Giants and Skylanders SWAP Force that emit a damaging shockwave when placed on the Portal of Power.

SWAP FORCE — SWAP Force™ Skylanders can mix and match their torsos and legs, combining abilities and elemental affinities in the process. Each half has its own Upgrade Paths.

MINI — Minis are fully playable smaller versions of Skylander figures. These tiny powerhouses join the adventure for *Skylanders Trap Team*!

TRAP MASTER — Trap Team Skylanders are more powerful when fighting against Villains and are also the only Skylanders that can open *Traptanium* Elemental gates.

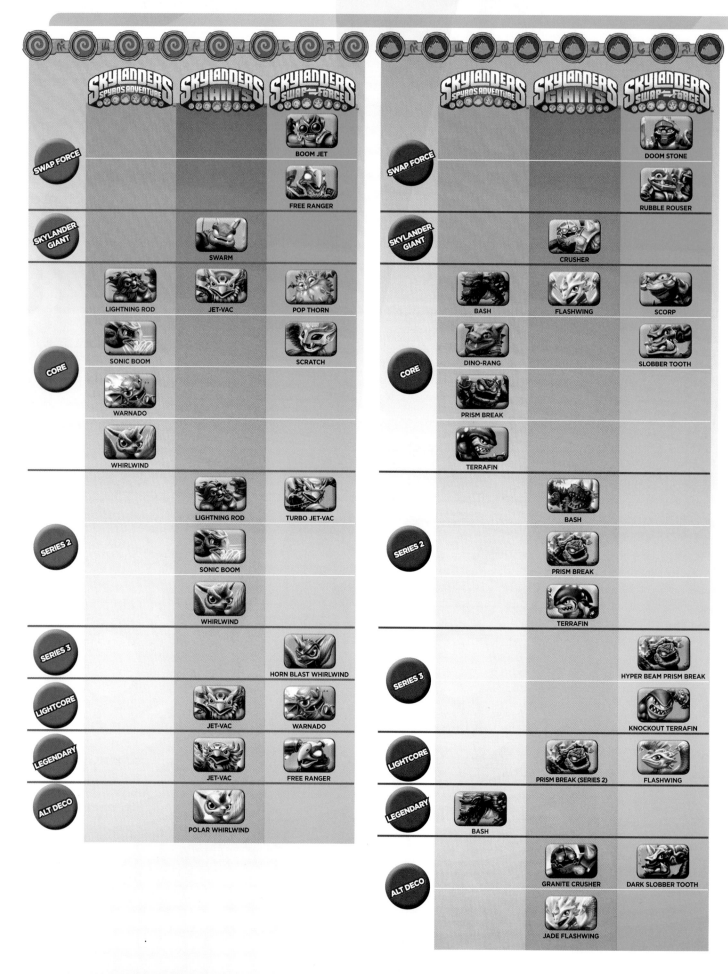

Left chart

	SKYLANDERS SPYRO'S ADVENTURE	SKYLANDERS GIANTS	SKYLANDERS SWAP FORCE
SWAP FORCE			BOOM JET / FREE RANGER
SKYLANDER GIANT		SWARM	
CORE	LIGHTNING ROD / SONIC BOOM / WARNADO / WHIRLWIND	JET-VAC	POP THORN / SCRATCH
SERIES 2		LIGHTNING ROD / SONIC BOOM / WHIRLWIND	TURBO JET-VAC
SERIES 3			HORN BLAST WHIRLWIND
LIGHTCORE		JET-VAC	WARNADO
LEGENDARY		JET-VAC	FREE RANGER
ALT DECO		POLAR WHIRLWIND	

Right chart

	SKYLANDERS SPYRO'S ADVENTURE	SKYLANDERS GIANTS	SKYLANDERS SWAP FORCE
SWAP FORCE			DOOM STONE / RUBBLE ROUSER
SKYLANDER GIANT		CRUSHER	
CORE	BASH / DINO-RANG / PRISM BREAK / TERRAFIN	FLASHWING	SCORP / SLOBBER TOOTH
SERIES 2		BASH / PRISM BREAK / TERRAFIN	
SERIES 3			HYPER BEAM PRISM BREAK / KNOCKOUT TERRAFIN
LIGHTCORE		PRISM BREAK (SERIES 2)	FLASHWING
LEGENDARY	BASH		
ALT DECO		GRANITE CRUSHER / JADE FLASHWING	DARK SLOBBER TOOTH

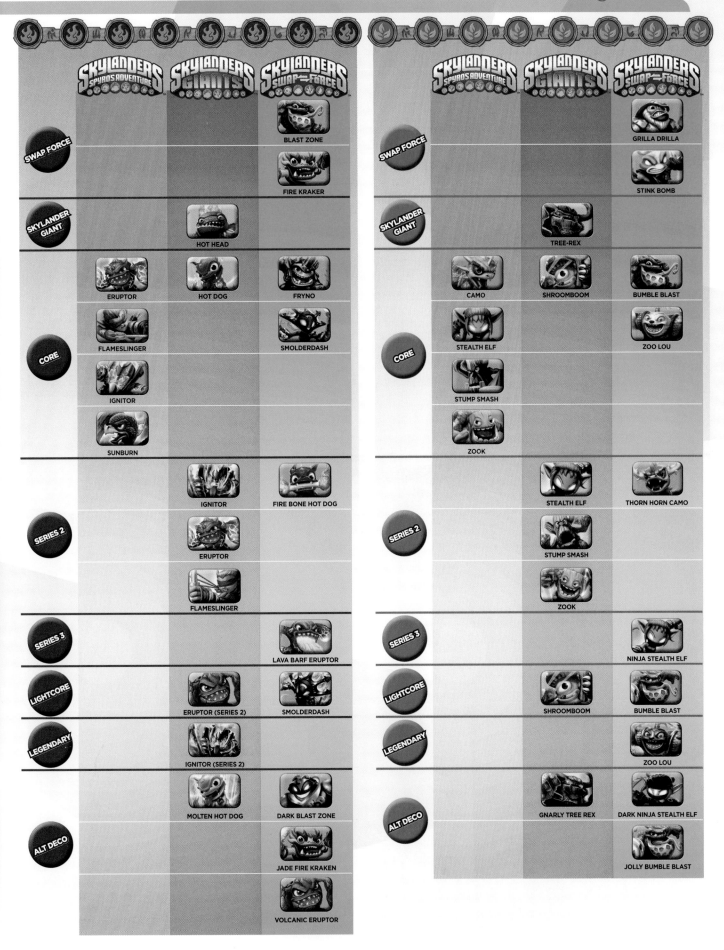

Fire Element

	SKYLANDERS SPYRO'S ADVENTURE	SKYLANDERS GIANTS	SKYLANDERS SWAP FORCE
SWAP FORCE			BLAST ZONE
			FIRE KRAKER
SKYLANDER GIANT		HOT HEAD	
CORE	ERUPTOR	HOT DOG	FRYNO
	FLAMESLINGER		SMOLDERDASH
	IGNITOR		
	SUNBURN		
SERIES 2		IGNITOR	FIRE BONE HOT DOG
		ERUPTOR	
		FLAMESLINGER	
SERIES 3			LAVA BARF ERUPTOR
LIGHTCORE		ERUPTOR (SERIES 2)	SMOLDERDASH
LEGENDARY		IGNITOR (SERIES 2)	
ALT DECO		MOLTEN HOT DOG	DARK BLAST ZONE
			JADE FIRE KRAKER
			VOLCANIC ERUPTOR

Life Element

	SKYLANDERS SPYRO'S ADVENTURE	SKYLANDERS GIANTS	SKYLANDERS SWAP FORCE
SWAP FORCE			GRILLA DRILLA
			STINK BOMB
SKYLANDER GIANT		TREE-REX	
CORE	CAMO	SHROOMBOOM	BUMBLE BLAST
	STEALTH ELF		ZOO LOU
	STUMP SMASH		
	ZOOK		
SERIES 2		STEALTH ELF	THORN HORN CAMO
		STUMP SMASH	
		ZOOK	
SERIES 3			NINJA STEALTH ELF
LIGHTCORE		SHROOMBOOM	BUMBLE BLAST
LEGENDARY			ZOO LOU
ALT DECO		GNARLY TREE REX	DARK NINJA STEALTH ELF
			JOLLY BUMBLE BLAST

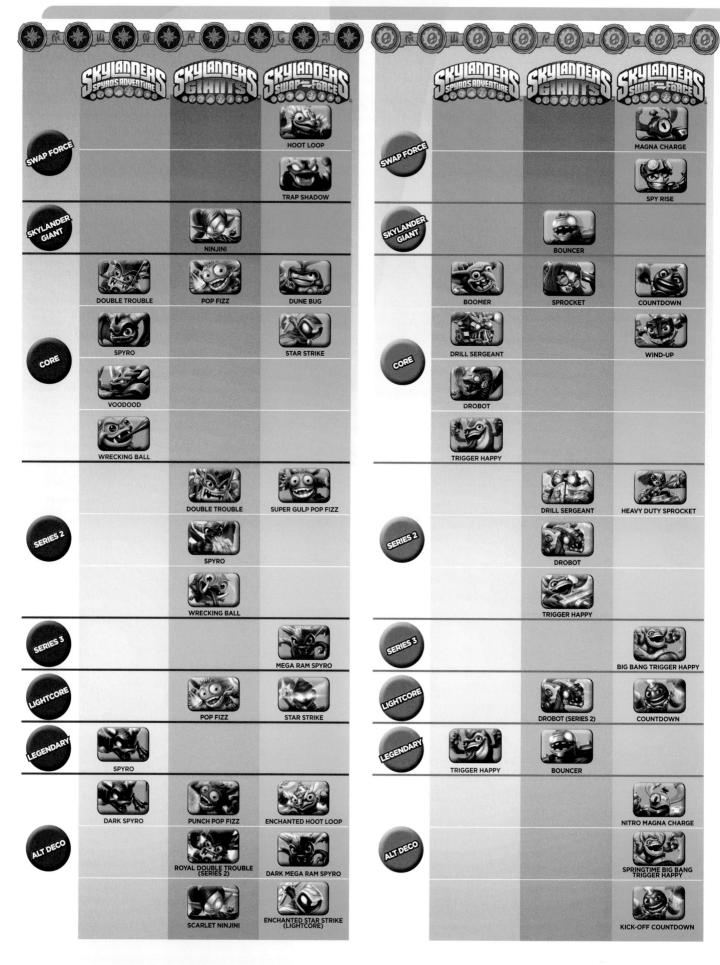

	SKYLANDERS SPYRO'S ADVENTURE	SKYLANDERS GIANTS	SKYLANDERS SWAP FORCE		SKYLANDERS SPYRO'S ADVENTURE	SKYLANDERS GIANTS	SKYLANDERS SWAP FORCE
SWAP FORCE			HOOT LOOP	**SWAP FORCE**			MAGNA CHARGE
			TRAP SHADOW				SPY RISE
SKYLANDER GIANT		NINJINI		**SKYLANDER GIANT**		BOUNCER	
CORE	DOUBLE TROUBLE	POP FIZZ	DUNE BUG	**CORE**	BOOMER	SPROCKET	COUNTDOWN
	SPYRO		STAR STRIKE		DRILL SERGEANT		WIND-UP
	VOODOOD				DROBOT		
	WRECKING BALL				TRIGGER HAPPY		
SERIES 2		DOUBLE TROUBLE	SUPER GULP POP FIZZ	**SERIES 2**		DRILL SERGEANT	HEAVY DUTY SPROCKET
		SPYRO				DROBOT	
		WRECKING BALL				TRIGGER HAPPY	
SERIES 3			MEGA RAM SPYRO	**SERIES 3**			BIG BANG TRIGGER HAPPY
LIGHTCORE		POP FIZZ	STAR STRIKE	**LIGHTCORE**		DROBOT (SERIES 2)	COUNTDOWN
LEGENDARY	SPYRO			**LEGENDARY**	TRIGGER HAPPY	BOUNCER	
ALT DECO	DARK SPYRO	PUNCH POP FIZZ	ENCHANTED HOOT LOOP	**ALT DECO**			NITRO MAGNA CHARGE
		ROYAL DOUBLE TROUBLE (SERIES 2)	DARK MEGA RAM SPYRO				SPRINGTIME BIG BANG TRIGGER HAPPY
		SCARLET NINJINI	ENCHANTED STAR STRIKE (LIGHTCORE)				KICK-OFF COUNTDOWN

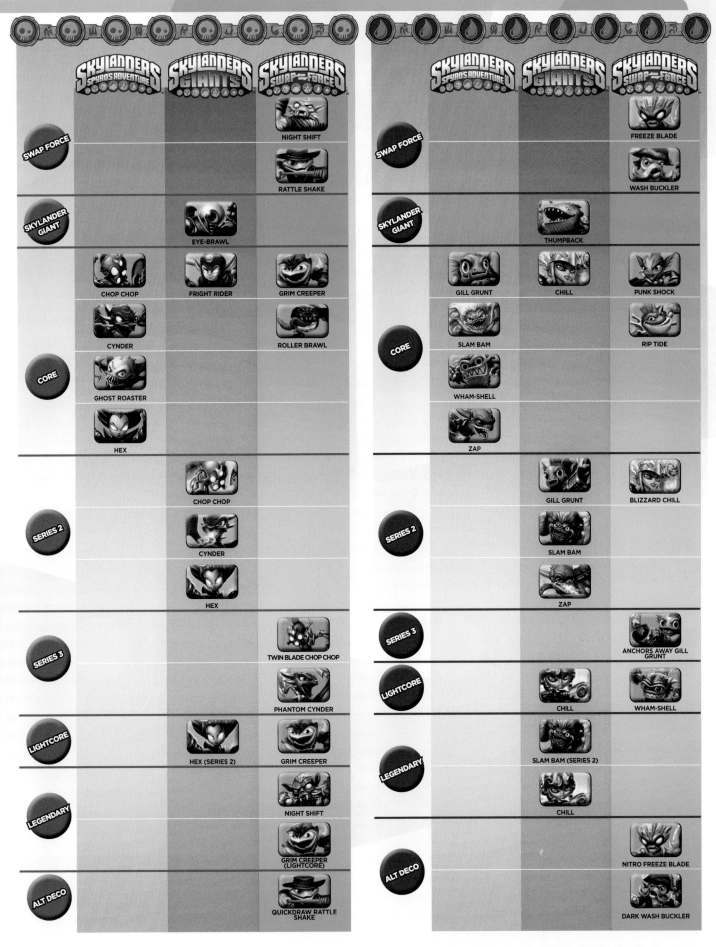

	SKYLANDERS SPYRO'S ADVENTURE	SKYLANDERS GIANTS	SKYLANDERS SWAP FORCE
SWAP FORCE			NIGHT SHIFT
			RATTLE SHAKE
SKYLANDER GIANT		EYE-BRAWL	
CORE	CHOP CHOP	FRIGHT RIDER	GRIM CREEPER
	CYNDER		ROLLER BRAWL
	GHOST ROASTER		
	HEX		
SERIES 2		CHOP CHOP	
		CYNDER	
		HEX	
SERIES 3			TWIN BLADE CHOP CHOP
			PHANTOM CYNDER
LIGHTCORE		HEX (SERIES 2)	GRIM CREEPER
LEGENDARY			NIGHT SHIFT
			GRIM CREEPER (LIGHTCORE)
ALT DECO			QUICKDRAW RATTLE SHAKE

	SKYLANDERS SPYRO'S ADVENTURE	SKYLANDERS GIANTS	SKYLANDERS SWAP FORCE
SWAP FORCE			FREEZE BLADE
			WASH BUCKLER
SKYLANDER GIANT		THUMPBACK	
CORE	GILL GRUNT	CHILL	PUNK SHOCK
	SLAM BAM		RIP TIDE
	WHAM-SHELL		
	ZAP		
SERIES 2		GILL GRUNT	BLIZZARD CHILL
		SLAM BAM	
		ZAP	
SERIES 3			ANCHORS AWAY GILL GRUNT
LIGHTCORE		CHILL	WHAM-SHELL
LEGENDARY		SLAM BAM (SERIES 2)	
		CHILL	
ALT DECO			NITRO FREEZE BLADE
			DARK WASH BUCKLER

New Skylanders

Legendary Trap Team Skylanders

Bushwack

Blades

Déjà Vu

Jawbreaker

Alt Deco

Dark Food Fight

Dark Snap Shot

Dark Wildfire

Nitro Head Rush

Nitro Krypt King

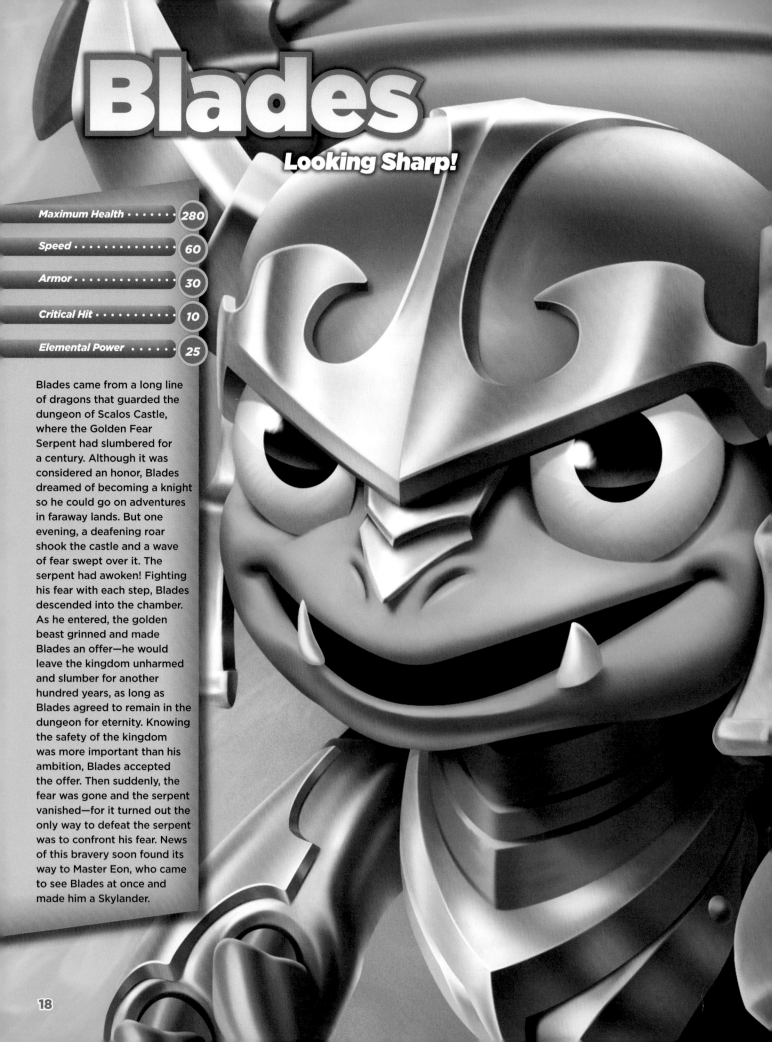

Blades

Looking Sharp!

Maximum Health	280
Speed	60
Armor	30
Critical Hit	10
Elemental Power	25

Blades came from a long line of dragons that guarded the dungeon of Scalos Castle, where the Golden Fear Serpent had slumbered for a century. Although it was considered an honor, Blades dreamed of becoming a knight so he could go on adventures in faraway lands. But one evening, a deafening roar shook the castle and a wave of fear swept over it. The serpent had awoken! Fighting his fear with each step, Blades descended into the chamber. As he entered, the golden beast grinned and made Blades an offer—he would leave the kingdom unharmed and slumber for another hundred years, as long as Blades agreed to remain in the dungeon for eternity. Knowing the safety of the kingdom was more important than his ambition, Blades accepted the offer. Then suddenly, the fear was gone and the serpent vanished—for it turned out the only way to defeat the serpent was to confront his fear. News of this bravery soon found its way to Master Eon, who came to see Blades at once and made him a Skylander.

Basic Attack Guide

▶ **Wing Slice**
Jumping Attack 1 is a back flip into the ground that does more damage than Wing Slice.

▶ **Blade Shards**
Can have two sets of shards in the ground at a time. Shards last longer if shot directly into Cyclone Swirl.

▶ **Cyclone Swirl**
Cyclone Swirl picks up Blade Shards already in the ground. With a cyclone active, press Attack 3 to cancel it and send Blade Shards flying.

Upgrade Profiles

Wind Wielder

When fully upgraded, Cyclone Swirl does double duty, punishing enemies caught in it and acting as a shield from ranged enemy projectile attacks. When you see a group of melee enemies ahead, summon a Cyclone Swirl and fill it with Blade Shards. If enemies are caught in the winds, jump before using Attack 1. The back flop does more damage and doesn't knock Wing Blades out of the cyclone.

Shard Shooter

The Shard Shooter Path boosts the power of Blade Shards considerably. The Shards added to Wing Slice appear randomly and fly straight, meaning they never bury themselves in the ground. The biggest boost in this path is Shard Shrapnel. It allows you to stay on the move to avoid attacks and still damage enemies.

⭕ SOUL GEM ABILITY

INSTANT SWIRL SHARDS! `4000`

Cyclone Swirls automatically contain Blade Shards.

Instant Swirl Shards! allows you to skip the step of covering the ground with Blade Shards before starting a Cyclone Swirl. To eradicate nearby enemies, add additional Blade Shards to the cyclone and then cancel it. Prerequisite: Find Blades' Soul Gem in CH 1: Soda Springs

Basic Attacks

WING SLICE

Press **Attack 1** for a Wing Slice attack.
Press **Attack 1**, **Attack 1**, HOLD **Attack 1** for a Tail Stab combo.

BLADE SHARDS

Press **Attack 2** to shoot Blade Shards into the ground; perform a Wing Slice to send them flying!

Upgrades

CYCLONE SWIRL `500`

Press **Attack 3** to create a Cyclone Swirl attack, damaging anything nearby.

SHARPENED WINGS `700`

Wing Slice attacks do increased damage.

SHARD HARDER `900`

Shoot more Blade Shards and at a farther distance.

WIND AT YOUR BACK `1200`

Cyclone Swirl now follows you around and does extra damage. Prerequisite: Purchase Cyclone Swirl

Wind Wielder

Improve Cyclone Swirl attacks.

FOLLOW LIKE THE WIND `1700`

Cyclone Swirl follows you more closely and spins Blade Shards faster.

CRUSHING CYCLONES `2200`

Enemies inside the Cyclone Swirl take increased damage from other attacks.

SHIELDING SWIRL `3000`

Cyclone Swirl is bigger and can deflect enemy projectiles.

Shard Shooter

Improve Blade Shard attacks.

SLICE SHARDS `1700`

Wing Slice attacks occasionally shoot Blade Shards.

CUTTING EDGE `2200`

Blade Shards do increased damage.

SHARD SHRAPNEL `3000`

Blade Shards stick to enemies, causing more damage over time.

Breeze

Twists of Fury!

Maximum Health	270
Speed	70
Armor	18
Critical Hit	50
Elemental Power	25

Basic Attack Notes

▷ **Rainbow of Doom**
Practice hitting Tempest Clouds with Rainbow of Doom while moving to get a feel for the right range. It's vital information!

▷ **Tempest Cloud**
Keep Tempest Cloud active at all times during fights. Lure pursuing enemies into the clouds when possible.

▷ **Dragon Flight**
Nice to have when you're dealing with a timed situation, such as carrying a bomb, or when you need to stay off damaging ground areas.

Upgrade Paths

Ultimate Rainbower

The first two upgrades in the Ultimate Rainbower Path are straightforward. The first doubles the number of rainbows fired and the second is a damage increase. Use Rainbow Singularity offensively by sending it into grouped enemies. It explodes after traveling a short distance or after touching an enemy. Rainbow Singularity is fully charged when the rainbow effect shrinks. Breeze walks slower while charging, so jump if you need to move a bit quicker.

Tempest Dragon

The upgrades of the Tempest Dragon Path allow Breeze to create a ring of clouds and electricity. Electricity arcs between Tempest Clouds, allowing Breeze to stay on the run and still damage pursuing enemies. Place Tempest Clouds near stationary enemies (the annoying ones with ranged abilities) to take them out as well. Aim Rainbow of Doom attacks at Breeze's clouds more often than enemies.

⬤ SOUL GEM ABILITY

RAINBOW OF HEALING (4000)
Rainbows HEAL your allies!
Rainbow of Healing is an amazing ability when playing with others. However, if you're playing solo, spend your gold on her other upgrades before buying this upgrade.

Basic Attacks

RAINBOW OF DOOM
Press **Attack 1** to fire an arced blast of rainbow energy.

TEMPEST CLOUD
Press **Attack 2** to send forth clouds that electrocute enemies. Hold **Attack 2** to make Tempest Clouds travel farther.

Upgrades

RAINBOW CHAIN (500)
Rainbows do extra damage—shoot a Tempest Cloud with a Rainbow of Doom and a second rainbow chains off of it.

TRIPLE TEMPEST (700)
Have three Tempest Clouds active at once. Tempest Clouds do extra damage.

DRAGON FLIGHT (900)
Press **Attack 3** to fly. Increased speed and armor while flying.

DUAL RAINBOWS (1200)
Hit a Tempest Cloud with a Rainbow of Doom and two rainbows will chain off of it. Prerequisite: Rainbow Chain

Ultimate Rainbower Path
Further develop Breeze's Rainbow of Doom Attack.

DOUBLE DOSE OF RAINBOW (1700)
Shoot two Rainbows of Doom at once.

ATOMIC RAINBOW (2200)
Rainbow of Doom attack does increased damage.

RAINBOW SINGULARITY (3000)
Hold **Attack 1** to charge up a super-powerful Rainbow of Doom black hole.

Tempest Dragon Path
Further develop Breeze's Tempest Cloud Attack.

TRIPLE RAINBOW, IT'S FULL ON (1700)
Hit a Tempest Cloud with a Rainbow of Doom and three rainbows will chain off of it.

TEMPEST TANTRUM (2200)
Bigger Tempest Cloud does increased damage with increased range.

TEMPEST MATRIX (3000)
Electricity forms between Tempest Clouds that hurts enemies.

Fling Kong

Monkey See, Monkey Doom!

Maximum Health	240
Speed	70
Armor	12
Critical Hit	70
Elemental Power	25

As a royal protector of the legendary monkey idol Kubla-Wa, Fling Kong trained seriously in the mysterious art of Monk-Ru, a form of fighting using the power of air. He was a devoted student, always the first to arrive to training and the last to leave. One day, a troop of foul-smelling, well-armed Gorilla-Goos appeared, led by the infamous General Snot. Snot had heard stories about the idol, particularly that it was made of solid gold. The villains quickly seized control of the temple that housed the idol and were on the verge of taking it. But suddenly the smelly gorillas found themselves face to face with Fling Kong—who attacked with the power of a true Monk-Ru master! Using his flying rug and powerful vortex discs, he expertly defeated the Gorilla-Goos and saved the idol. Soon after, word of his actions spread to Master Eon. Now a Skylander, Fling Kong knocks the wind out of evil throughout all of the Skylands!

Basic Attack Notes

▶ **Power Discs**

If there are enemies guarding a higher ledge, jump and throw Power Discs to take them out safely.

▶ **Magic Carpet Dash**

With the Mad Dash Upgrade, change the direction of the Dash by pressing a direction on the controller when you release Attack 2.

▶ **Cymbal Crash**

The Kong Klang upgrade allows Fling King to continue moving while charging the attack.

Upgrade Paths

Disc Jockey

The upgrades from the Disc Jocky Path are wonderful for battles in tight spaces. Trick Shot sends Power Discs through multiple enemies and bouncing off walls. Smash Hit is slightly less powerful than The Kong Klang, but does not require any charging. A Toss Up triples the damage of Power Discs and doesn't take too long to charge, but you don't control when it goes off.

Carpet Captain

The three abilities of the Carpet Captain Path turn Magic Carpet Dash into a destroyer of groups of enemies. Smash 'N' Dash extends the length of the dash, and Shock Treatment continues to damage enemies caught in Magic Carpet Dash's wake. Use Double Whammy to clear the path ahead or finish enemies that survived the initial dash and electricity. Tap the direction you want to throw the discs before pressing Attack 1.

⬤ SOUL GEM ABILITY

MAKE IT RAIN! — 4000

Hold **Attack 2** even longer and then release to fly up into the air, unleashing a rain of Power Discs from above. Prerequisite: Find Fling Kong's Soul Gem during Chapter 11: Wilikin Workshop

First, the bad news: Make it Rain! has a lengthy charge time (the violet flash of light tells you it's ready), and Fling Kong remains vulnerable to attacks. The upside is that he flies safely off screen while Make It Rain! demolishes everything within its range. It's dangerous to use when you don't know an area, but keep it in mind when you know a fight is coming and there's enough time to build a full charge (it doesn't begin until you release **Attack 2**).

Basic Attacks

POWER DISCS

Press **Attack 1** to fling Power Discs.

MAGIC CARPET DASH

Press **Attack 2** to dash forward and smash into enemies.

Upgrades

SPIKED! — 500

Fact: Power Discs with spikes do more damage.

CYMBAL CRASH — 700

Press **Attack 3** to smash Power Discs together and create sound waves to damage nearby enemies.

MAD DASH — 900

Hold **Attack 2** to charge up the Magic Carpet Dash to do more damage and last longer.

THE KONG KLANG — 1200

Hold **Attack 3** for a more powerful Cymbal Crash that also stuns enemies. Prerequisite: Cymbal Crash

Disc Jockey

Improve Power Discs attacks.

TRICK SHOT — 1700

Power Discs can go through enemies and bounce off walls.

SMASH HIT — 2200

Do a Cymbal Crash towards the end of a Magic Carpet Dash for a super smash combo.

A TOSS-UP — 3000

Hold **Attack 1** to charge up Power Discs for a massive overhead throw.

Carpet Captain

Improve Magic Carpet Dash attacks.

SMASH 'N' DASH — 1700

Hitting an enemy with a Magic Carpet Dash makes the dash last longer.

DOUBLE WHAMMY — 2200

Throw a Power Disc towards the end of a Magic Carpet Dash for a double-disc combo.

SHOCK TREATMENT — 3000

Leave a trail of electricity after a Magic Carpet Dash that damages enemies.

Gusto

Gusts and Glory!

Maximum Health	400
Speed	60
Armor	30
Critical Hit	50
Elemental Power	25

Gusto was once a cloud wrangler in the peaceful Thunderclap Kingdom, where he learned to master the wind under the guidance of the mysterious Cloud Dragon. But a day came when a fleet of dragon hunters appeared on the horizon, seeking to capture the fabled creature. Despite the danger, Gusto stepped forward to defend it. The hunters could see that Gusto was not a soldier and didn't even have a real weapon—just a "curved stick." However, he was no coward! And, throwing his large boomerang, Gusto hit his surprised opponents again and again—until the hunters surrendered and were forced to retreat. For standing up for himself and protecting the Cloud Dragon, Gusto was given a new Traptanium Boomerang and made part of the Trap Team!

Basic Attack Notes

▶ **Traptanium Boomerang**

After throwing a Traptanium Boomerang, press Attack 1 to recall it faster.

▶ **Inhaler**

Gusto must be stationary while inhaling or exhaling (jumping cancels both). If he's moving, he stops immediately. He can spin in place, but he can't advance.

▶ **Twistin' in the Wind**

Hold button to extend spinning time up to 3 seconds. You can still steer Gusto while he spins.

Upgrade Paths

Air Ace

Rang Me Like a Hurricane's hurricanes spawn only when an enemy or object takes damage and you can't control where they go. Boomerang Buddies appears each time Gusto throws a Traptanium Boomerang, with up to three appearing at the same time. The three buddies orbit him, damaging enemies (they ignore objects). Buddies exist for a brief time or until Gusto throws a Traptanium Boomerang when three Buddies are already out.

Dizzy Destroyer

Gusto must deal damage with Twistin' in the Wind to spawn hurricanes with the Spin Like the Wind upgrade. When Gusto earns Lightning Ball, you can roll through packs of enemies, leaving them shocked (if he has the Shocking Twist upgrade) and pummeled with hurricanes. Gusto isn't invulnerable while in lightning form, so watch out for ranged attacks and other hazards in the area.

⃝ SOUL GEM ABILITY

BOOMERANGS 4 BREAKFAST `4000`

Inhale a Traptanium Boomerang in the air for a super-powered attack. Prerequisite: Find Gusto's Soul Gem in Chapter 3: Chompy Mountain

Throw the Traptanium Boomerang and press **Attack 2** when it returns to inhale it. Exhaling with the boomerang in his belly triples the damage the attack does normally. While the Boomerang is in his belly, Gusto can't throw it, but he can still use Twistin' in the Wind.

Basic Attacks

TRAPTANIUM BOOMERANG

Press **Attack 1** to throw a Traptanium Boomerang.

INHALER

Press **Attack 2** to inhale enemies and press **Attack 2** again to spit them out.

Upgrades

THE BREATH OF LIFE `500`

Regain HP by inhaling enemies.

TWISTIN' IN THE WIND `700`

Press **Attack 3** to spin around and whack enemies with the boomerang.

ELECTRO-RANG `900`

Hold **Attack 1** to charge up the Traptanium Boomerang attack.

LOTS OF LUNGPOWER `1200`

Can inhale more enemies at a time.

Air Ace

Improve Traptanium Boomerang attacks.

BOOM-ERANG `1700`

Traptanium Boomerang and Electro-Rang do more damage.

RANG ME LIKE A HURRICANE `2200`

Traptanium Boomerang attack creates mini hurricanes.

BOOMERANG BUDDIES `3000`

Boomerang attack releases additional rangs that orbit and protect Gusto.

Dizzy Destroyer

Improve Twistin' in the Wind attacks.

SPIN LIKE THE WIND `1700`

Can perform Twistin' in the Wind attack for longer and spawn mini hurricanes.

SHOCKING TWIST `2200`

Twistin' in the Wind attack electrocutes enemies.

LIGHTNING BALL `3000`

Hold **Attack 3** to turn into an unstoppable Lightning Ball.

Full Blast Jet-Vac

Hawk and Awe!

Maximum Health	240
Speed	70
Armor	30
Critical Hit	30
Elemental Power	25

Jet-Vac was the greatest, most daring flying ace in all of Windham. He was given his magical wings when he was young, as was the tradition for all Sky Barons. But when his homeland was raided, he chose to sacrifice his wings to a young mother so she could fly her children to safety. This act of nobility caught the attention of Master Eon, who sought out the young Sky Baron and presented him with a gift—a powerful vacuum device that would allow him to soar through the skies once again. Jet-Vac accepted the gift with gratitude, and now daringly fights evil alongside the other Skylanders.

Basic Attack Notes

▶ **Vac-Blaster**
Rapid fire rate and good range. Available while jumping and when Jet-Vac Jet Pack is active.

▶ **Suction Gun**
Use Suction Gun to pull in nearby treasure, food, and smaller enemies. Larger enemies take damage but are not pulled closer.

▶ **Jet-Vac Jet Pack**
Limited duration flight time. Use Suction Gun to recharge the tank faster.

Upgrade Paths

Bird Blaster
The Bird Blaster Path boosts the strength of Vac-Blaster considerably. Piercing Winds and Vac Master-Blaster 20X increase the number of enemies hit and how much damage is dealt by each blast. The real gem in this path is Super Suction Air Blaster. Use Suction Gun to finish off enemies to charge a super shot. The Vac-Blaster can store up to eight super shots at a time. Take out smaller enemies with Suction Gun and use the super shots on more powerful foes.

Vac-Packeteer
The Vac-Packeteer Path gives Pet Vac more time in the air before a recharge is required. While Suction Gun doesn't work in the air, the final upgrade of this path, Flying Corkscrew, adds a devastating new attack. Tap Attack 2 and a direction to carve a path through enemies. You can perform up to four Flying Corkscrews from one full tank.

◯ SOUL GEM ABILITY

EAGLE-AIR BATTLE GEAR `4000`
Jet-Vac gets enhanced resistances and a pretty sweet visor.

Eagle-Air Battle Gear boosts Jet-Vac's armor to 120. That's a huge increase, so consider this a high-priority purchase.

Basic Attacks

VAC-BLASTER
Press **Attack 1** to shoot enemies with a powerful blast of air.

SUCTION GUN
Hold **Attack 2** to suck enemies into the spinning fan blades.

Upgrades

FEISTIER FAN `500`
Bigger spinning fan blades on the Suction Gun do increased damage to enemies.

JET-VAC JET PACK `700`
Press **Attack 3** to fly and perform new attacks in the air.

VAC BLASTER 9000 `900`
Vac-Blaster does increased damage.

TURBINE SUCTION FAN `1200`
Suction Gun attacks do even more increased damage. Prerequisite: Feistier Fan

Bird Blaster Path
Further develop Jet-Vac's Vac-Blaster attacks.

PIERCING WINDS `1700`
Vac-Blaster does even more increased damage and pierces multiple enemies.

VAC MASTER-BLASTER 20X `2200`
Vac-Blaster does maximum damage.

SUPER SUCTION AIR BLASTER `3000`
Suck up enemies with the Suction Gun and it gives the Vac-Blaster a super shot.

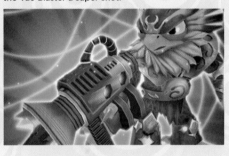

Vac-Packeteer Path
Further develop Jet-Vac's Suction and Flight attacks.

TANK RESERVES `1700`
Can remain in flight longer and recharge faster.

THE MULCHER `2200`
Suction Gun attacks do maximum damage.

FLYING CORKSCREW `3000`
While flying, press **Attack 2** to blast forward and perform a powerful corkscrew attack.

WOW POW!

DOUBLE BARREL `5000`
While flying, swap the Vac Blaster for two superpowered guns and hold **Attack 1** to fire continuously until they overheat. Prerequisite: Jet-Vac Jet Pack

Hold **Attack 1** (or tap it rapidly) to increase Vac Blaster's firing rate, but don't let the guns overheat. They don't simply power down, they explode, knocking Jet-Vac backward and down to the ground where he's stunned momentarily. A great ability for a brief burst of focused fire, so long as you remember to stop firing at the first sound of trouble.

Pet Vac

Hawk and Awe!

Maximum Health	240
Speed	70
Armor	12
Critical Hit	20
Elemental Power	25

Basic Attack Notes

▶ **Vac Blaster**

Rapid fire rate and good range. Available while jumping and when Jet-Vac Jet Pack is active.

▶ **Suction Gun**

Use Suction Gun to pull in nearby treasure and smaller enemies. Larger enemies take damage but are not pulled closer.

▶ **Jet-Vac Jet Pack**

Limited duration flight time. Use Suction Gun to recharge the tank faster.

Upgrade Paths

Bird Blaster

The Bird Blaster Path boosts the strength of Vac-Blaster considerably. Piercing Winds and Vac Master-Blaster 20X increase the number of enemies, and how much damage is dealt, hit by each blast. The real gem in this path is Super Suction Air Blaster. Use Suction Gun to finish off enemies to charge a super shot. The Vac-Blaster can store up to eight super shots at a time. Take out smaller enemies with Suction Gun and use the super shots on more powerful foes.

Vac-Packeteer

The Vac-Packeteer Path gives Pet Vac more time in the air before a recharge is required. While Suction Gun doesn't work in the air, the final upgrade of this path, Flying Corkscrew, adds a devastating new attack. Tap Attack 2 and a direction to carve a path through enemies. You can perform up to four Flying Corkscrews from one full tank.

⬤ SOUL GEM ABILITY

EAGLE-AIR BATTLE GEAR — 4000

Enhanced armor and a pretty sweet visor.

Eagle-Air Battle Gear boosts Pet Vac's armor to 102. That's a huge increase, so consider this a high-priority purchase.

Basic Attacks

VAC BLASTER

Press **Attack 1** to shoot enemies with a powerful blast of air.

SUCTION GUN

Hold **Attack 2** to suck enemies into the spinning fan blades.

Upgrades

FEISTIER FAN — 500

Bigger spinning fan blades on the Suction Gun do increased damage to enemies.

JET-VAC JET PACK — 700

Press **Attack 3** to fly and perform new attacks in the air.

VAC BLASTER 9000 — 900

Vac-Blaster does increased damage.

TURBINE SUCTION FAN — 1200

Suction Gun attacks do even more increased damage. Prerequisite: Feistier Fan

Bird Blaster Path

Further develop Pet Vac's Vac-Blaster attacks.

PIERCING WINDS — 1700

Vac Blaster does even more increased damage and pierces multiple enemies.

VAC MASTER-BLASTER 20X — 2200

Vac Blaster does maximum damage.

SUPER SUCTION AIR BLASTER — 3000

Suck up enemies with the Suction Gun and it gives the Vac Blaster a super shot.

Vac-Packeteer Path

Further develop Pet Vac's Suction and Flight attacks.

TANK RESERVES — 1700

Can remain in flight longer and recharge faster.

THE MULCHER — 2200

Suction Gun attacks do maximum damage.

FLYING CORKSCREW — 3000

While flying, press **Attack 2** to blast forward and perform a powerful corkscrew attack.

Thunderbolt

A Storm is Coming!

Maximum Health	410
Speed	60
Armor	48
Critical Hit	30
Elemental Power	25

Epically strong and heroically competitive, Thunderbolt grew up on legendary Mount Cloudpierce. Every year, his people held a contest to determine who would wield the Storm Sword—a legendary blade with the power to change the seasons in Skylands. To Thunderbolt, this would be a great honor. But on the day he won the contest and was about to be presented with the sword, a Frost Mage snatched it and plunged all of Skylands into a wintery deep-freeze. Undaunted, Thunderbolt bravely took chase. Riding twin bolts of chained lightning, he overtook the mage, reclaimed the sword, and restored balance to the weather systems in Skylands. For his heroic actions, Thunderbolt was made a member of the Trap Team, and he now uses his Traptanium Storm Sword to strike evil at every turn!

Basic Attack Notes

▶ **Traptanium Thundersword**
Press Attack 1 three times to perform a combo. Jumping Attack 1 is an overhead Traptanium Thundersword swing.

▶ **Storm Clouds**
Thunderbolt can summon up to three Storm Clouds at a time. Can't be done while jumping.

▶ **Hurricane Pain**
Thunderbolt can't move while creating a Twister. Only one Twister can exist at a time.

Upgrade Paths

Power Conductor

The Power Conductor Path begins by adding two combo attacks and ends by strengthening all Traptanium Thundersword combos. Direct Current ends with the Traptanium Thundersword buried in the ground, damaging nearby enemies. Thunder Thrust looks similar to Thunderbolt's initial combo, but is slightly quicker. Just Add Lightning changes the look of the Traptanium Thundersword and allows you to extend the last swing of each combo by holding down the Attack button.

I of the Storm

The lightning attacks from Traptanium Thundersword swings and Storm Clouds hit harder and travel farther with the initial upgrade in the I of the Storm Path. With the Exploding Clouds upgrade, you can cause a Storm Cloud to explode with two or three swings with the Traptanium Sword.

⬤ SOUL GEM ABILITY

LIGHTNING RAIN! — 4000
Hold **Attack 1** and then press **Attack 2** to call in a lightning storm. Prerequisite: Find Thunderbolt's Soul Gem in Chapter 12: Time Town

Save Lightning Rain! for areas filled with lower-health enemies. The lightning storm deals considerable damage overall, but individual lightning strikes aren't exceptionally strong.

Basic Attacks

TRAPTANIUM THUNDERSWORD
Press **Attack 1** to swing the Traptanium Thundersword.

STORM CLOUDS
Press **Attack 2** to summon a cloud that rains pain down on enemies.

Upgrades

LIGHTNING CLOUDS — 500
Charge up Storm Clouds with the Thundersword, causing them to shoot lightning.

HURRICANE PAIN — 700
Press **Attack 3** to summon a Twister.

MORE THUNDER — 900
Traptanium Thundersword does more damage.

HURRICANE PAIN REMAINS — 1200
Twister lasts longer, does more damage, and sucks in clouds. Prerequisite: Hurricane Pain.

Power Conductor
Improve Traptanium Thundersword attacks.

DIRECT CURRENT — 1700
Press **Attack 1**, **Attack 1** HOLD **Attack 2** for Power Conductor combo.

THUNDER THRUST — 2200
Press **Attack 1**, **Attack 1**, HOLD **Attack 3** for a Thunder Thrust combo.

JUST ADD LIGHTNING — 3000
Press **Attack 1**, **Attack 1**, HOLD **Attack 1** to add some lightning power to your sword slam.

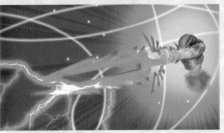

I of the Storm
Improve Lightning attacks.

STORMIER AND STORMIER — 1700
All lightning attacks have extra range and do increased damage.

CHARGE IT UP! — 2200
Charge up Storm Clouds with the Thundersword with extra power.

EXPLODING CLOUDS — 3000
Storm Clouds can be overcharged with lightning and explode for maximum damage.

Bop
Rock and Roll!

Maximum Health	310
Speed	50
Armor	12
Critical Hit	20
Elemental Power	25

Basic Attack Notes

▶ **Tail Swipe**

A powerful 360-degree tail attack that can also deflect incoming projectiles.

▶ **Rock and Roll**

A charging attack that is somewhat slow but it does a lot of damage.

▶ **Summoning: Stone Projection**

A wall attack that can be hit with a Tail Swipe to launch rocks as a long-range attack.

Upgrade Paths

Granite Dragon

Bop's mace tail is his strongest feature and is powerful before any upgrades. Choosing this path further upgrades Tail Swipe to massive damage. Gaia Hammer is one of the highest-damage attacks in the game. It can dish out nearly 1000 damage! The charge takes a moment, but against bosses, it should be your primary attack. Summoning: Stone Uppercut increases the damage of Stone Projection for long range attacks but the Tail Swipe is all you really need.

Pulver Dragon

For a dash-type attack, Rock and Roll dishes out serious damage. While it's not as fast as other dash attacks, the extra damage more than makes up for it. After buying all the upgrades on this path, Rock and Roll becomes a dash-type attack that does more damage than the base Tail Swipe. The upgrades on this path give Rock and Roll excellent range, superior damage, and the ability to roll right through enemies.

● SOUL GEM ABILITY

TRICERATOPS HONOR GUARD `4000`

New armor makes you harder to hit.

One of Bop's weaknesses is his low armor rating. When you purchase this ability, Bop's base armor stat increases four fold! That's a huge improvement and lets him hang in tough close-range combat situations for a lot longer.

Basic Attacks

TAIL SWIPE

Press **Attack 1** to swing your tail around to **attack** 360 degrees of enemies.

ROCK AND ROLL

Hold **Attack 2** to roll into a ball and then over your enemies.

Upgrades

TENNIS TAIL `500`

Deflect incoming objects with your Tail Swipe.

IRON TAIL `700`

Tail Swipe does increased damage.

SUMMONING STONE PROJECTION `900`

Hold **Attack 3** to summon a rock wall; hit it with your Tail Swipe to launch rocks.

DOUBLE ROLL `1200`

Use the Roll attack for twice as long.

Granite Dragon

Further develop Tail Swipe & Summoning attacks.

MACE OF DESTRUCTION `1700`

Tail Swipe does MORE increased damage.

SUMMONING: STONE UPPERCUT `2200`

Stone Projection does increased damage.

GAIA HAMMER `3000`

Hold **Attack 1** to charge up the Tail Swipe and do extra damage. Prerequisite: Mace of Destruction

Pulver Dragon

Further develop Roll attack.

PULVER ROLL `1700`

Roll attack does increased damage.

EARTHEN FORCE ROLL `2200`

Roll does MORE damage and can roll right through enemy attacks.

CONTINENTAL BOULDER `3000`

Becomes a giant ball while rolling—roll faster and do even MORE damage. Prerequisite: Pulver Roll

Fist Bump

Knock Knock...Too Late!

Maximum Health	280
Speed	60
Armor	30
Critical Hit	20
Elemental Power	25

Fist Bump had long been the sleeping protector of the Bubbling Bamboo Forest, but awoke from a long hibernation when a horde of nasty purple Greebles arrived with gigantic rock-smashing machines. Intent on building a new base, their machines wreaked havoc—chewing up the land and spitting out billowing clouds of smoke into the enchanted air. Seeing this, Fist Bump was furious. Using his enormous stone fists, he hammered the ground with all his strength, creating a massive earthquake that sent huge shockwaves towards the Greeble camp. This reduced the machines to mere scrap and sent the Greebles running off in a panic. The act of bravery caught the attention of Terrafin, who brought Fist Bump to meet Master Eon. Now as a Skylander, Fist Bump makes evil quake wherever he goes!

Basic Attack Notes

▶ **Panda Pound**

Smashing attack that activates Fault Lines. When done in the air he smashes into the ground causing a Fault Line.

▶ **Fault Line Slam**

Create a Fault Line in a straight line causing low damage. Fault lines remain and can be activated, causing spikes to spring forth.

▶ **Seismic Slide**

A charging attack that also creates small Fault Lines.

Upgrade Paths

Rowdy Richter

Fault Lines are Fist Bump's bread and butter attack and this path adds damage through several methods. Quake 'N' Bake should be the first choice to increase Fault Lines' power and damage. Fault Lines in Glass Houses and A Bolder Boulder provide extra damage from projectiles shooting out of the Fault Lines. Fault Lines initial attack does low damage but they can be used many ways. What makes them so effective is that they stay around for so long that you can set up traps or continually damage enemies. Create Fault Lines constantly during battle and activate them when enemies step near them.

Bamboo Bonanza

Instead of adding simple damage increases, this path focus on bamboo for both damage and health regeneration. Healing Bamboo spawns health-boosting plants while Bamboo Harvest turns the plants into bombs. Jump For It! Speeds up the aerial Panda Pound attack to quickly trigger the exploding bamboo and create lots of Fault Lines. With the dual nature of bamboo Fist Bump should use Fault Lines for long range attacks and save the bamboo if he is running low on health or explode them if they enemies are really tough.

⬤ SOUL GEM ABILITY

RIDING THE RAILS　4000

Walking creates Fault Lines and mini fault cracks. Prerequisite: Find Fist Bump's Soul Gem in CH 7: Monster Marsh

This ability passively creates Fault Lines to further fill the battlefield with these deadly cracks. A simple stroll can create damaging traps for enemies to run into once they are activated. This ability is especially powerful on the Rowdy Richter path.

Basic Attacks

PANDA POUND

Press **Attack 1** to smash the ground and also activate Fault Lines.

FAULT LINE SLAM

Press **Attack 2** to slam the ground so hard, it creates Fault Lines.

Upgrades

SEISMIC SLIDE　500

Press **Attack 3** to slide across the ground and ram into enemies.

PANQUAKE　700

Panda Pound attack creates mini fault cracks and performing it in the air creates Fault Lines.

HOLD THE LINE　900

Fault Lines travel further and farther.

DON'T BUMP FIST BUMP　1200

All Fault Lines are automatically activated when you take damage.

Rowdy Richter

Improve Fault Line attacks.

FAULT LINES IN GLASS HOUSES　1700

When Fault Lines are activated, some of them shoot stones at enemies.

QUAKE 'N' BAKE　2200

Activated Fault Lines are more powerful and do extra damage.

A BOLDER BOULDER　3000

When Fault Lines are activated, some shoot spikey boulders at enemies.

Bamboo Bonanza

Grow Bamboo from your Fault Lines.

HEALING BAMBOO　1700

When Fault Lines are activated, some of them spawn bamboo. Slide into them to regain HP.

BAMBOO HARVEST　2200

Perform a Panda Pound in the air and bamboo plants explode, damaging enemies.

JUMP FOR IT!　3000

Can perform a Panda Pound in the air much quicker and create an extra Fault Line.

Head Rush

Taking Charge!

Maximum Health	340
Speed	60
Armor	48
Critical Hit	10
Elemental Power	25

Head Rush was raised in a small village that had fallen under the spell of a powerful Harvest Sphinx, who forced the frightened villagers to plow the vast fields of golden grass for his own benefit. Although there were many villagers, no individual was brave enough to confront the Sphinx and put an end to its rule. But Head Rush believed there was a chance to fight back if she could somehow inspire her people to stand together. Charging through her village, Head Rush shouted a mighty yodel that woke the villagers from their spell! With the village behind her, she then led the charge to drive the Sphinx from the island for good. For her leadership and bravery, she was made part of the Trap Team, where she uses her giant Traptanium horns to take charge of evil!

Basic Attack Notes

▶ **Traptanium Horns**
Can be used to head bash enemies up close or to charge at foes. When upgraded she is able to turn while using the charge attack.

▶ **Stomp!**
The stomp has a small area of effect and when upgraded it can be done three times in a combo or in the air.

▶ **Yodel**
An echoing attack continues to damage enemies in earshot but Head Rush is unable to move.

Upgrade Paths

Lungs of Steel

High Note transforms the yodel from a single forward wave into a mid-range 360-degree attack. Modulate Yodel increase damage and allows fine tuning the attack by controlling the pitch. To further increase damage of Yodel purchase Forget Breaking Glass to add falling rocks and several spinning waves when she stops singing. The range of the Yodel is surprisingly far and can reach enemies at long-range. Although Head Rush cannot move while using Yodel, when it is fully powered up it is capable of stopping most enemies before they can close in. Be careful of remaining stationary against very tough enemies, charging foes, and long range projectile attacks.

Stomp Harder

Power Steering makes the charge attack more powerful, adding damage with each turn. Before running into enemies do a few quick turns to maximize its effect. This becomes one of her most effective abilities to deal with large groups of enemies and it also provides a great speed boost. Stomp! receives two damage increases on this path and it is the best choice to take out any foe foolish enough to get in too close. This attack can be performed three times to create a combo with a devastating final blow. Also, the attack hurts all enemies in a small radius and doesn't need to directly hit one enemy.

⬤ SOUL GEM ABILITY

HORNS APLENTY! — 4000

New Traptanium Horns do ultimate damage.
Prerequisite: Find Head Rush's Soul Gem in CH 11: Wilikin Workshop

This is one of the most practical abilities gained from a Soul Gem. The Traptanium Horns instantly get maxed out with this ability and significantly increase damage to her head bash and charge attacks.

Basic Attacks

TRAPTANIUM HORNS

Press **Attack 1** to head bash enemies, hold **Attack 1** to charge ahead.

STOMP!

Press **Attack 2** to stomp the ground so hard, anything nearby takes damage.

Upgrades

MEGA STOMP — 500

Press **Attack 2**, **Attack 2**, **Attack 2** for a Mega Stomp combo.

YODEL — 700

Press **Attack 3** to perform a powerful yodel attack, damaging all enemies within earshot.

STOMPING ON AIR — 900

While in the air, press **Attack 2** to stomp down with more power.

CHARGE CONTROL — 1200

Can turn while performing a charge attack, which also does extra damage.

Lungs of Steel

Improve Yodel attacks.

HIGH NOTE — 1700

Yodel attack does extra damage.

MODULATE YODEL — 2200

Yodel attack does even MORE damage, and you can control the pitch.

FORGET BREAKING GLASS — 3000

Yodel attack is so loud, it destroys the ground beneath you.

Stomp Harder

Improve Stomp attacks.

A STOMP TO REMEMBER — 1700

Stomp attack does extra damage.

POWER STEERING — 2200

Turning during a charge attack makes it do additional extra damage with each turn.

OMEGA STOMP — 3000

Stomp attack does extra damage and destroys the ground beneath you.

Rocky Roll

Roll With It!

Maximum Health	270
Speed	60
Armor	30
Critical Hit	40
Elemental Power	25

Rocky was a rock digger who wanted to make a difference, and Roll was a boulder that wanted to see the world. The two of them had known each other since they were young and in mining school together. They had shared the same goal—making the sacred journey to Peek's Peak, where it was said that one's destiny reveals itself. But time went on, and it wasn't until many years later that they found each other traveling the same path towards the mythical peak. The connection that was established years before had finally taken shape, and the two realized they were meant to journey far and wide together—as Rocky Roll. After several adventures together, they met Master Eon by chance, who recognized that their connection was special. Now as an awesome Skylander duo, Rocky Roll will crush anything that threatens Skylands!

Basic Attack Notes

▶ **Spit Ball**
Shoot out a bouncing rock projectile.

▶ **Boulder Dash**
A charging attack that bowls over enemies.

▶ **Boulder Barrier**
Forms a protective Boulder Barrier and can launch the boulders out. Upgrades to enter Bouncy Attack Mode.

Upgrade Paths

Geological Grandmaster

Start out with Rock Hardest to gain the damage increase for Spit Ball and Boulder Barrier. Super Spit Ball can charge up a giant boulder and hold it until you're ready to launch it. This attack does twice the damage of a single boulder and is best against smaller clusters of tough foes. It is effective at long range to allow time to charge. For groups of enemies Triple Spit Balls is ideal since it adds a wider area to the attack. The triple shot should be used at mid range as the boulders continue to spread out as they travel and might miss enemies at long range.

Rolling Rumbler

This path is more geared towards melee damage and close combat. Let's Roll gives the Boulder Dash more speed and damage to use hit and run tactics. The other two upgrades require using Boulder Barrier to go into Bouncy Attack Mode. Rocky Boxing provides a dashing punch that is quick and does a good amount of damage. Roll With the Punches is another Bouncy Mode attack option but it is not as effective as the dashing punch attack.

SOUL GEM ABILITY

BOULDER POSSE — 4000

Press **Attack 3** to increase the amount of boulders in the Boulder Barrier all the way up to nine. Prerequisite: Find Rocky Roll's Soul Gem in CH 12: Time Town

Creates a huge arsenal of rocks that orbit Rocky Roll. The boulders provide protection and damage anything that gets close. Keep the protective barrier when surrounded. When they are not immediately in demand, continue to create and shoot them to hit enemies around Rocky Roll.

Basic Attacks

SPIT BALL
Press **Attack 1** to have Roll spit out a bouncing rock projectile.

BOULDER DASH
Press **Attack 2** to perform a Boulder Dash charge attack.

Upgrades

BOULDER BARRIER — 500
Press **Attack 3** to form a protective Boulder Barrier, then press **Attack 3** again to launch the boulders out.

ROCK ON — 700
Spit Ball and Boulder Barrier attacks do more damage.

BOUNCY ATTACK MODE — 900
Press **Attack 3** to create Boulder Barriers, then hold **Attack 2** to enter Bouncy Attack Mode.

MOH BOULDERS — 1200
Press **Attack 3** to increase the amount of boulders in the Boulder Barrier from 3 to 6. Prerequisite: Boulder Barrier

Geological Grandmaster
Improve Spit Ball attacks.

SUPER SPIT BALL — 1700
Hold **Attack 1** to charge up your Spit Ball attack into a giant boulder projectile.

ROCK HARDEST — 2200
Spit Ball and Boulder Barrier attacks do maximum damage.

TRIPLE SPIT BALLS — 3000
Shoot 3 Spit Balls at once that ricochet into smaller boulders.

Rolling Rumbler
Improve Roll attacks.

LET'S ROLL! — 1700
Rapidly press **Attack 2** to rev up the Boulder Dash for more damage and speed.

ROLL WITH THE PUNCHES — 2200
In Bouncy Attack Mode, press **Attack 1** to perform a spinning fist attack.

ROCKY BOXING — 3000
In Bouncy Attack Mode, press **Attack 2** to throw a dashing punch attack.

Terrabite

It's Beatin' Time!

Maximum Health	310
Speed	50
Armor	18
Critical Hit	30
Elemental Power	25

Basic Attack Notes

▷ Punch
A fast and powerful attack that can be repeated in a combo and upgrades to hit multiple enemies.

▷ Earth Swim
Terrabite burrows underground and is immune to harm. He can steer underground and emerge with a belly flop attack.

▷ Feeding Frenzy
A long-range attack of mini-sharks that burrow and latch onto enemies, causing a small amount of damage over time.

Upgrade Paths

Sand Hog
Initially, Terrabite doesn't get any extra speed from burrowing, but Master Earth Swimmer takes care of that. This allows him to sneak up on enemies and belly flop for high damage or quickly evade level hazards. Keep in mind that belly flop does a lot of damage but it has small range and Terrabite can't move momentarily after the attack. Razorfin gives Earth Swim the ability to do a small amount of damage while burrowed and immune to damage. Another damage enhancement on this path is Homing Frenzy that adds increased damage for homing mini-sharks that can be performed above or underground.

Brawler
This path is mainly devoted to Punch but don't mistake a lack of complexity for lack of effectiveness. Punch is deadly at close range, and comes out faster than attacks from most melee Skylanders. Also, his punches have a slight knockback effect that can temporarily stun enemies, interrupting their attacks. Terrabite's Body Slam combo ends with a belly flop, shocking any enemies at close range. The Uppercut combo is great up-close on tough foes due to its nearly double damage uppercut. Frenzy Shield adds a passive retaliation attack that unleashes mini-sharks against anyone that damages him.

⬤ SOUL GEM ABILITY

SURFACE FEEDER — 4000
Collect power-ups while burrowed.

This is a nice little addition to Terrabite's arsenal, but you can hold off buying it until other upgrades have been purchased. Surface Feeder gives Terrabite immunity from enemy attacks while he is underground collecting all types of power-ups, including food and gold.

Basic Attacks

PUNCH
Press **Attack 1** to punch the enemy. Press **Attack 1**, **Attack 1**, HOLD **Attack 1** to perform a combo.

EARTH SWIM
Press **Attack 2** to burrow underground, press **Attack 1** to perform a belly flop.

Upgrades

BRASS KNUCKLES — 500
Punch attacks do increased damage.

MEGA BELLYFLOP — 700
Belly flop does increased damage and affects a larger area.

FEEDING FRENZY — 900
Press **Attack 3** to spawn mini-sharks that burrow and latch onto enemies.

MULTI TARGET PUNCHES — 1200
Punch attack hits multiple enemies.

Sand Hog
Further develop burrowing abilities.

MASTER EARTH SWIMMER — 1700
Increased speed while burrowing.

HOMING FRENZY — 2200
Mini-sharks home in on enemies and do extra damage.

RAZORFIN — 3000
While burrowed, your dorsal fin does damage to enemies.

Brawler
Further develop punching abilities.

PUGILIST — 1700
Press **Attack 1**, **Attack 1**, HOLD **Attack 2** for Body Slam. Press **Attack 1**, **Attack 1**, HOLD **Attack 3** for Uppercut.

SPIKED KNUCKLES — 2200
All punch attacks do even more damage!

FRENZY SHIELD — 3000
You launch mini-sharks at enemies who damage you.

Wallop

Hammer It Home!

Maximum Health	300
Speed	60
Armor	18
Critical Hit	50
Elemental Power	25

For generations, Wallop's people used the volcanic lava pits of Mount Scorch to forge the most awesome weapons in all of Skylands. And Wallop was the finest apprentice any of the masters had ever seen. Using hammers in both of his mighty hands, he could tirelessly pound and shape the incredibly hot metal into the sharpest swords or the hardest axes. But on the day he was to demonstrate his skills to the masters of his craft, a fierce fire viper awoke from his deep sleep in the belly of the volcano. The huge snake erupted forth, attacking Wallop's village. But, bravely charging the beast with his two massive hammers, Wallop was able to bring down the creature and save his village. Now with his Traptanium-infused hammers, he fights with the Skylanders to protect the lands from any evil that rises to attack!

Basic Attack Notes

▶ **Traptanium Hammer**
Powerful dual hammer attack that can upgrade damage and be used in Tantrum Mode by rapidly pressing Attack 1.

▶ **Hammer Toss**
Each hammer is individually hurled in the air and lands on enemies.

▶ **When Hammers Collide**
Both hammers spin into the battlefield, doing light damage, and smash together for heavy damage.

Upgrade Paths

Tantrum Thrower

It's hammer time on this path and Wallop gets the ability to instantly enter Tantrum Mode. Total Meltdown allows him to remain enraged longer and do extra damage. These upgrades give Wallop the ability to hold down the attack button and go on a rampage to smash through groups of enemies or take on just about any foe face-to-face. Aftershock Wave adds a long-range attack that damages enemies in a straight line. However, Hammer Toss and When Hammers Collide are his best tools to deal damage at mid and long range. Weaken enemies with those two attacks and charge in with hammers swinging!

Hammer Handler

This path focuses on using the Traptanium Hammer at mid and long range. Better with Shrapnel adds Traptanium shards that do additional damage from Tossed Hammers. The shrapnel becomes even more effective with Traptanium Splitters that allow those shards to stick to enemies and continue to damage over time. What a Collision! gives When Hammers Collide a bigger explosion and even more damage to deal with tougher enemies at a distance. Alternate between these attacks but keep in mind the thrown hammers take some time to reach their target. Use them at long range to keep enemies away and wear down tough foes. Yet, if enemies get in melee range switch to Traptanium Hammer attacks.

⬤ SOUL GEM ABILITY

NOW THAT'S A HAMMER! `4000`

Hold **Attack 2** to charge up the Hammer Toss and make super hammers. Prerequisite: Find Wallop's Soul Gem in CH 3: Chompy Mountains.

After one or both of the hammers are tossed into the air, hold **Attack 2** to power them up. The longer the button is held the bigger they grow and will do more damage. They can grow three times their normal size providing nearly four times the damage. Wallop is free to move around while the hammers are charging in midair.

Basic Attacks

TRAPTANIUM HAMMER
Press **Attack 1** to swing the mighty Traptanium Hammers.

HAMMER TOSS
Press **Attack 2** to toss Traptanium Hammers, which smash down with mighty force.

Upgrades

TANTRUM MODE `500`
Rapidly press **Attack 1** to enter Tantrum Mode.

HAMMER SLAMMER `700`
Hammer Toss attack does extra damage.

WHEN HAMMERS COLLIDE `900`
Press **Attack 3** to spin both hammers into the battlefield, which then smash together.

CUTTING EDGE `1200`
New Traptanium Hammers do extra damage.

Tantrum Thrower
Improve Tantrum Mode attacks.

INSTANT TANTRUM `1700`
Hold **Attack 1** to instantly enter Tantrum Mode.

TOTAL MELTDOWN `2200`
Hold **Attack 1** to remain in Tantrum Mode for longer and do extra damage.

AFTERSHOCK WAVE `3000`
Release a powerful wave of Earth energy after coming out of Tantrum Mode.

Hammer Handler
Improve Hammer Toss attacks.

BETTER WITH SHRAPNEL `1700`
Tossed Hammers shoot out Traptanium shrapnel on impact.

WHAT A COLLISION! `2200`
When Hammers Collide attack creates a bigger explosion that does extra damage.

TRAPTANIUM SPLINTERS `3000`
Traptanium shrapnel from Hammer Toss stick to enemies and do damage over time.

Hog Wild Fryno

Crash and Burn!

Maximum Health	330
Speed	60
Armor	6
Critical Hit	20
Elemental Power	25

Fryno was once a member of the notorious Blazing Biker Brigade and spent most of his youth riding around Skylands with the rest of his crew. But what Fryno did not realize was that, while he enjoyed a life of freedom and adventure, his crew was responsible for acts of burglary throughout Skylands. When Fryno discovered that he had been riding around with a bunch of villains, he burned with rage and demanded that they make amends for the wrong they had done. This resulted in an epic fight, which Fryno won, and the disbanding of the Blazing Biker Brigade. Fryno was in the midst of returning the valuables his crew had stolen when he met Master Eon, who was impressed with his good character and fighting abilities, and offered him a membership to a new crew—the Skylanders.

Basic Attack Notes

▶ **Brawl**
Rapid punches that propel Fryno forward unless he's hitting something.

▶ **Heated**
Keep Heated whenever possible. Don't go into fights without building Heat first.

▶ **The Horn and The Hog**
Good for closing distance quickly, especially when his motorcycle is involved.

Upgrade Paths

Brawler

The Brawler Path punishes enemies limited to melee attacks. Remember to stay Heated as often as possible. The more Heated Fryno is, the more swings he gets from Hot Hands. Spiked Up increases the damage done, and Temperature Tantrum damages more enemies. The Brawler Path does not require much thinking. It only needs enough enemies to punch.

Hot Shop

Fryno's Hot Shop Path is a big help when dealing with ranged opponents. The Horn and The Hog is the best way to reach ranged enemies quickly, and what's faster than throwing a motorcycle at them? It's the closest thing he has to a ranged attack. Once Fryno gets his Wow Pow! ability, you can choose to throw the motorcycle (by pressing Attack 3 to end the ride early) to blow it up where he's Burning Rubber.

⬤ SOUL GEM ABILITY

MADNESS MAXED `4000`

Press **Attack 2** rapidly to make Fryno even more heated. So angry!

Madness Max builds Fryno's heat from orange to yellow. Heated affects almost everything Fryno does. He rides his hog when heated, he does more damage when heated, and so on. Madness Maxed is a priority purchase. Get it as soon as you can!

Basic Attacks

BRAWL

Press **Attack 1** to punch nearby enemies. Speed and damage of punches is increased depending on heat.

HEATED

Press **Attack 2** repeatedly to smash the ground and increase heat level.

Upgrades

THE HORN AND THE HOG `500`

Press **Attack 3** to dash forward dealing damage to enemies in the way. When heated, Fryno jumps on a motorcycle to deal damage to nearby enemies.

BUILT TOUGH `700`

Health is increased. Probably from punching the ground so much...

FIRED UP! `900`

Press **Attack 2** repeatedly to throw a tantrum and become heated. Tantrums now have increased range and damage.

MOTLEN FURY `1200`

All attacks do increased damage when heated.

Brawler Path

HOT HANDS `1700`

Hold **Attack 1** to rapidly punch nearby enemies and release heat.

SPIKED UP `2200`

New metal gloves cause Hot Hands to do increased damage. Prerequisite: Hot Hands

TEMPERATURE TANTRUM `3000`

Nearby enemies take damage while Fryno is heated.

Hot Shop Path

BORN TO RIDE `1700`

The Horn and The Hog will always summon a molten motorcycle.

HOT ROD `2200`

All attacks with the motorcycle do increased damage.

CRASH AND BURN `3000`

Fryno throws the motorcycle at the end of a dash, causing a massive explosion that damages nearby enemies. Who's paying for that...?

WOW POW!

BURNING RUBBER `5000`

While riding the motorcycle, hold **Attack 2** to go into a power drift, blasting enemies with molten rocks

You must hold **Attack 3** until Burning Rubber begins. Fryno spins in place, flinging burning rocks in every direction. The wheels of the motorcycle damage whatever they hit as well. Once Burning Rubber begins, there's no way to cut it short.

Ka-Boom

Boom Time!

Maximum Health	250
Speed	60
Armor	12
Critical Hit	80
Elemental Power	39

Ka-Boom hails from an ancient volcanic island known as Munitions Forge, where he and his people crafted machinery that was used all throughout Skylands. But the ruthless Captain Ironbeard wanted the forge for himself so he could build an unstoppable pirate armada. With a fleet of pirate ships approaching, Ka-Boom went to work, creating the greatest anti-pirate weapon ever forged—The Boom Cannon! When Ironbeard arrived with his invaders, Ka-Boom met them at the edge of the docks with his cannon lowered, still smoldering red hot from having just come out of the fire. One by one, he sank their ships until Captain Ironbeard finally retreated. Now as a valued member of the Trap Team, Ka-Boom uses his Red Hot Traptanium Cannon to blast evil in the broadsides!

Basic Attack Notes

▶ **Traptanium Cannonballs**
A single giant cannonball attack that can be charged for double damage after upgrading to Cannon Charge.

▶ **Cannon Jump**
Leap towards enemies causing a large damaging explosion and create a fiery earthquake with Jumpquake.

▶ **Mortar Strike**
Cannonballs land where the white crosshairs are placed. This can be held to charge and release them all at once.

Upgrade Paths

Cannonball Runner

Bouncing Balls and Super Bouncing Balls add a ricochet effect that bounces the cannonballs off walls and between enemies. In closed off areas these powers can send shots bouncing around like pinballs. Triple Shot launches three cannonballs at once that spread out in a wide pattern providing more long-range coverage. The increase in shots and the bouncing abilities allow Ka-Boom to continually fire off cannonballs and overwhelm most enemies before they can even touch him. Each cannonball does a fair amount of damage but what makes them very effective is their speed and the pure number that can be on-screen at once.

Jumping Juggernaut

Fire Fly burns all enemies in the path of the jump while Big Air adds a larger area of effect and stun ability. Both of these add a good amount of damage, but Triple Jump makes the most of attack by allowing three jumps in a row. Cannon Jump is Ka-Boom's single most powerful attack and with the added upgrades he can jump in and out of enemy hordes, leaving a deadly fire trail behind. The attack is most effective at mid range as the initial landing attack does the most damage. Jump from enemy to enemy to do heavy damage and leave the flames behind to finish them off.

◯ SOUL GEM ABILITY

MISSILE RAIN — 4000

Mortar Strike attack now rains down fiery Traptanium Missiles. Prerequisite: Find Ka-Boom's Soul Gem in CH 18: The Ultimate Weapon

The only downside to Mortar Strike is that Ka-Boom is unable to move while targeting enemies. The best time to use this attack is when he is in a safe place or at long range where enemies can't reach him. Send a big barrage of missiles into a group of enemies to wipe them out.

Basic Attacks

TRAPTANIUM CANNONBALLS
Press **Attack 1** to shoot Traptanium Cannonballs.

CANNON JUMP
Press **Attack 2** to blast the ground and leap towards an enemy, leaving a big explosion.

Upgrades

JUMPQUAKE — 500
Cannon Jump now creates an earthquake that damages nearby enemies over time.

MORTAR STRIKE — 700
Press **Attack 3** to fire exploding cannonballs into the air, Hold **Attack 3** to aim your shot.

THE LONG RANGER — 900
Increases the range of the Mortar Strike attack.

CANNON CHARGE — 1200
Hold **Attack 1** to charge up the cannon and release to fire a more powerful Traptanium Cannonball.

Cannonball Runner
Improve Traptanium Cannonball attacks.

BOUNCING BALLS — 1700
Traptanium Cannonballs ricochet off of walls.

SUPER BOUNCING BALLS — 2200
Traptanium Cannonballs bounce between enemies.

TRIPLE SHOT — 3000
Shoot 3 Traptanium Cannonballs at once.

Jumping Juggernaut
Improve Cannon Jump attacks.

FIRE FLY — 1700
Scorch all enemies in the path of Ka-Boom's Cannon Jump.

BIG AIR — 2200
Cannon Jump has a greater area of effect and stuns enemies.

TRIPLE JUMP — 3000
Can do 3 Cannon Jump attacks in a row without having to rest.

Small Fry

Crash and Burn!

Maximum Health	330
Speed	60
Armor	6
Critical Hit	20
Elemental Power	25

Basic Attack Notes

▶ ## Brawl
Rapid punches that propel Small Fry forward unless he's hitting something.

▶ ## Heated
Keep Heated whenever possible. Don't go into fights without building Heat first.

▶ ## The Horn and The Hog
Good for closing distance quickly, especially when his motorcycle is involved.

Upgrade Paths

Brawler

The Brawler Path punishes enemies limited to melee attacks. Remember to stay Heated as often as possible. The more Heated Small Fry is, the more swings he gets from Hot Hands. Spiked Up is a basic damage increase that makes his punches more effective. Temperature Tantrum damages nearby enemies giving him the ability to hurt enemies in a slightly larger area. The Brawler Path does not require much thinking. Always get Heated before entering a battle and let the fists fly!

Hot Shop

Small Fry's Hot Shop Path is a big help when dealing with ranged opponents. Born to Ride and Hot Rod both provide a damage increase to make the attack even more effective. Use hit and run tactics to dart in and out of enemy groups. The upgraded Horn and The Hog is the best way to reach ranged enemies quickly and escape before they can retaliate. Crash and Burn is his only long-range attack but it is tough to aim when tossing a motorcycle. Stay on the bike and charge through enemies using superior speed to catch them off guard.

⬤ SOUL GEM ABILITY

MADNESS MAXED   4000

Press **Attack 2** rapidly to make Small Fry even more heated. So angry!

Madness Maxed builds Small Fry's heat from orange to yellow. Heated affects almost everything Small Fry does. He rides his hog when heated, he does more damage when heated, and so on. Madness Maxed is a priority purchase. Get it as soon as you can!

Basic Attacks

BRAWL

Press **Attack 1** to punch nearby enemies. Speed and damage of punches is increased depending on heat.

HEATED

Press **Attack 2** repeatedly to smash the ground and increase heat level.

Upgrades

HORN AND THE HOG   500

Press **Attack 3** to dash forward, dealing damage to enemies in the way. When heated, Small Fry jumps on a motorcycle to deal damage to nearby enemies.

BUILT TOUGH   700

Health is increased. Probably from punching the ground so much...

FIRED UP   900

Press **Attack 2** repeatedly to throw a tantrum and become heated. Tantrums now have increased range and damage.

MOLTEN FURY   1200

All attacks do increased damage when heated.

Brawler Path

HOT HANDS   1700

Hold **Attack 1** to rapidly punch nearby enemies and release heat.

SPIKED UP   2200

New metal gloves causes Hot Hands to do increased damage.

TEMPERATURE TANTRUM   3000

Nearby enemies take damage while Small Fry is heated.

Hot Shop Path

BORN TO RIDE   1700

The Horn and The Hog will always summon a molten motorcycle.

HOT ROD   2200

All attacks with the motorcycle do increased damage.

CRASH AND BURN   3000

Small Fry throws the motorcycle at the end of a dash, causing a massive explosion that damages nearby enemies. Who's paying for that...?

Torch

Fire It Up!

Maximum Health	230
Speed	60
Armor	12
Critical Hit	40
Elemental Power	25

Torch's childhood was spent working with her grandfather as a dragon keeper, where she helped tend to a stable of dragons that protected her village. One year, an evil Snow Dragon unleashed a terrible blizzard that trapped her entire homeland inside a massive ice glacier! Torch was the only one to escape. Having always been fearless, she set out at once to rescue the villagers and her dragons from their chilly fate. Armed with her Firespout Flamethrower, she fought hard through the treacherous conditions and bravely defeated the Snow Dragon in an epic battle. After the village was free from its icy doom, Torch returned home to find her grandfather missing. The only token left behind was his lucky flaming horseshoe. Now as a member of the Skylanders, Torch wields her powerful flamethrower as well as her lucky horseshoe in hopes it will one day lead her to the grandfather she lost.

Basic Attack Notes

▶ ## Blazing Bellows

Press and hold to shoot continuous flames that can be upgraded to a Blue Flame for extra damage and piercing effect.

▶ ## Flaming Horseshoes

Pitch a giant horseshoe that sticks to foes and can cause extra damage from fire when used with Pyro Pendant.

▶ ## Flaming Hair Whip

A circular attack of flaming hair the burns and knocks back enemies that are in close.

Upgrade Paths

Forged in Flames

Hair's Getting Long is a great power to use when surrounded due to its knock back from Flaming Hair Whip plus the extra damage and range from this upgrade. The other two upgrades on this path increase the damage of Blazing Bellows. It gets a direct two-fold increase with Double Barrel Bellows. The other upgrade, Scorched Earth Policy, adds a low amount of damage to anyone that walks into the residual flames. Use Flaming Horseshoes at long range and possibly Flaming Hair for very close contact, but all other situations can be taken care of by the boosted Blazing Bellows.

Maid of Metal

Extra Hot Shoes and Fireworks Display both increase damage through added time and explosive effects respectively. Hopping Mad Horseshoes brings the giant horseshoes to life and lets it loose on enemies. All of these upgrades increase the damage and functionality of Flaming Horseshoes and going down this path means they should become the primary source of attack. Note that Flaming Horseshoes excels at mid to long range. However, use Flaming Hair Whip if a mob overwhelms you. Also, alternate attacks with Blazing Bellows. It has great damage potential and it further enhances the effectiveness of Flaming Horseshoes nearly acquired powers.

○ SOUL GEM ABILITY

THE INCINERATOR — 4000

Press **Attack 1** rapidly to create the ultimate flamethrower. Prerequisite: Find Torch's Soul Gem in CH 9: Mystic Mill

This attack does almost three times the damage of the regular Blazing Bellows. Once the ultimate flamethrower is activated it continues to stay in effect as long as the attack button is pressed. Movement becomes very slow while this is active but its massive damage roasts anything nearby.

Basic Attacks

BLAZING BELLOWS

Press and hold **Attack 1** to roast enemies with a flamethrower attack.

FLAMING HORSESHOES

Press **Attack 2** to pitch Flaming Horseshoes that stick to enemies.

Upgrades

HEATING UP — 500

Blazing Bellows attack shoots farther and does extra damage.

FLAMING HAIR WHIP — 700

Press **Attack 3** to whip flaming hair around and knock back nearby enemies.

PYRO PENDANT — 900

Enemies with Flaming Horseshoes stuck to them take extra damage from fire.

BLUE FLAME — 1200

Hold **Attack 1** for a little longer and flames turn blue, doing extra damage and going through enemies.

Forged In Flames

Improve Blazing Bellows and Flaming Hair attacks.

SCORCHED EARTH POLICY — 1700

Blazing Bellows attack now sets the ground on fire, damaging anyone who touches it.

HAIR'S GETTING LONG — 2200

Flaming Hair Whip has increased range and does extra damage.

DOUBLE BARREL BELLOWS — 3000

Bigger Blazing Bellows flames.

Maid of Metal

Improve Flaming Horseshoe attacks.

EXTRA HOT SHOES — 1700

Flaming Horseshoes stuck to enemies do additional damage them over time.

FIREWORKS DISPLAY — 2200

Flaming Horseshoes will explode upon wearing off.

HOPPING MAD HORSESHOES — 3000

Use a fire attack on a Flaming Horseshoe and it comes to life, attacking enemies.

Trail Blazer

The Mane Event!

Maximum Health	270
Speed	85
Armor	18
Critical Hit	30
Elemental Power	25

Trail Blazer was always hot tempered, especially when he saw anything as being unfair. One day, he came across another unicorn that was trapped in a net. But it wasn't just any unicorn. It was the mythical Unocorn—a magical creature with a Churro Horn that sprinkled enchanted cinnamon throughout Skylands. Trail Blazer freed it at once. Soon after, the Dark Wizards who had set the trap returned, and were very angry to find their dastardly deed had been thwarted. But Trail Blazer was much more fired up—for it turned out the spicy cinnamon from the Churro Horn had somehow rubbed off on him and mixed with his elemental fire. So he was literally set ablaze with fury! He then ran fiery circles around the wizards, forcing them to flee and never return. After realizing his newfound fury could be used to fight evil everywhere, Trail Blazer sought out the Skylanders, who immediately welcomed him as a member.

Basic Attack Notes

▶ **Fireball**
A fireball attack that hits single foes but can be upgraded twice.

▶ **Roundhouse Kick**
A backwards kick which shoots a fireball and upgrades to Bucking Bronco that adds multiple kicks and fireballs.

▶ **Stampede!**
A charging attack that shoots fire while rushing into enemies.

Upgrade Paths

Equine Excellence

All three attacks get significant upgrades. The Stampede attack adds two flaming forms that greatly increase the area covered in the charge. Kick It Up a Notch is a straightforward boost to the power and duration of the both Roundhouse Kick and Bucking Bronco. These attacks are great up close but keep in mind Bucking Bronco can be difficult to control or aim. Triple Fireballs covers a huge area and is an excellent choice against groups of enemies. Note that the trio of fireballs spreads out fairly wide and covers a lot of ground but they are lobbed a short distance away.

Fireballer

Not His 1st Rodeo extends the time in Bucking Bronco Mode, but more importantly it adds extra flames that increase damage by covering a wider area. Kick It Up a Notch further extends the duration of Roadhouse Kick and Bucking Bronco plus the damage boost maxes out the attack. These two upgrades work together to increase the effectiveness of the kicking attacks at close and mid range. Bouncing Fireballs extend not only the range of the attack but the flaming shots damage several enemies in a straight line following the bouncing fireball.

⬤ SOUL GEM ABILITY

HEAT WAVE — 4000

Hold **Attack 1** to charge up the Fireball attack, then release for a wave of fire. Prerequisite: Find Trail Blazer's Soul Gem in CH 13: The Future of Skylands

Unlike the Fireball attacks, the wave of fire built up from this ability travels through enemies. This move is best used as a mid-range weapon since the wave disappears after a while.

Basic Attacks

FIREBALL

Press **Attack 1** to shoot Fireballs.

ROUNDHOUSE KICK

Press **Attack 2** to deliver a Roundhouse Kick.

Upgrades

BRING THE HEAT — 500

Fireball attack does extra damage.

STAMPEDE! — 700

Press **Attack 3** for a charge attack, shooting fire out of your horn.

BUCKING BRONCO — 900

Hold **Attack 2** to go into Bucking Bronco Mode, kicking in every direction.

FUEL THE FIRE — 1200

All attacks do extra damage.

Equine Excellence
Improve Stampede attacks.

FLAMING FORMS — 1700

Two flaming forms accompany you during the Stampede attack.

FIREWALKER — 2200

Stampede attack leaves behind a trail of fiery footprints that damage enemies.

TRIPLE FIREBALLS — 3000

Shoot three Fireballs at a time.

Fireballer
Improve Fireball attacks.

KICK IT UP A NOTCH — 1700

Roundhouse Kick and Bucking Bronco attacks have increased power and duration.

BOUNCING FIREBALLS — 2200

Fireballs now bounce along the ground and travel further.

NOT HIS 1ST RODEO — 3000

Hold **Attack 2** to stay in Bucking Bronco Mode for longer and kick up extra flame dust.

Weeruptor

Born to Burn!

Maximum Health	290
Speed	50
Armor	18
Critical Hit	30
Elemental Power	25

Basic Attack Notes

▶ **Lava Lob**

A fast attack but with relatively short range. It is great for hitting opponents above Weeruptor.

▶ **Eruption**

This attack has to build up for a bit before it explodes, hitting enemies in a small radius.

▶ **Magma Ball**

A powerful attack that moves slowly and can be tricky to aim.

Upgrade Paths

Magmantor

If you decide to pursue the Magmantor Path, the Lava Lob gets much better. Keep in mind the lava balls are quick but they have a high arching path with limited range. To help remedy that, Heavy Duty Plasma increases the range of the attack, making it more viable as a long-range tactic. Once you unlock Beast of Conflagration, the damage of the power is increased by about 60%! For even more damage, get Lava Blob Bomb to add splash damage to nearby enemies, affecting more foes at once.

Volcanor

Eruption is a tricky power to master. It requires you to charge the attack for a second or two, which leaves Weeruptor vulnerable. Once the magma has erupted, it can hit enemies within range multiple times. The most important upgrade for Eruption is Quick Eruption. Quick Eruption makes the power much more useful since Weeruptor barely needs to slow down to release a powerful eruption full of seeping magma, volcanoes, and magma balls. The other two powers on this path each increase damage. The boost in speed and damage on this path turn Eruption into an excellent weapon for crowd control.

⬤ SOUL GEM ABILITY

MEGA MAGMA BALLS   4000

Shoot up to three Magma Balls at a time that do extra damage.

Mega Magma Balls dramatically improves Weeruptor's regular Magma Balls attack. The balls are about twice the size and do about 25% more damage. They're still slow and hard to aim, but since the balls are bigger it's easier to hit enemies.

Basic Attacks

LAVA LOB

Press **Attack 1** to lob blobs of lava at your enemies.

ERUPTION

Press **Attack 2** to erupt into a pool of lava, damaging enemies all around you.

Upgrades

BIG BLOB LAVA THROW   500

Lava Blob attack gets bigger and does increased damage.

FIERY REMAINS   700

Lava Blobs leave behind pools of flame when they hit the ground.

ERUPTION—FLYING TEPHRA   900

Lava balls shoot out while performing the Eruption attack.

MAGMA BALL   1200

Press **Attack 3** to spit out Magma Balls.

Magmantor

Further develop Weeruptor's Lava Blobs and Magma Balls.

HEAVY DUTY PLASMA   1700

Lava Blobs bounce and travel further.

LAVA BLOB BOMB   2200

Lava Blobs explode and damage nearby enemies.

BEAST OF CONFLAGRATION   3000

Lava Blobs do increased damage in the form of a fiery beast.

Volcanor

Further develop Weeruptor's Eruption attacks.

QUICK ERUPTION   1700

It takes much less time to perform an Eruption attack.

PYROXYSMAL SUPER ERUPTION   2200

Eruption attack does increased damage.

REVENGE OF PROMETHEUS   3000

Eruption causes small volcanoes to form, doing extra damage. Prerequisite: Pyroxysmal Super Eruption

Wildfire

Bringing the Heat!

Maximum Health	330
Speed	60
Armor	30
Critical Hit	30
Elemental Power	25

Wildfire was once a young lion of the Fire Claw Clan, about to enter into the Rite of Infernos—a test of survival in the treacherous fire plains. However, because he was made of gold, he was treated as an outcast and not allowed to participate. But this didn't stop him. That night, Wildfire secretly followed the path of the other lions, carrying only his father's enchanted shield. Soon he found them cornered by a giant flame scorpion. Using the shield, he protected the group from the beast's enormous stinging tail, giving them time to safely escape. And though Wildfire was injured in the fight, his father's shield magically changed him—magnifying the strength that was already in his heart—making him the mightiest of his clan. Now part of the Trap Team, Wildfire uses his enormous Traptanium-bonded shield to defend any and all who need it!

Basic Attack Notes

▶ **Traptanium Shield Bash**
Has a downward slam attack and gains proximity damage plus protection from Heat Shield.

▶ **Chains of Fire**
Burns enemies as well as pulling them in closer.

▶ **Fire Roar**
A high damage mid range flaming breath attack.

Upgrade Paths

Shield Slasher

Searing Slam is a great desperation move to use when feeling overwhelmed by a crowd of enemies. It hits all foes in the immediate area for decent damage. The other two powers on this path are combo enhancements for the Traptanium Shield Bash. Burning Bash is best against strong single enemies or foes in a straight line due to final downward strike at the end of the combo. On the other hand, Fire Spin ends with a circular fire attack that is very effective against a bunch of swarming enemies.

Chain Champion

Lots of Chains can pull five enemies at once and No Escape increases the area of effect, allowing Wildfire to become an enemy magnet. The goal behind these powers is to pull enemies in close to unleash a Traptanium Shield Bash combo or use the Fire Roar. Blazing Breath gives extra damage to Fire Roar and it's a great choice after pulling in foes. However, the upgrade also significantly increases range—providing Wildfire with a powerful burst attack from close to mid range.

⬤ SOUL GEM ABILITY

LION FORM	4000

Hold **Attack 1** to enter Heatshield Mode, then press **Attack 1** again to transform into a wild, Fire Lion. Prerequisite: Find Wildfire's Soul Gem in CH 8: Telescope Towers

Transform into a powerful charging Fire Lion that races along on all fours. Use **Attack 2** to perform a leaping attack that causes massive damage to a large group of enemies. Unfortunately, the attack can only be used once and it returns Wildfire to normal.

Basic Attacks

TRAPTANIUM SHIELD BASH

Press **Attack 1** for a single Shield Bash attack. Press **Attack 1**, **Attack 1** and **Attack 1**, **Attack 1**, **Attack 1** for Shield Bash combos.

CHAINS OF FIRE

Press **Attack 2** to summon Chains of Fire that not only burn but pull enemies closer.

Upgrades

HEAT SHIELD	500

Hold **Attack 1** to use the Heat Shield for protection and damage to nearby enemies.

EXTRA CHAINS	700

Chains of Fire can now pull four enemies at once.

FIRE ROAR	900

Press **Attack 3** to unleash a Fire Roar attack.

HOTTER HEAT SHIELD	1200

Heatshield now burns brighter and does extra damage. Prequisite: Heat Shield

Shield Slasher
Improve Traptanium Shield Bash attacks.

BURNING BASH	1700

Press **Attack 1**, **Attack 1** HOLD **Attack 2** for a Heat Wave combo.

FIRE SPIN	2200

Press **Attack 1**, **Attack 1**, HOLD **Attack 3** for a Fire Spin combo.

SEARING SLAM	3000

Press **Attack 1** in the air for a Searing Slam attack.

Chain Champion
Improve Chains of Fire attacks..

LOTS OF CHAINS	1700

Chains of Fire can now pull five enemies at once

BLAZING BREATH	2200

Fire Roar has longer range and does extra damage.

NO ESCAPE!	5000

Chains of Fire has a wider area of effect and can pull five enemies at once. Prerequisite: Lots of Chains

Barkley

Be Afraid of the Bark!

Maximum Health	430
Speed	40
Armor	24
Critical Hit	40
Elemental Power	60

Basic Attack Notes

▷ **Shockwave Slam**
A powerful attack that has a good area of effect from shockwaves.

▷ **Sequoia Stampede**
Charge through enemies and obstacles.

▷ **Photosynthesis Cannon**
A projectile attack that can be upgraded to fire three burst shots.

Upgrade Paths

Treefolk Charger

Sequoia Stampede starts off as a useful ability mostly for the extra speed it provides. However, on this path it gains many extra benefits; including damage as good as Barkley's slams, and speed that makes him one of the fastest Minis in the game. Lightfooted and Ultimate Stampede boost the attack to maximum damage. The Titanic Elbow Drop upgrade inflicts massive damage on any enemy unfortunate enough to get caught in the seismic blast where Barkley lands.

Lumbering Laserer

Photosynthesis Cannon is not as damaging as Barkley's Slam attacks, but it makes up for lack of power with massive range. A fully upgraded Cannon with the Lumbering Laserer Path empowers the weapon to wreak havoc on the battlefield. Super-Charged Vaporizer is one of the most damaging powers in the game. It can be hard to hit enemies with it, but even the mightiest foes fall to the blast. This works in conjunction with the Pod Maker power. After Barkley defeats an enemy with Super-Charged Vaporizer they turn into Plant Pods which explode, dealing even more damage to nearby foes.

⬤ SOUL GEM ABILITY

WOODPECKER PAL · 4000

A woodpecker buddy joins Barkley in battle.

This fun Soul Gem gives Barkley a woodpecker that hangs out on his back. When there are enemies nearby, the woodpecker swoops down and attacks for a moderate amount of damage.

Basic Attacks

SHOCKWAVE SLAM

Press **Attack 1** to slam the ground with massive fists, causing shockwaves.

SEQUOIA STAMPEDE

Press and hold **Attack 2** to charge through enemies and obstacles.

Upgrades

PHOTOSYNTHESIS CANNON · 500

Press **Attack 3** to harness the power of the sun and shoot light beams.

BIG THORN SHOCKWAVE SLAM · 700

Hold **Attack 1** for a bigger, more powerful Shockwave Slam.

SUPER STAMPEDE · 900

Sequoia Stampede attack does increased damage.

TREEFOLK TRIPLESHOT · 1200

Photosynthesis Cannon fires triple burst shots.
Prerequisite: Photosynthesis Cannon

Treefolk Charger

Provides more upgrades for the Sequoia Stampede attacks.

TITANIC ELBOW DROP · 1700

Press **Attack 1** while charging to perform one serious elbow drop move.

LIGHTFOOTED · 2200

Charge longer and faster, doing more damage in the process.

ULTIMATE STAMPEDE · 3000

Sequoia Stampede attack does maximum damage.

Lumbering Laserer

Provides more upgrades for the Photosynthesis Cannon.

SUPER-CHARGED VAPORIZER · 1700

Hold down **Attack 3** to charge up the Photosynthesis Cannon for more damage.

SUN SKEWER · 2200

Photosynthesis Cannon blasts through enemies and explodes for more damage.

THE POD MAKER · 3000

Vaporized enemies turn into exploding plant pods.
Prerequisite: Super-Charged Vaporizer

Bushwhack

Axe to the Max!

Maximum Health	290
Speed	60
Armor	18
Critical Hit	60
Elemental Power	39

Born to a race of tree elves who were protectors of the rich Arcadian Timberland, Bushwack was supposed to be a ranger. But being the smallest of his clan, he was sent deep into the woods by the Chieftain to study with Arbo, known for helping the Skylanders rebuild the Core of Light. The tree spirit looked beyond Bushwhack's size, and seeing that he had the heart of a warrior, taught him many secrets. Arbo even gifted him with an enchanted axe. So when a legion of Lumberjack Trolls invaded the forest and overpowered the elves, it was Bushwhack who set out to stop them. Drawing out the trolls, he used his enchanted axe and knowledge of the forest to capture them and destroy their tree cutting machines. Afterward, Bushwhack not only was made a ranger, but a Skylander. As part of the Trap Team, he now uses his Traptanium axe to whack evil wherever it grows!

Basic Attack Notes

▶ Traptanium Axe

Can perform a combo by holding the last attack and gets an upgrade leaving a thorny trail that damages enemies.

▶ Mystic Acorn

A long-range attack that stuns and can explode when upgraded with Nut Grenade!

▶ Headbash

A powerful leaping attack that damages anything in the immediate area.

Upgrade Paths

Axe Avenger

All the powers on this path upgrade the Traptanium Axe, and An Axe to Grind is a basic damage boost. However, the most impressive upgrades are from Combo Attacks. Head First is the best choice against really tough enemies that are clustered together. The Spin and Slash combo ends in a spinning assault that can be steered slightly to guide it into more enemies. Go Nuts! further improves the Spin and Slash combo with Mystic Acorns that shoot out in all directions. This combo is the best choice to use when surrounded by a group of enemies.

Armor Awesomeness

Bushwhack can heal himself at a good pace using Bush's Shack. The healing hut does very little damage, and he is still susceptible to harm, so perform healing in between battles. Primal Warrior further reduces damage and adds more power to Headbash. After increasing damage from the Primal Warrior, Spring Forward becomes even more effective by adding a damaging dash that hurts anything in its path. The Traptanium Axe is still a good weapon for quick attacks, but the dash and heavy damage from Headbash are a pretty obvious choice for dealing a lot of damage even at mid-range.

⬤ SOUL GEM ABILITY

TIMBER! `4000`

Jump and hold **Attack 1** to plant a giant tree, which is then cut down to smash whatever's below. Prerequisite: Find Bushwhack's Soul Gem in CH 3: Chompy Mountains

Create a giant tree with an in-air slam attack, and when it is cut down, it does devastating damage to whatever the tree lands on. The attack takes a while to launch, but the massive damage and large area of effect is worth the wait!

Basic Attacks

TRAPTANIUM AXE

Press **Attack 1** to swing the Traptanium Axe.
Press **Attack 1**, **Attack 1**, HOLD **Attack 1** for a combo attack.

MYSTIC ACORN

Press **Attack 2** to throw a Mystic Acorn that stuns enemies.

Upgrades

HEADBASH `500`

Press **Attack 3** for a powerful Headbash move, damaging anything nearby.

NUT GRENADE! `700`

Acorns now explode on impact, doing more damage.

IN A NUT SHELL `900`

Get some new armor, taking reduced damage.

THORN TRAIL `1200`

Traptanium Axe attack now leaves a trail of thorns that damage enemies.

Axe Avenger

Improve Traptanium Axe attacks.

AN AXE TO GRIND `1700`

Traptanium Axe attack does extra damage.

COMBO ATTACKS `2200`

Press **Attack 1**, **Attack 1**, HOLD **Attack 2** for the Spin and Slash combo.

Press **Attack 1**, **Attack 1**, HOLD **Attack 3** for Head First combo.

GO NUTS! `3000`

Keep holding **Attack 2** after a Spin and Slash combo to shoot nuts in all directions. Prerequisite: An Axe to Grind

Armor Awesomeness

Improve armor for protection and attack.

BUSH'S SHACK `1700`

Hold **Attack 1** to create a leafy hut for protection and healing.

PRIMAL WARRIOR `2200`

Get new armor, taking reduced damage and doing extra damage with the Headbash attack.

SPRING FORWARD `3000`

Hold **Attack 3** to dash forward and perform a super Headbash attack.

Food Fight

Eat This!

Maximum Health	260
Speed	60
Armor	18
Critical Hit	30
Elemental Power	46

Food Fight does more than just play with his food, he battles with it! This tough little Veggie Warrior is the byproduct of a troll food experiment gone wrong. When the Troll Farmers Guild attempted to fertilize their soil with gunpowder, they got more than a super snack—they got an all-out Food Fight! Rising from the ground, he led the neighborhood Garden Patrol to victory. Later, he went on to defend his garden home against a rogue army of gnomes after they attempted to wrap the Asparagus people in bacon! His courage caught the eye of Master Eon, who decided that this was one veggie lover he needed on his side as a valued member of the Skylanders. When it comes to Food Fight, it's all you can eat for evil!

Basic Attack Notes

▶ **Tomato Launcher**
Exploding tomatoes can be upgraded with Green Thump to create plants that provide a powered-up shot.

▶ **Blooms of Doom**
Create artichoke traps that explode after a short time causing heavy damage.

▶ **Zucchini Blast**
A short-range attack that does a lot of damage in a wide area.

Upgrade Paths

Tomatologist

Heavy Harvest turns tomatoes into even more powerful projectiles. HeirBOOM Tomatoes and Bad Aftertaste work together to use the Blooms of Doom to explode Tomato Plants that damage enemies over time. Use the Tomato Launcher to constantly shoot foes or simply to create plants. Blooms of Doom deals heavy damage, and when not under attack, use them near Tomato Plants to make deadly traps. To deal with long range foes create a few plants to power up the Tomato Launcher and open fire.

Bloomer and Boomer

Zucchini Blast was already a heavy damage attack, but Special Squash adds a charge ability that does nearly double the damage. Keep in mind that this attack covers a lot of area but only at close range and it also has a bit of a delay between shots. Zucchini Goo adds an important slow down effect to prevent enemies swarming up close. Use 'Choke Chain's detonating ability to space out the Blooms of Doom so each one can trigger the others but also cover the most amount of ground. This added power is ideal for setting massive traps and even useful when on the run.

⚪ SOUL GEM ABILITY

THAT'S HOW I ROLL 4000
Hold **Attack 1** to charge up a Super Tomato, release **Attack 1** to ride it and run over enemies. Prerequisite: Find Food Fight's Soul Gem in CH 2: Know-It-All Island

It takes a while to charge up the Super Tomato but it is a sight to be seen as Food Fight runs on top of a giant tomato, crushing enemies beneath him. Charge the attack in a safe place and roll over smaller enemies.

Basic Attacks

TOMATO LAUNCHER
Press **Attack 1** to launch exploding tomatoes.

BLOOMS OF DOOM
Press **Attack 2** to plant artichoke traps, which also explode!

Upgrades

EXTRA RIPE TOMATOES 500
Tomatoes do more damage.

GREEN THUMB 700
Tomatoes that hit the ground grow into plants. Collect them for more powerful shots.

ZUCCHINI BLAST 900
Press **Attack 3** to deliver a Zucchini Blast. Does heavy damage over a wide area.

BLOOMS OF BIGGER DOOM 1200
Blooms of Doom make bigger explosions.

Tomatologist
Improves Tomato Launcher attacks.

HEAVY HARVEST 1700
Tomatoes picked up from plants are bigger and do even MORE damage.

HEIRBOOM TOMATOES 2200
Detonate Tomato Plants with a Zucchini Blast.

BAD AFTERTASTE 3000
Enemies damaged by exploding Tomato plants will take damage over time. Prerequisite: HeirBOOM Tomatoes

Bloomer and Boomer
Improves Zucchini Blast and Blooms of Doom attacks.

SPECIAL SQUASH 1700
Hold **Attack 3** to charge up the Zucchini Blast for extra damage.

ZUCCHINI GOO 2200
Enemies hit by the Zucchini Blast are slowed down.

CHOKE CHAIN 3000
Blooms of Doom detonate each other.

High Five
Buzz Off!

Maximum Health	270
Speed	60
Armor	6
Critical Hit	70
Elemental Power	53

Growing up, High Five was one of the most skilled racers of all the dragonflies. But as the fifth son of the Royal High Flying Dragonflies, he was not allowed to enter any of the racing tournaments that took place each year because of his age. Instead he was forced to watch from the sidelines as his four older brothers competed for the coveted Trophy of Sparx, which legend has said holds magical properties. One year, during the biggest racing event of the season, High Five learned that the Troll Racing Team had stolen the valuable trophy and were going to use the race to cover their escape. He quickly took action, jumping into the race and using his amazing flying skills to weave and dodge his way to the front of the pack, where he caught up to the trolls and brought them down. For his actions, High Five was given the Trophy of Sparx. Even more importantly, he was made a Skylander, where he now helps protect Skylands from any evildoers!

Basic Attack Notes

▶ **Poison Pellets**

Can be shot one at a time or in rapid fire, plus it can leave behind a poisonous cloud when upgraded.

▶ **Buzz Dash**

A speedy dash attack darts past enemies spinning them around.

▶ **Fly Slam**

A powerful slam attack that can be done in air and can be upgraded to a charge attack that does more damage for HP.

Upgrade Paths

Pollen Prince

Start out with Cloud Control to get five Poison Clouds at once that do more damage and move faster. Next, get extra damage with extra large clouds from Power Clouds. High Five's quick shot speed can now pepper enemies from afar and fill an entire area with large damaging Poisonous Clouds. After filling the screen with purple clouds use the Buzz 'Em Up Power to dash through the clouds to make them even more powerful and extend their life.

Speedy Slammer

Fly Slam receives two upgrades on this path. Spin Cycle makes the most of the damaging attack by sucking in enemies. Fly Slam can be charged to do massive damage and now this extends its use by sweeping foes into the damage radius. Slam Apples is a welcomed health boost to the draining Fly Slam attack and reduced the HP cost making it usable more often. Buzz Dash can be used continuously with Buzz Buzz Buzz. The speedy attack can be used to run into groups of enemies or simply to retreat to set up a charged Fly Slam attack.

◯ SOUL GEM ABILITY

ORGANIC SLAM APPLES 4000

Fly Slam Apples heal more HP. Prerequisite: Find High Five's Soul Gem in CH 10: The Secret of Sewers of Supreme Stink

Fly Slam can be charged up to do massive damage but it costs HP. However, with this Soul Gem ability the apples that appear after the slam heal even more HP. The boost in HP makes the attack a great option as the apples can replenish nearly all HP that was lost.

Basic Attacks

POISON PELLETS

Press **Attack 1** to shoot Poison Pellets. Hold **Attack 1** for rapid fire.

BUZZ DASH

Press **Attack 2** for a speedy dash attack.

Upgrades

POISON CLOUD 500

Poison Pellets attack leaves behind a poisonous cloud, damaging nearby enemies.

FLY SLAM 700

Press **Attack 3** to slam down on enemies around you.

BUZZ CHARGE 900

Hold **Attack 2** to charge up a stronger Buzz Dash.

BUZZERKER OVERDRIVE 1200

For the cost of HP, hold **Attack 3** to REALLY power up the Fly Slam. Also move faster with lower HP. Prerequisite: Fly Slam

Pollen Prince

Improve Poison Pellets attacks.

CLOUD CONTROL 1700

Have up to five Poison Clouds active at a time, moving faster and doing more damage.

BUZZ 'EM UP 2200

Buzz Dash through Poison Clouds to power them up and extend their life.

POWER CLOUDS 3000

Extra big Poison Clouds do extra big damage.

Speedy Slammer

Improve Buzz Dash and Fly Slam attacks.

SPIN CYCLE 1700

While holding **Attack 3**, enemies will be sucked up into the Fly Slam zone.

BUZZ BUZZ BUZZ 2200

Hold **Attack 2** for consecutive Buzz Dashes.

SLAM APPLES 3000

Hold **Attack 3** to charge up the Fly Slam attack even further and release apples that heal you.

Sure Shot Shroomboom

He Shoots, He Spores!

Maximum Health	260
Speed	60
Armor	18
Critical Hit	20
Elemental Power	25

Shroomboom was most unfortunate to have been born in a pizza topping garden belonging to Kaos. Growing up among his fellow fungi, he knew it was only a matter of time before a late night craving would bring about their demise. So Shroomboom took a twig and a strand of spider web and made a slingshot. One by one, he launched all of his friends over the garden fence before flinging himself over to join them. Then he guided them all to the edge of the island and leapt to freedom, using his mushroom cap to catch a friendly breeze. Now as a member of the Skylanders, Shroomboom continues to perform courageous deeds... but he can be hard to find on pizza night.

Basic Attack Notes

▶ **Slingshot**
Lob attack that bounces around until contacting a target, or three seconds pass.

▶ **Mushroom Ring**
Shroomboom can pass between mushrooms without destroying them, even with Self-Slingshot.

▶ **Launch Paratroopers**
Hold Attack 3 to launch rapidly, but walk slowly.

Upgrade Paths

Barrier Boost

The Barrier Boost Path turns Mushroom Ring into a powerful defensive tool, and Shroomboom into a tough nut to crack. He can Launch Paratroopers or use Self-Slingshot without removing the barrier. When every upgrade is active, Shroomboom can remain safely behind a large ring of mushrooms that emit a damaging cloud, and even escape underground should the need arise.

Paramushroom Promotion

The Paramushroom Promotion Path boosts Launch Paratroopers and gives Slingshot an extra, explosive kick. Go with this path if you prefer to play Shroomboom on the move. You're surrendering significant defensive upgrades, so be aggressive. You need to overwhelm enemies, so fill the area with Paratroopers and bouncing, exploding mushrooms.

⬤ SOUL GEM ABILITY

SELF-SLINGSHOT — 4000
Hold **Attack 1** to slingshot Shroomboom towards enemies.

The old command (press **Attack 2** while holding **Attack 1**) brings up the Self-Slingshot quicker (and the mushrooms from High Spore!) if you're in a rush. There's no delay for firing Shroomboom, either. As soon as the slingshot appears, he's ready to go.

Basic Attacks

SLINGSHOT
Press **Attack 1** to shoot exploding mushrooms.

MUSHROOM RING
Press **Attack 2** to spawn a ring of mushrooms that damage enemies.

Upgrades

LAUNCH PARATROOPERS — 500
Press **Attack 3** to shoot mushroom paratroopers who drop down from the sky.

SUPER SHROOMS — 700
Mushroom Ring gets bigger.

BIGGER BOOMSHROOMS — 900
Hold **Attack 1** to charge up a giant exploding mushroom.

BOUNCING BOOMSHROOMS — 1200
Exploding mushrooms bounce on the ground and do increased damage.

Barrier Boost
Upgrades Mushroom Ring for better protection.

SPORE POWER — 1700
Mushroom Ring creates a damaging spore cloud.

ULTIMATE RING — 2200
Mushroom Ring is the biggest it gets.

BACK TO THE BEGINNING — 3000
Hold **Attack 2** to remain underground, where you can move around freely.

Paramushroom Promotion
Provides more upgrades for the Paratrooper and Slingshot attacks.

LOCK 'N' LOAD — 1700
Can fire exploding mushrooms faster that do increased damage.

FUNGAL INFESTATION — 2200
Mushroom Paratroopers stick to enemies and do damage over time.

PARATROOPER INVASION — 3000
Shoot three Mushroom Paratroopers at once.

WOW POW!

HIGH SPORE! — 5000
Hold **Attack 1** to create mushroom bumpers and play pinball with enemies. Prerequisite: Self-Slingshot

The mushroom bumpers appear close to Shroomboom's location, so you need to lure enemies in close to use High Spore!. Blue mushrooms are good for two bounces, yellow mushrooms for one.

Tuff Luck

It's Your Lucky Day!

Maximum Health	310
Speed	85
Armor	48
Critical Hit	80
Elemental Power	39

For many years, Tuff Luck and her tribe guarded the Fortunata Springs—the source of all good luck in Skylands. Though it was hidden in the Random Canyons, which move without warning to cover the hidden entrance to the magical waters, minions of Kaos located the springs and flew in sponge-tankers to drain every drop of the lucky liquid. Fortunately, Tuff Luck was patrolling the area and immediately jumped into action when she saw what was happening. Between her awesome skill and unbeatable good luck, she single-handedly drove off the minions. She then drank from the magical waters, as was custom for her tribe. Sensing a greater calling, Tuff Luck decided to leave her tribe to join the Trap Team, where she could do even more to help protect Skylands. Armed with her Traptanium Warblades, she always beats the odds—and evil—at every turn!

Basic Attack Notes

▶ **Traptanium Warblades**

A slicing attack that can be used three times in a combo and gains an energy wave ability from Glaive Wave.

▶ **Pounce Mode**

Become invisible in Pounce Mode then leap out to attack, plus the Clover Patches do damage.

▶ **Warblade Stab**

A leaping attack that can be upgraded to control where Warblade Stab lands.

Upgrade Paths

Pouncy Pouncer

Clover Patches become a lot more effective on this path. Poison Ivy adds more damage to the green patches and can be used as a trap or simply to re-enter Pounce Mode. On the other hand, using 4-Leafed Clover allows the clover to heal Tuff Luck when entering Pounce Mode. To further reinforce the effectiveness of Pounce Mode, Powerful Pounce adds extra damage when springing out to attack. The plan on this path is to keep using Pounce Mode to create clover patches to take advantage of its abilities. However, don't ignore the Warblade Stab that is her most damaging attack and can be launched from Pounce Mode as well.

Warblade Whacker

Waive Goodbye is a straightforward increase to the Traptanium Warbaldes, adding some needed damage to the already extended range this attack has. The other two upgrades are devastating combos made to take advantage of that damage boost. Lucky Spin ends with a whirling attack that links right into Pounce Mode. Hoping into the clover is a great way to escape after this combo or set up a surprise attack. When enemies are closer together use the Wingin' Warblade combo to deliver a powerful Warblade Stab at the end. This combo is also a great choice to use on very tough single enemies.

⬤ SOUL GEM ABILITY

GARDEN OF PAIN   4000

Hold **Attack 3** and press **Attack 1** to grow spiky blades of grass that do massive damage. Prerequisite: Find Tuff Luck's Soul Gem in CH 16: The Golden Desert.

Garden of Pain is a powerful attack with a good area of effect to deal with any enemies in the immediate area. The best part is that move doesn't require any charge time and can be pulled off quickly to deal with bad guys that are trying to overwhelm you.

Basic Attacks

TRAPTANIUM WARBLADES

Press **Attack 1** to swipe with Traptanium Warblades. Press **Attack 1**, **Attack 1**, **Attack 1** for a combo strike.

POUNCE MODE

Press **Attack 2** to enter Pounce Mode, invisible to enemies. Then press **Attack 1** to pounce!

Upgrades

WARBLADE STAB   500

Press **Attack 3** to spring forward with a powerful Warblade Stab attack.

GREEN THUMB   700

Stay in Pounce Mode longer.

CONTROL YOUR DESTINY   900

Hold **Attack 3** to control where Warblade Stab lands. Prerequisite: Warblade Stab.

GLAIVE WAVE   1200

Traptanium Warblade attack now shoots an energy wave.

Pouncy Pouncer

Improve Pounce Mode attacks.

POISON IVY   1700

Clover patches in Pounce Mode stun enemies.

POWERFUL POUNCE   2200

Traptanium Warblade attack from Pounce Mode does more damage.

4-LEAFED CLOVER   3000

Touching clover in Pounce Mode restores HP.

Warblade Whacker

Improve Traptanium Warblade attacks.

WAIVE GOODBYE   1700

Energy wave released from Traptanium Warblade attack does more damage.

LUCKY SPIN   2200

Press **Attack 1**, **Attack 1** HOLD **Attack 2** for Lucky Spin combo.

WINGIN' WARBLADE   3000

Press **Attack 1**, **Attack 1**, HOLD **Attack 3** for Wingin' Warblade combo.

Whisper Elf

Silent but Deadly!

Maximum Health	270
Speed	70
Armor	12
Critical Hit	50
Elemental Power	25

Basic Attack Notes

▶ **Blade Slash**
A quick and powerful melee attack.

▶ **Stealthier Decoy**
Disappear and leave behind a decoy. Upgrades to place a scarecrow in place of the decoy to distract enemies.

▶ **Arboreal Acrobatics**
A quick acrobatic move performed as a tumbling leap.

Upgrade Paths

Pook Blade Saint

Whisper Elf's Blade Slash melee attack is a powerful one. She attacks with blinding speed while moving in and out of range to avoid counterattacks. The Elf Jitsu upgrade adds two combos to the base attack. Poison Spores combo sprays enemies in front her with a poison cloud. Blade Flurry combo temporarily turns her into a blinding ball of blades, hitting enemies even more rapidly. Shadowsbane Blade Dance is a very effective passive power. Whenever Whisper Elf attacks, the blades automatically attack her target as well. Additionally, the blades make her Arboreal Acrobatics deal a small amount of damage.

Forest Ninja

Stealthier Decoy can be confusing at first. Whisper Elf appears to keep running in place, but if you look closely, you can see her green eyes as you move her about. Stealthier Decoy has two benefits. First, once you upgrade it to leave Scarecrows, it creates major distractions for enemies. Second, Whisper Elf's attack does increased damage when first leaving Stealthier Decoy. This path increases the number of Scarecrows, adds serious damaging effects, and makes them sturdier.

○ SOUL GEM ABILITY

SYLVAN REGENERATION   4000

Regenerate health over time.

Approximately every five seconds, Whisper Elf automatically regains five health. This isn't huge health restoration, but every bit helps. If you're low on health, try to find a quiet spot in the level and let your health build back up.

Basic Attacks

BLADE SLASH

Press **Attack 1** to slice enemies up with a pair of sharp blades. Press **Attack 1**, **Attack 1**, HOLD **Attack 1** to perform a special combo.

STEALTHIER DECOY

Press **Attack 2** to disappear completely but leave behind a decoy image that enemies are drawn to.

Upgrades

STRAW POOK SCARECROW   500

A Scarecrow appears in place of your decoy and distracts enemies.

DRAGONFANG DAGGER   700

Blade attacks do increased damage.

STURDY SCARECROW   900

Scarecrows last longer and take more damage to destroy. Prerequisite: Straw Pook Scarecrow

ARBOREAL ACROBATICS   1200

Press **Attack 3** to perform a quick acrobatic move. Hold **Attack 3** and flip in any direction using the left control stick.

Pook Blade Saint Path

Further develop Whisper Elf's blade attacks.

ELF JITSU   1700

Press **Attack 1**, **Attack 1**, HOLD **Attack 2** for Poison Spores. Press **Attack 1**, **Attack 1**, HOLD **Attack 3** for Blade Flurry.

ELVEN SUNBLADE   2200

Blade attacks deal even MORE increased damage.

SHADOWSBANE BLADE DANCE   3000

Magical Blades fight alongside you.

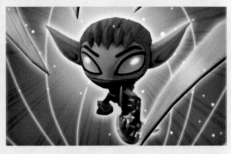

Forest Ninja Path

Further develop Whisper Elf's Scarecrow skills.

SCARE-CRIO TRIO   1700

Three Scarecrows are created in place of your decoy.

SCARECROW BOOBY TRAP   2200

Scarecrows explode and damage enemies.

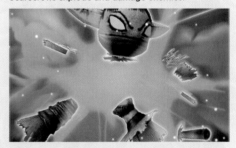

SCARECROW SPIN SLICER   3000

Scarecrows have axes and do extra damage.

Blastermind

Mind Over Matter!

Maximum Health	240
Speed	70
Armor	30
Critical Hit	50
Elemental Power	39

Blastermind was once the "hide and sheep" champion of the Sardonic Mountains, where he and his friends played regularly. But when he was about to set a new Skylands record, the ground collapsed and Blastermind fell into a deep, mysterious cavern filled with shimmering crystals. As his friends circled the hole up top, they suddenly found themselves face to face with a dangerous Ham Dragon, who had felt the rumble of the collapse. Down below, Blastermind felt helpless. But fortunately, the cavern was filled with Psionic Power Crystals once used by the Ancients to amplify their thoughts. When the crystals "heard" Blastermind's worried thoughts about saving his friends, they found him worthy—and bestowed upon him awesome psionic powers, which he used to get out of the hole and mentally blast the circling Ham Dragon. Soon after, Blastermind joined the Skylanders as part of the Trap Team, using his new Traptanium Psionic Helmet to fight evil everywhere!

Basic Attack Notes

▶ Brainwaves

Has a 360-degree area of effect, and when upgraded, can be held for a continuous effect and area blast.

▶ Levitation

Damages enemies on contact and provides additional damage when slammed to the ground.

▶ Brain Freeze

Slows enemies hit by this attack.

Upgrade Paths

Psychokinetic

Blastermind uses mental powers to damage foes at close range with Brainwaves. Levitation is a great long-range attack and should be used with Brain Freeze to control and manipulate enemies before they close in. This path takes Levitation to a whole new level with three new options. Brain Blowout can get rid of enemies, knocking them out of the immediate area. Remote Control takes a while to charge, but it can turn levitating enemies into a weapon by slamming the captive foe into other enemies. For direct damage, use Mind Mash to repeatedly smash levitated enemies over and over. However, not all enemies can be levitated.

Mentalist

Mind Control and Mind Blown work together to take over enemies and make them your minions. The initial attack takes a while to charge, but Brain Freeze attacks should slow them down and provide a good opportunity. Note that not all foes are susceptible to these mind control attacks. This path is mostly geared towards Brain Freeze boosts, but don't overlook The More the Merrier which is a significant upgrade to Levitation. This levitating power allows more enemies to be caught in Levitation, both removing them from the battlefield and damaging them in the process.

○ SOUL GEM ABILITY

LOCK PUZZLE PSYCHIC — 4000

Hold **Attack 2** to charge up Levitation attack and shoot Lock Puzzles with it to solve them instantly. Prerequisite: Find Blastermind's Soul Gem in CH 15: Skyhighlands

This ability isn't focused on damage or defense; instead it is rooted in mental discipline. Using Blastermind's psychic ability, any Lock Puzzle can be solved instantly. However, these puzzles are an excellent challenge and should be attempted before letting the Skylander solve it for you.

Basic Attacks

BRAINWAVES

Press **Attack 1** to blast nearby enemies with powerful Brainwaves.

LEVITATION

Press **Attack 2** to levitate enemies and smash them to the ground.

Upgrades

TASTY WAVES — 500

Hold **Attack 1** to use the Brainwave attack for a longer duration.

BRAIN FREEZE — 700

Press **Attack 3** to create energy balls that slow enemies down.

BRAIN STORM — 900

Hold **Attack 1** to charge up the Brainwave attack, and release for a super-powered Brain Storm. Prerequisite: Tasty Waves

DOWN TO EARTH — 1200

Levitated enemies damage other nearby foes during the smashdown.

Mentalist

Improve Brain Freeze attacks.

MIND CONTROL — 1700

Hold **Attack 3** to create an energy ball that takes control of enemies' minds.

THE MORE THE MERRIER — 2200

Levitation Field passes through enemies and can levitate multiple foes. Prerequisite: Mind Control

MIND BLOWN — 3000

Mind-Controlled enemies damage others after going back to normal.

Psychokinetic

Improve Brainwaves attacks.

BRAIN BLOWOUT — 1700

Press **Attack 1** near levitating enemies for a massive knockback.

REMOTE CONTROL — 2200

Hold **Attack 2** to charge up the Levitation attack and control enemies you levitate.

MIND MASH — 3000

While levitating an enemy, press **Attack 1**, **Attack 2**, or **Attack 3** to slam them down repeatedly. Prerequisite: Remote Control

Cobra Cadabra

Charmed and Ready!

Maximum Health	290
Speed	70
Armor	36
Critical Hit	40
Elemental Power	46

Though Cobra Cadabra was an assistant to The Great Mabuni, a traveling magician that performed all over Skylands, he wanted more than anything to become a magician himself. Unfortunately, the guild of Mysteriously Mad Magic Masters of Mystery, who for centuries taught all of the greatest magicians, would not permit it. And so Mabuni decided to teach the cobra himself, even through it was forbidden. They studied everything together, from vanishing acts to snake charming. But when the guild discovered this, they sent a team of magic rabbit enforcers to punish them both. Although the beastly hares were the most powerful of their kind in Skylands, Cobra Cadabra remained brave. Playing an enchanted tune on his flute, he used what he had learned to cast a spell over the rabbits and lead them away. Upon hearing this, this guild was impressed by such a display of skill, and accepted the snake charmer as a member. Soon after, Cobra Cadabra was made a member of another group—the Skylanders!

Basic Attack Notes

▶ **Magic Flute**
Musical blasts can increase in range and damage when the flute is timed to the beat of the music.

▶ **Cobra Basket**
Damages nearby enemies and can be upgraded to activate ten at once.

▶ **Launch Cobra!**
Hold to aim the attack which passes through foes and each time it is used it creates a Cobra Basket.

Upgrade Paths

Concerto Cobra

The first two upgrades add maximum damage to the Magical Flute as well as a useful ricochet effect from Reverb Riff. With a fully powered Magic Flute, drop Cobra Baskets to slow enemies' approach and fire off a barrage of musical blasts from mid to long range. Snake Charmer's Solo is an interesting attack that damages foes as it passes over them and can enchant them to fight on your side. However, the enchantment is only temporary and does not work on all enemies. It takes a while to put foes under your spell so make sure you're in a safe spot when attempting to charm them.

Master of Baskets

Basket Quintet can launch five baskets at a time, and after upgrading to ten baskets from Basket Party, they can cover the battlefield in no time. Once all ten are out, use Call and Response to shoot them and do nearly twice the damage to enemies that touch them. The first two upgrades can make a defensive barrier of baskets that can keep enemies at bay while it slowly wears them down. However, they are also powerful offensive weapons when tossed into a group of bad guys and detonated using A Tisket, A Tasket. This is a great approach for a hit and run strategy.

⬤ SOUL GEM ABILITY

BIG BASKET BOMB	**4000**

Press **Attack 3** to launch into active Cobra Baskets to create a massive explosion. Prerequisite: Find Cobra Cadara's Soul Gem in CH 14: Operation: Troll Rocket Steal

The Cobra Launch receives a big boost from this ability by triggering a massive explosion when jumping into an active Cobra Basket. This is a great weapon to deal with groups of enemies and can also be used to quickly dart from foe to foe, causing a lot of damage.

Basic Attacks

MAGIC FLUTE
Press **Attack 1** to musically blast enemies with your Magic Pungi Flute.

COBRA BASKET
Press **Attack 2** to lob Cobra Baskets, which damage nearby enemies to the beat.

Upgrades

KEEP THE BEAT!	**500**

Magic Flute attack does more damage when played to the beat of the music.

LAUNCH COBRA!	**700**

Press **Attack 3** to launch forward out of the basket, damaging anything in your path.

BASKET PARTY	**900**

Can have up to 10 Cobra Baskets active at once.

PUNGI POWER	**1200**

Magic Flute attack travels further and does more damage.

Concerto Cobra
Improve Magic Flute attacks.

REVERB RIFF	**1700**

Magic Flute music notes bounce off walls and enemies and can do extra damage.

ULTIMATE FLUTE ROCK	**2200**

Magic Flute attack does maximum damage.

SNAKE CHARMER'S SOLO	**3000**

Hold **Attack 1** to play an enchanting song that charms enemies to fight for your cause.

Master of Baskets
Improve Cobra Basket attacks.

BASKET QUINTET	**1700**

Throw five Cobra Baskets at once.

CALL AND RESPONSE	**2200**

Shoot Cobra Baskets with your Magic Flute to power them up.

A TISKET, A TASKET	**3000**

Hold **Attack 2** to detonate all active Cobra Baskets.

Déjà Vu

Did That Just Happen?

Maximum Health	210
Speed	60
Armor	18
Critical Hit	60
Elemental Power	46

On a remote island in Skylands, Déjà Vu tirelessly worked on a machine that would make the perfect three-minute egg in half the time. After pouring over countless magic tomes, and even consulting the lost plans used to create the legendary Tower of Time, she finally completed construction of the huge machine. Unfortunately, a gang of evil giant sea slugs, searching for a way to acquire super speed, learned of her machine and set about to take it at all costs. Slow, but well armed, the massive slugs bore down on the island. But rather than allow her work to be used for evil, Déjà Vu quickly jumped into action and set the clock's hands to thirteen—causing a time overload. Caught up in the blast, she was given an amazing power over time, which she then used to stop the evil slugs in their tracks and spin them home. Now as a Skylander, Déjà Vu uses her incredible powers to turn back the clock on evil!

Basic Attack Notes

▶ **Space-Time Shots**
A magical ball that seeks out enemies and can be fired by Past Selves.

▶ **Past Selves**
A copy that relives recent actions of the Skylander, including attacks, and can swap places

▶ **Time Rift**
Attacks foes and Space-Time Shots, damages foes that touch it, turns into a black hole when shot

Upgrade Paths

Remember to Live

Space-Time Duality is a priority as it literally doubles Déjà Vu's firepower. When used with several Time Rifts this greatly increases firepower, especially since these shots home in on enemies. Past Selves get a damage boost from Explosion Déjà Vu in the form of a triple explosion. However, the Past Self also gains a great new ability from Time Heals All Wounds. This healing upgrade restores a decent amount of health each time the Past Self takes damage. Both of the Past Self upgrades are passive abilities, so create a copy and let it run wild while focusing on firing off a constant barrage of Space-Time Shots and Time Rifts.

Live to Remember

Past Selves gain a lot of functionality that all work together on this path. Start with Past Self Paralysis to gain extra damage plus the defensive ability to freeze enemies. When added along side Warp Field, enemies can be pulled into the Past Selves to distract them as well as freeze foes that touch the Past Self. Finally, Go Out With a Bang adds extra Space-Time Shots when the copy expires. Obviously the tactic should be to keep a Past Self at all time and swap with them to use their effects. This allows them to draw enemies in, freeze them, and then unleash extra damage while you are free to focus on Time-Space Shots.

⚪ SOUL GEM ABILITY

BLACK HOLE BEDLAM 4000
Time Rifts now turn into massive black holes, releasing unstable time power. Prerequisite: Find Déjà Vu's Soul Gem in CH 6:Rainfish Rivera

The Time Rifts become black holes that explode with energy and cover a medium area. Three Time Rifts can be created at the same time to essentially create several time bombs. Lure enemies into these unstable rifts to do heavy damage to groups of foes.

Basic Attacks

SPACE-TIME SHOTS
Press **Attack 1** to shoot a magical ball of time energy that homes in on enemies

PAST SELVES
Press **Attack 2** to bring a version of your past self that explodes. Press **Attack 2** again to switch places with it.

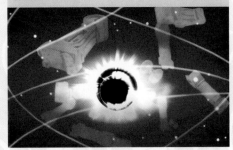

Upgrades

TIME RIFT 500
Press **Attack 3** to create a Time Rift, damaging all who touch it. Shoot the Time Rift to create a black hole.

LONG-TERM MEMORY 700
Past Selves last longer and replay a longer history, as well as damage anything nearby.

TIME RIFTS APLENTY 900
Have more Time Rifts active at once. Time Rifts now attract Space-Time Shots. Prerequisite: Time Rift

Live to Remember
Take a different path to improve Past Selves attacks.

WARP FIELD 1700
Shoot a Past Self to create a warp field, pulling enemies towards the Past Self.

PAST SELF PARALYSIS 2200
Past Selves do extra damage and freeze all nearby enemies.

GO OUT WITH A BANG 3000
When a Past Self explodes or when you switch with it, it releases Space-Time Shots.

CIRCULAR LOGIC 1200
Past Selves fire Space-Time Shots.

Remember to Live
Improve Past Selves attacks.

EXPLOSION DÉJÀ VU 1700
When a Past Self explodes, the explosion is repeated two more times.

TIME HEALS ALL WOUNDS 2200
When a Past Self takes damage, you are healed by an equal amount.

SPACE-TIME DUALITY 3000
Press **Attack 1** to shoot two Space-Time Shots at once.

Enigma

Out of Sight!

Maximum Health	310
Speed	60
Armor	30
Critical Hit	60
Elemental Power	32

Summoned by a Mabu Mystic, Enigma comes from a nameless place "between the worlds." Though the Mystic was really just looking for someone to play Skystones, he was quickly enraptured by Enigma's stories about his mysterious homeland. Unfortunately, the Darkness got wind of these stories, and seeking another realm to conquer, sent minions to lay siege on the gateway that remained open. Making matters worse, the Mabu had no idea how to close it. So, with a legion of minions fast approaching, Enigma chose to use his Sigil of Mystery to seal the doorway—cutting him off from his home forever. This large sacrifice caught the attention of the Trap Team, who welcomed Enigma and gave him a new home as a protector of Skylands. He now uses his Traptanium Sigil to put a world of hurt on evil everywhere!

Basic Attack Notes

▶ **Mystic Staff**
Can attack three times for a combo and performs a downward slam while jumping.

▶ **Invisibility Mode**
Creates a Magic Mist while invisible and can be canceled by pressing Attack 2.

▶ **Paradox Pound**
Attack effects area where it lands and can be used in air to quickly land and slam the ground.

Upgrade Paths

Chief of Staff

The Mystic Staff becomes a more versatile and deadly weapon on this path. The basic combo is a great start but now there are two more choices for dealing with groups of enemies. Magic Eye Combo ends with a dashing move that covers a lot of ground and hurts enemies in its wake. Use the Teleport Slam Combo for some crowd control with its final slam move that hurts enemies in the vicinity. The Paradox Pound gets a boost from It's Raining Eyes? but it has a long charge time and is best used before enemies are up close.

Invisible Invader

Make the most of Enigma's invisibility by confusing foes with ghost versions and they'll never know what's coming. Becoming a stealthy and strategic warrior is essential on this path by using invisibility to take out the targets you want, while avoiding enemy attention. To aid in this endeavor, Ninja Style adds a big damage boost to further enforce using sneak attacks while invisible. Mindboggling adds more damage to Paradox Pound and knocks back foes, making it the perfect weapon to deal with groups of enemies. This attack has a large area of effect and is great to use with invisibility to sneak into a large group and multiple foes before they know what hit them.

⬤ SOUL GEM ABILITY

AN EYE FOR SEVERAL EYES — 4000

Hold **Attack 3** and press **Attack 1** to fire eye beams and rain down eye balls. Requires Paradox Pound. Prerequisite: Find Enigma's Soul Gem in CH 14: Operation: Troll Rocket Steal

An incredible ability that shoots a continuous beam from the Mystic Staff. Enigma can't move while the beam is in use but it can be rotated in a full circle to cut through foes around him. The beam does a lot of damage but it has a slightly longer launch window than the Paradox Pound.

Basic Attacks

MYSTIC STAFF

Press **Attack 1** to swing the Mystic Staff. **Attack 1**, **Attack 1**, HOLD **Attack 1** for a combo.

INVISIBILITY MODE

Press **Attack 2** to turn invisible and move around in total stealth.

Upgrades

PARADOX POUND — 500

Press **Attack 3** to slam the staff into the ground and damage all nearby enemies.

MAGIC MIST — 700

Magic Mist released in Invisibility Mode damages enemies over time.

CLOAK AND DAGGER — 900

Invisibility Mode lasts longer and freezes enemies; cloak can do damage well.

PARADOX POWER — 1200

Paradox Pound does more damage. Prerequisite: Paradox Pound.

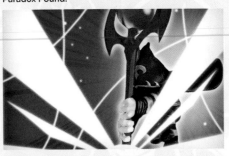

Invisible Invader
Improve the Invisibility Mode attacks.

NINJA STYLE — 1700

Attacks coming out of Invisibility Mode do extra damage.

MINDBOGGLING — 2200

Paradox Pound does even MORE damage and blasts enemies back.

GIVE UP THE GHOST — 3000

Ghost version of yourself appear while in Invisibility Mode.

Chief of Staff
Improve the Mystic Staff attacks.

EYE DASH COMBO — 1700

Press **Attack 1**, **Attack 1**, **Attack 2** for a Cloak Dash combo.

CLOAK DASH COMBO — 2200

Press **Attack 1**, **Attack 1**, **Attack 3** for an Eye Slam combo.

IT'S RAINING EYES? — 3000

Hold **Attack 3** to charge up the Paradox Pound attack and rain down magic eyeballs.

Mini Jini

Any Last Wishes?

Maximum Health	410
Speed	85
Armor	48
Critical Hit	80
Elemental Power	60

Basic Attack Notes

▶ **Wishblades**

A whirling blade attack that can be used in a combo and can be upgraded to a charge attack with an explosive blast.

▶ **Bottle Blast**

Hide inside the bottle and launch rockets. Press Attack 2 to blast out in a magical explosion.

▶ **Surrealistic Spheres**

Summon magical orbs that can be upgraded to four that can damage multiple enemies.

Upgrade Paths

Swords of Might

Mini-Jini's Wishblades turn her into a whirling dervish of destruction. While the blades don't initially do much damage, they are extremely fast and can slice through foes quickly. Ultimate Wishblade maxes out the blade's damage and should be purchased as soon as possible. The sword combos are excellent at extending Mini-Jini's melee range. The Fling Blade combo causes Mini-Jini to throw her sword, and the Enchanted Blade combo summons a sword to Mini-Jini's side. Once the sword is summoned, she can follow up with Bottle and Sphere attacks. Wishbladesplosion is an immensely damaging attack. Charge the attack, and any enemies standing in front of her take major damage.

Ancient Djinn Magic

This path specializes in using mid and long range attacks. Buy a Better Bottle and Ultimate Bottle Rockets provide needed boosts to make Bottle Blast a viable offensive weapon. Also, once you get to the Buy a Better Bottle power, the bottle becomes a great defensive tactic. Going inside the bottle dramatically increases Mini-Jini's armor, allowing her to completely deflect a significant number of attacks. Stay in the bottle, and blast the enemies with the upgraded rockets. To further enhance long-range attacks, Super Surrealistic Spheres adds more damage and wider area of effect for her magic orbs. However, the spheres can be difficult to control.

● SOUL GEM ABILITY

DAZZLING ENCHANTMENT `4000`

While inside the bottle, hold down **Attack 3** to put enemies into a trance.

This power makes Mini-Jini's bottle attacks more practical. When you activate Dazzling Enchantment, purple smoke pours out of the top of the bottle, putting nearby small and medium sized enemies to sleep. It's important to note that this trance effect does not work against large enemies.

Basic Attacks

WISHBLADES

Press **Attack 1** to swing dual swords for hacking and slashing enemies. Press **Attack 1, Attack 1,** HOLD **Attack 1** for a special combo.

BOTTLE BLAST

Press **Attack 2** to hide inside the bottle. Press **Attack 2** again to blast out in a magical explosion.

Upgrades

SURREALISTIC SPHERES `500`

Press **Attack 3** to summon magical orbs and cast them towards the enemies.

ABRA-CA-STAB-BRA `700`

Wishblades do increased damage.

JUGGLING ACT `900`

Hold **Attack 3** to summon four magical orbs and damage multiple enemies. Prerequisite: Surrealistic Spheres

BOTTLE ROCKETS `1200`

While inside the bottle, press **Attack 1** to launch rockets.

Swords of Might

Empowers Mini-Jini's swords to wreak destruction upon her foes!

WISHBLADE COMBOS `1700`

Press **Attack 1, Attack 1,** HOLD **Attack 2** for Fling Blade. Press **Attack 1, Attack 1,** HOLD **Attack 3** for Enchanted Blade.

WISHBLADESPLOSION `2200`

Hold the **Attack 1** button to charge up the swords into an explosive blast.

ULTIMATE WISHBLADE `3000`

Wishblades do maximum damage.

Ancient Djinn Magic

Harness ancient Djinn magic to improve Mini-Jini's bottle and Surrealistic Sphere attacks.

SUPER SURREALISTIC SPHERES `1700`

Magical orbs do more damage and affect a greater area.

ULTIMATE BOTTLE ROCKETS `2200`

Bottle rockets launch faster, do more damage, and affect a greater area.

BUY A BETTER BOTTLE `3000`

Bottle is stronger and moves faster.

Fizzy Frenzy Pop Fizz

The Motion of the Potion!

Maximum Health	270
Speed	60
Armor	18
Critical Hit	30
Elemental Power	25

Nobody is quite sure who Pop Fizz was before he became an alchemist, least of all Pop Fizz himself. After many years of experimenting with magical potions, his appearance has changed quite significantly. In fact, no one even knows his original color. But it's widely known that he is a little crazy, his experiments are reckless, and the accidents they cause are too numerous to measure. Understandably, he has had a difficult time finding lab partners, or anyone that even wants to be near him. In hopes of making himself more appealing to others, he attempted to create the most effective charm potion ever—but that just turned him into a big, wild, berserker. Or maybe that's just how he saw the potion working in the first place...

Basic Attack Notes

▶ **Potion Lob**

Undehand toss at distant enemies, downward smash when a target is extremely close.

▶ **Beast Form**

Limited duration, slow start, and has a cooldown. Don't activate this in a crowd!

▶ **New Concoction**

Starts with one potion and learns two others, each with different effects.

Upgrade Paths

Mad Scientist

The Mad Scientist Path is all about the Mixologist upgrade. Learn how to combine the potion effects (such as putting a green potion puddle on the ground and guiding mobile purple potions vials into it) and what the effects are (continuing the previous example, it's poisoned vials chasing down enemies).

Best of the Beast

The Best of the Beast Path allows Pop Fizz to stay in Beast Form longer and adds potion-based attacks, with Attack 3. Yellow is a flame attack, green is a flailing attack that hits multiple times, and purple is a lunging ground pound. If you like mixing it up in close quarters, this is the path for you.

⬤ SOUL GEM ABILITY

SHAKE IT! `4000`

Repeatedly press **Attack 3** to shake the potion bottle until it explodes. Prerequisite: New Concoction

Big build up, big payoff ability. You must press **Attack 3** rapidly and fill the on-screen meter before you get the massive explosion. Being hit by enemies does not reduce the amount of meter that has been filled. If Pop Fizz is at full health, don't be shy about using this in a crowd.

Basic Attacks

POTION LOB

Press **Attack 1** to launch Pop Fizz's currently equipped potion.

BEAST FORM

Press **Attack 2** to drink a potion and temporarily change into a beast form.

Upgrades

NEW CONCOCTION `500`

Press **Attack 3** to switch to a new potion that can walk on two legs and fight by your side when thrown.

PUDDLE OF PAIN `700`

Press **Attack 3** again to switch to a new potion that leaves a damaging puddle of acid when thrown. Prerequisite: New Concoction

RAGING BEST `900`

All attacks in Beast Form do additional damage.

DEXTROUS DELIVERY `1200`

Throw potions and grab new ones much faster.

Mad Scientist Path

Further Develop Pop Fizz's potion attacks.

MASTER CHEMIST `1700`

All potions do increased damage and have improved effects.

MIXOLOGIST `2200`

Mix the effects of different colored potions for brand new effects.

ALL IN `3000`

Hold **Attack 1** to pull up to three potions out and release to throw them all at once.

Best of the Beast Path

Further develop Pop Fizz's Beast Form attacks.

MORE BEAST! `1700`

Beast Form meter drains slower and recharges faster.

MUTANT BEAST `2200`

In Beast Form, Press **Attack 3** to perform a special attack based on which potion is active.

BESERKER BOOST `3000`

In Beast Form, damaging enemies recharges the Beast Form meter.

WOW POW!

OVERSIZE ME! `5000`

Repeatedly press **Attack 2** to swallow a potion whole and become a Super Beast with overloaded attacks

Oversize ME! almost makes Best of the Beast Path mandatory for Fizzy Frenzy Pop Fizz. Every upgrade from that Path works when Pop Fizz is oversized. Pop Fizz's speed increases as the amount of meter left decreases.

Spry
All Fired Up!

Maximum Health	280
Speed	70
Armor	18
Critical Hit	30
Elemental Power	60

Basic Attack Notes

▶ **Flameball**
A fiery projectile attack that can be upgraded to shooting three projectiles at once.

▶ **Charge**
A charging attack that needs to be charged up and can be upgraded to increase distance.

▶ **Spry's Flight**
Gain the ability to fly as well as increased speed and armor.

Upgrade Paths

Sheep Burner

Flameball is slower than most ranged attacks, but it deals better damage than most projectiles and has an excellent knockback. On this path it also has plenty of upgrades to increased range, damage, and number of Flameballs. Exploding Fireblast should be the first choice because it adds damage and an explosive Flameball. On the defensive end Fire Shield adds a protective flaming barrier. Save Daybringer Flame upgrade for last. Attacking with regular Flameballs actually deals more damage in the amount of time it takes to charge and release Daybringer Flame. It is a great option to do maximum damage when there is lull in the battle.

Blitz Spry

Charge is one of the best dash-type attacks in the game. Once Spry hits full speed, the damage from the attack more than doubles. Charge also has two great secondary effects. Stun Charge unlocks a stun effect and any enemy hit by the Charge cannot move for approximately three seconds. The second effect is a huge knockback. Charge is a fantastic power for crowd control and knocking enemies off of ledges. Both Comet Dash and Ibex'sath Charge add much needed damage to the attack. However, due to its relatively low damage, it should be used in conjunction with other attacks.

⬤ SOUL GEM ABILITY

SPRY'S EARTH POUND `4000`

In flight, press **Attack 1** to Dive Bomb.

This dive bomb attack is a great addition to Spry's arsenal. It's not quite as good as Fireslam, but it's a great area-of-effect attack with excellent range.

Basic Attacks

FLAMEBALL

Press **Attack 1** to breathe balls of fire at your enemies.

CHARGE

Press and hold **Attack 2** to lower your horns and charge forward, knocking over anything in your way.

Upgrades

LONG RANGE RAZE `500`
Flameball attacks travel farther.

SPRY'S FLIGHT `700`
Press **Attack 3** to fly. Increased speed and resistance while flying.

SPRINT CHARGE `900`
Can perform Charge attack for increased distance.

TRIPLE FLAMEBALLS `1200`
Shoot three Flameballs at once.

Sheep Burner Path
Further develop Spry's Flameball attacks.

FIRE SHIELD `1700`
A fire shield appears when using the Flameball attack.

EXPLODING FIREBLAST `2200`
Flameballs do extra damage and the middle one explodes.

THE DAYBRINGER FLAME `3000`
Hold **Attack 1** to charge up Flameball attack for maximum damage.

Blitz Spry Path
Further develop Spry's Charging attacks.

STUN CHARGE `1700`
Enemies hit by Charge Attack become stunned.

COMET DASH `2200`
Charge attack does increased damage.

IBEX'S WRATH CHARGE `3000`
Charge longer to do extra damage.

Chopper
Dino Might!

Maximum Health	250
Speed	60
Armor	6
Critical Hit	50
Elemental Power	25

Growing up, Chopper was much smaller than the rest of his dinosaur kin. But this didn't bother him because he had big ideas. Ahead of the annual hunting competition to honor the village idol, Roarke Tunga, Chopper spent weeks building himself a super Gyro-Dino-Exo-Suit. When the competition began, he took to the air—firing his missiles and chomping everything in his path. With Chopper on the verge of victory, the competition came to a sudden halt when the nearby volcano erupted, flooding the village with lava. Seeing the residents of his village trapped, Chopper quickly flew into action. One at a time, he airlifted everyone to safety. And was even able to save the village idol. For heroically using his head, Chopper was made a Skylander!

Basic Attack Notes

▶ **Raptor Rockets**

A single rocket attack that can be upgrading to a homing missile. Can be performed while flying.

▶ **Chopper Blades**

A charge attack that travels a decent distance and can be performed in air while flying.

▶ **Roar!**

A powerful roar with short range that renders Chopper immobile. This attack can only be performed on the ground.

Upgrade Paths

Roar Like Never Before

Roar! starts out with a short range of attack and relatively low damage. Call of the Wild and King of the Jurassic Jungle will max out the attack giving it the range and damage it needs. Remember that Roar! can not be performed in the air and Raptor Rockets should be used in that case. Speaking of rockets, R.O.A.R Missiles charges the rockets to launch a pair of high damage projectiles, but these don't home in and must be aimed. The upgraded Roar! is the best choice against groups of enemies as it hits all foes in a straight line, but use the Raptor Rockets when retreating.

Blaster From the Past

Chopper Blades get a maximum damage boost from Props to You but otherwise this path is all about rockets. More Missiles can charge up the rockets releasing two at a time but these travel in a straight line and don't track enemies. Save the big rockets for tough single enemies or close groups of foes. Get Bigger the Boom first to create larger rockets for extra damage, then weaken foes at a distance with constant rocket fire. If enemies get too close use the upgraded Chopper Blades to cut through them and get to a safe distance to continue a barrage of rocket fire.

⬤ SOUL GEM ABILITY

ULTIMATE DINO DESTRUCTION — 4000

Press Jump twice to enter Flight Mode, then press **Attack 3** to release a rocket strike of epic proportions. Prerequisite: Find Chopper's Soul Gem in CH 5: Chef Zeppelin

Surprisingly Flight Mode doesn't add a lot of speed to Chopper's movement. Yet, this barrage of rockets makes it worth flying around since they home in on enemies, allowing him to fire them off from a safe distance and guarantee they hit.

Basic Attacks

RAPTOR ROCKETS

Press **Attack 1** to shoot Raptor Rockets.

CHOPPER BLADES

Press **Attack 2** to fly into enemies with Chopper Blades.

Upgrades

ROAR! — 500

Press **Attack 3** to unleash a powerful roar attack.

REV'D UP ROCKETS — 700

Raptor Rockets do extra damage.

HOMING MISSILES — 900

Raptor Rockets seek out enemies for a sure hit.

BETTER BLADES — 1200

Chopper Blades do extra damage.

Roar Like Never Before

Improve Roar attacks.

CALL OF THE WILD — 1700

Roar Attack does extra damage and travels further.

R.O.A.R. MISSILES — 2200

Hold **Attack 1** to charge up Raptor Rockets to release super, Rage of All Raptor Missiles.

KING OF THE JURASSIC JUNGLE — 3000

Roar Attack does maximum damage, with maximum range. Prerequisite: Call of the Wild.

Blaster From the Past

Improve Raptor Rocket and Chopper Blades attacks.

THE BIGGER THE BOOM — 1700

Raptor Rockets create bigger explosions doing extra damage.

PROPS TO YOU — 2200

Chopper Blades do maximum damage.

MORE MISSILE — 3000

Hold **Attack 1** to charge up Raptor Rockets to release bigger missiles doing more damage.

Drobit
Blink and Destroy!

Maximum Health	290
Speed	60
Armor	24
Critical Hit	20
Elemental Power	25

Basic Attack Notes

▶ Mega Blasters

Rapid-fire laser eye blasts are low in damage but extremely quick.

▶ Tactical Bladegears

Spinning gears that ricochet off walls and continue to damage enemies. Two are shot at a time and they spread out as they travel.

▶ Thruster Flight

When airborne Drobit has increased speed and armor. The attack button can be held to allow him to hover without changing direction.

Upgrade Paths

Master Blaster

Initially the eye blasts do low damage, but they fire very quickly. This path is focused on the Mega Blasters and makes them one of the best projectile attacks. Dendrite Focus Crystals give a direct increase in damage. Antimatter Charges boost damage by damaging nearby enemies with exploding beams. The final upgrade, Quadratic Blasters, allows lasers to be shot from the wings as well, giving Drobit four shots at once. Although the damage from each laser is not very high, the incredible speed and number of beams give him a high efficiency of damage per second.

Clockwork Dragon

This path is focused exclusively on Tactical Bladegears. Depleted Uranium Bladegears is a straightforward damage increase. Explosive Bladegears is similar to Antimatter Charges by adding damage to nearby enemies from contact explosions. Even though these both add damage perhaps the most important upgrade is Tri-spread Bladegear that shoots three at once. The reason this last ability is so crucial is that although the blades ricochet they are initially hard to aim. With three Bladegears shot at the same time it is a lot easier to hit your targets. Remember that they spread out over time so at long distances they can entirely miss their mark.

● SOUL GEM ABILITY

AFTERBURNERS — 4000

Fly faster and afterburners damage enemies.

It's hard to hit the enemies directly with the Afterburners once you take off. The trick is to target them before you take off and then take flight to inflict plenty of damage. This is a great way not only to escape a bad situation, but also to dish out some serious damage on the way out.

Basic Attacks

MEGA BLASTERS

Press **Attack 1** to shoot rapid-fire laser blasts out of your eyes.

TACTICAL BLADEGEARS

Press **Attack 2** to deploy Bladegears that ricochet off of walls and pummel enemies.

Upgrades

THRUSTER FLIGHT — 500

Hold **Attack 3** to have Drobit fly. Drobit gets increased speed and armor while flying.

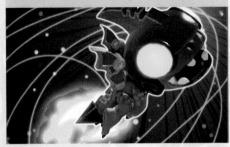

GALVANIZED BLADEGEARS — 700

Bladegears do increased damage.

AXON FOCUS CRYSTALS — 900

Eye Blasters do increased damage.

HOVER MODE — 1200

Hold **Attack 3** to have Drobit hover. Prerequisite: Thruster Flight

Master Blaster

Further develop Drobit's Blaster attacks.

DENDRITE FOCUS CRYSTALS — 1700

Eye Blasters do even more increased damage.

ANTIMATTER CHANGES — 2200

Eye Blaster beams explode on contact, doing damage to enemies.

QUADRATIC BLASTERS — 3000

Press **Attack 1** to shoot lasers out of your wings as well.

Clockwork Dragon

Further develop Drobit's Bladegear attacks.

DEPLETED URANIUM BLADEGEARS — 1700

Bladegears do even more increased damage.

EXPLOSIVE BLADEGEARS — 2200

Bladegears explode on contact, doing damage to nearby enemies.

TRI-SPREAD BLADEGEARS — 3000

Press **Attack 2** to shoot three Bladegears at once.

Gearshift

All Geared Up!

Maximum Health	300
Speed	70
Armor	24
Critical Hit	40
Elemental Power	39

Gearshift was created on the Tech island of Metallana by King Mercurus, who considered the young robot to be his own daughter. But rather than performing royal duties, Gearshift preferred to spend her time in the oily depths of the kingdom among its workers, secretly tending to the huge subterranean machines. When her father discovered this, he was furious—but then a squadron of Undead Stormriders suddenly attacked. Learning that these marauders wanted to capture her father, Gearshift used her knowledge of the labyrinth below to hide him. Seizing the emblem of her people—The Great Gear—she used it to fight the Stormriders, inspiring the workers to rise up. Together, they drove the Stormriders out of Metallana and saved the kingdom. For this, Gearshift was made part of the Trap Team, using her new awesome Traptanium-forged gear to help defend Skylands!

Basic Attack Notes

▶ **Traptanium Gear**

Have three unique attacks. Hoop Mode uses a spin attack for the highest damage. Dual Mode has gears in each hand for mid damage. Fragment Mode provides a projectile attack.

▶ **Mode Toggle**

Toggle between modes and provide a small amount of damage. When upgraded it releases a Gear Saw.

▶ **Gear Grind**

A cartwheel attack that upgrades to drop Mini-Gears which can be knocked into enemies while in Hoop Mode.

Upgrade Paths

Dual Mode Duelist

All of the powers on this path require Gearshift to be in Dual Mode so make sure you are conformable with that mode. Gear Saw receives several upgrades to provide an effective long-range attack to accompany the dual wielding melee ability. Start out with Spare Parts to create a Gear Saw at the end of a three-button string. Note that Gear Saws don't do a ton of damage but they hang around continuing to damage enemies. Several Gear Saws can be out at a time and to extend their life use Keep 'Em Spinning. Continually attack to send out Gear Saws for long-range damage and try to keep as many spinning as possible.

Fragment Mode Freak

Gearshift must be in Fragment Mode to fully utilize the upgrades on this path. Enhanced Fragmentation fires out more fragments and the other two upgrades release Mini-Gears. This path is centered around mid to long range attacks. Stay on the move, firing out fragments as fast a possible and if you have to retreat, enemies take damage as they trample over the Mini-Gears. Use Gear Grind for quick mobility to dash out of danger and always try to keep a safe distance to continue to fire off fragments.

⬤ SOUL GEM ABILITY

SWING SHIFT `4000`

Traptanium Gear is more powerful and can switch modes much faster. Prerequiste: Find Gearshift's Soul Gem in CH 13: The Future of Skylands

Swing Shift provides two essential upgrades! It makes switching between modes much faster to take advantage of her unique abilities in each mode. It also increases damage to all modes by making the Traptanium gear more powerful. Get this ability as soon as possible!

Basic Attacks

TRAPTANIUM GEAR

Press **Attack 1** to perform a Traptanium Gear attack, depending on which Mode you are in.

MODE TOGGLE

Press **Attack 2** to toggle between Hoop Mode, Dual Mode, and Fragment Mode, all with different attacks.

Upgrades

GEAR GRIND `500`

Press **Attack 3** to cartwheel forward damaging anything in your path.

GEAR SAW `700`

Press **Attack 2** to switch modes and release a Gear Saw. Gear Grind into it to make it spin again.

MANY MINI-GEARS `900`

Press **Attack 3** to Gear Grind and release a bunch of dangerous Mini-Gears. Prerequiste: Gear Grind

MINI-GEAR DISTRIBUTION `1200`

After Mini-Gears are released, press **Attack 1** in Hoop Mode to knock Mini-Gears into enemies. Prerequiste: Many Mini-Gears

Dual Mode Duelist

Improve attacks in Dual Mode.

SPARE PARTS `1700`

In Dual Mode, press **Attack 1**, **Attack 1**, **Attack 1** to release a Gear Saw.

KEEP 'EM SPINNING `2200`

In Dual Mode, press **Attack 1** to hit a Gear Saw and make it spin longer.

GEARED UP `3000`

Gear Saws are larger and occasionally release Mini-Gears.

Fragment Mode Freak

Improve attacks in Fragment Mode.

ENHANCED FRAGMENTATION `1700`

In Fragment Mode, press **Attack 1** to fire more fragments out.

KICK IT INTO HIGH GEAR `2200`

In Fragment Mode, press **Attack 1** to also release Mini-Gears.

HARDWARE OVERLOAD `3000`

In Fragment Mode, repeatedly press **Attack 1** to lob out a ton of Mini-Gears.

Jawbreaker

Down for the Count!

Maximum Health	340
Speed	50
Armor	12
Critical Hit	70
Elemental Power	25

Jawbreaker hailed from a race of robots that operated and maintained a vast underground complex of enormous machines that powered the legendary Sky Train, which traveled between a thousand different islands daily. Like many of his fellow robots, Jawbreaker led an ordered existence—full of rules and regulations—which he followed happily. However, one day a huge army of Gear Trolls invaded the subterranean complex. Known for being major train enthusiasts, they were set on taking over the Sky Train for their own evil use. Jawbreaker quickly jumped into action and used his massive fists to beat the trolls into retreat. His quick action and ability to think for himself made him an individual. For this he was made part of the Trap Team, where he now uses his Traptanium powered fists to deliver mighty blows to evil!

Basic Attack Notes

▷ **Traptanium Punch**
Quick damaging jabs that can gain a shocking effect from Robo Rage Mode.

▷ **Robo Rage Mode**
An empowering mode that lasts for a short time and grants increased speed, punching power, and more damage.

▷ **Spark Shock**
The ground punch does damage up close and releases several electric sparks that shoot out in all directions.

Upgrade Paths

High Voltage

The upgrades on this path are focused on doing a lot of damage from shocking electric sparks. These blue projectiles are his only long-range attack and can be effective, especially in large numbers. Robo Rage Mode is Jawbreaker's unique ability that boosts his speed and power. Sparking Interest further enhances this mode by constantly releasing sparks. Anytime Jawbreaker is in combat he should continue to active Robo Rage Mode! While in this mode Static Cling gives Spark Shot a spin attack and sticky sparks. To further fill the battlefield with sparks Hands Off! gives a passive retaliation that releases sparks whenever he is hit.

Out-RAGE-ous

Robo Rage Mode receives several upgrades on this path reinforcing how essential this mode is to Jawbreaker's tactics. While in this mode he gets speed/power boosts, and thanks to Defense Firmware Update, he takes less damage as well. Punch for Power and Jolting Jab work together when in Robo Rage Mode. These allow him to stay in that mode longer while landing punches and enhances the attacks by creating static bursts that damage other enemies. The extra defense and punching offense should make it obvious to trigger Robo Rage Mode and charge into melee range punching enemies into submission.

● SOUL GEM ABILITY

HYPERCHARGED HAYMAKER `4000`
Hold **Attack 3** to charge up a powerful, electromagnetic punch. Prerequisite: Find Jawbreaker's Soul Gem in CH 1: Soda Springs

To perform this attack enter Robo Rage Mode and continue holding **Attack 3** for a short time to charge up a single power punch. Based on the short charge, it makes sense to use the Hypercharged Haymaker every time Jawbreaker goes into Robo Rage Mode.

Basic Attacks

TRAPTANIUM PUNCH
Press **Attack 1** to throw a powerful punch with big, Traptanium fists.

ROBO RAGE MODE
Press **Attack 3** to enter Robo Rage Mode, moving faster, punching harder, and doing more damage.

Upgrades

RAGIN' ROBO RAGE `500`
Robo Rage Mode lasts even longer.

SPARK SHOCK `700`
Press **Attack 3** to punch the ground and release a wave of electric sparks.

ALTERNATING CURRENT `900`
Punching in Robo Rage Mode shocks enemies, doing extra damage over time.

HEAVY HANDS `1200`
Traptanium Punches do more damage.

High Voltage
Improve Spark Shock attacks.

STATIC CLING `1700`
Spark Shock attack sticks to enemies, doing damage over time.

HANDS OFF! `2200`
Getting hit by an enemy automatically releases a wave of electric sparks.

SPARKING INTEREST `3000`
Constantly release electric sparks in Robo Rage Mode.

Out-RAGE-ous
Improve Robo Rage Mode attacks.

JOLTING JAB `1700`
Punching in Robo Rage Mode creates static bursts, which damage other enemies.

DEFENSE FIRMWARE UPDATE `2200`
Take less damage while in Robo Rage Mode.

PUNCH FOR POWER `3000`
Stay in Robo Rage Mode longer by landing punches.

Tread Head

Tread and Shred!

Maximum Health	270
Speed	85
Armor	18
Critical Hit	20
Elemental Power	25

As an orphan from the Dizzying Dunes, Tread Head had always dreamed of racing. And after a summer of scavenging for parts, he finally managed to build a bike that would allow him to enter the local racing circuit. The other competitors laughed at the crudeness of his work, but Tread Head had built it for performance, not for style. So when the race began, he jumped out to a commanding lead. But as he entered a canyon, he suddenly found himself at a roadblock—of Goblin troops! Knowing the other racers were in danger, he pulled off the road and kicked up so much dust that the Goblins had no choice but to flee, allowing the other racers to pass safely. Tread Head may have lost the race that day, but he earned the respect of Master Eon, who would see to it that Tread Head would tread on evil wherever he goes!

Basic Attack Notes

▶ **Wheelie**

Pop a wheelie and hold attack to charge through enemies. Can upgrade tread for more damage and to ride the wheelie for longer.

▶ **Backfire Blast**

A backward attack that fires a blast at mid-range.

▶ **Spin Out!**

A spin attack that can upgrade damage and attack radius. While spinning damage taken is cut in half.

Upgrade Paths

Drag Racer

Tread Head is one of the most straightforward Skylanders to play. Simply hold down the attack button to perform a Wheelie and charge through enemies. Spike a Wheelie should be the first choice to add extra damage. This makes the Wheelie one of the most powerful charging attacks in the game. The other two upgrades, Go Out With a Bang and Burning Rubber, add extra attacks during the last stage of a Wheelie but these aren't easy to plan. Don't confuse the simplicity of this Skylander to mean he is not very effective. He is both easy and fun to play; and the speed and power of his Wheelie is essentially a melee and ranged attack in one.

Pavement Peeler

Wheelie Mode receives an increased area of effect thanks to Spray It, Don't Say It. This ability sprays dirt and rock during a tight turn to provide some mid-range damage. Spin Out! gets most of the attention on this path with upgrades that set the ground ablaze and slows enemies on contact. With these added effects Spin Out! becomes an even more effective melee attack. Wheelie is still a great ability to zip in and out of enemies. However, when space is limited or if you want to get close and personal, Spin Out! is the best choice due to its damage reduction and extra features on this path.

⬤ SOUL GEM ABILITY

ROCKET BOOST — 4000

Once you hit maximum speed in Wheelie Mode, press **Attack 3** to rocket boost off of a ramp. Prerequisite: Find Tread Head's Soul Gem in CH 9: Mystic Mill

The Rocket Boost attack does a lot of damage, but what do you expect when Tread Head flies into the air and comes crashing down? This move can be difficult to use since it can only be done at maximum speed. If you learn to pick up the visual cue when Tread Head's at top speed, this is a devastating attack.

Basic Attacks

WHEELIE

Press **Attack 1** to speed up and pop a wheelie right through enemies.

BACKFIRE BLAST

Press **Attack 2** to shoot enemies behind you with backfire from your cycle.

Upgrades

PEDAL TO THE METAL — 500

Perform the Wheelie attack for longer.

SPIN OUT! — 700

Press **Attack 3** for a spin attack—any damage you take while spinning is cut in half.

TREAD HEAVILY — 900

Bigger treads equals bigger damage from the Wheelie attack.

KICK UP SOME DUST — 1200

Spin Out attack does extra damage around a larger area. Prerequisite: Spin Out!

Drag Racer

Improve Wheelie attacks.

SPIKE A WHEELIE — 1700

Spiked wheels make Wheelie attack do extra damage.

GO OUT WITH A BANG — 2200

Shoot out a massive backfire during the last stage of a Wheelie.

BURNING RUBBER — 3000

Leave a fire trail during the last stages of a Wheelie.

Pavement Peeler

Improve Spin Out attacks.

EAT MY DUST — 1700

Enemies hit by the Spin Out attack are slowed down by a dust cloud.

SPRAY IT, DON'T SAY IT — 2200

In Wheelie Mode, make tight turns to spray enemies with dirt and rocks.

FIRE SPIN — 3000

Spin Out attack goes so fast that it sets the ground on fire.

Trigger Snappy

No Gold, No Glory!

Maximum Health	200
Speed	70
Armor	30
Critical Hit	50
Elemental Power	25

Basic Attack Notes

▶ ### Golden Pistols

Shoot coins out of both guns. Can upgrade to a charge attack that does nearly six times the damage.

▶ ### Lob Golden Safe

Lob a Golden Safe at mid range and upgrades to toss a larger Pot of Gold.

▶ ### Golden Machine Gun

A rapidfire attack from a stationary machine gun that can be rotated 360-degrees.

Upgrade Paths

Golden Frenzy

Golden Gun starts off as a weak, long-range attack. The trick to this power is the charge upgrades. Golden Mega Charge is a good start, but Golden Yamato Blast is amazing. Charge the attack for about five seconds to launch a beam that inflicts over 600 damage to everything in its path. This path can be difficult to master as the regular shots have a low damage per second rating. You must learn to charge the Golden Pistols at all times to release varying levels of power shots.

Golden Money Bags

Lob Golden Safe receives upgrades to damage and range on this path. It's a fantastic medium-range attack with an area-of-effect coin blast. Not only does it do high damage but it is easy to aim. Heads or Tails is the highlight of this power. The initial attack does a ton of damage but if the coin lands heads, it becomes a mine, blasting off as soon as an enemy approaches. The gun attacks are still the best bet for long range but for anything elese the massive damge of Lob Golden Safe is the obvious choice.

⬤ SOUL GEM ABILITY

INFINITE AMMO `4000`

Golden Machine Gun has unlimited Ammo.

Infinite Ammo is a great enhancement for the Golden Machine Gun. Unlimited ammo allows Trigger Snappy to more easily hold strategic positions and mow down advancing enemies.

Basic Attacks

GOLDEN PISTOLS

Press **Attack 1** to shoot rapid fire coins out of both Golden Pistols.

LOB GOLDEN SAFE

Press **Attack 2** to lob golden safes at your enemies.

Upgrades

GOLDEN SUPER CHARGE `500`

Hold **Attack 1** to charge up your Golden Pistols, then release to fire a bullet that does extra damage.

POT O'GOLD `700`

Throw a Pot of Gold, which deals increased damage.

GOLDEN MEGA CHARGE `900`

Charge up your Golden Pistols longer to do even MORE damage.

GOLDEN MACHINE GUN `1200`

Hold **Attack 3** to activate Golden Machine Gun and swivel its aim using the left control stick.

Golden Frenzy Path

Further develop Trigger Snappy's Golden Gun attacks.

HAPPINESS IS A GOLDEN GUN `1700`

Golden Pistols deal increased damage.

BOUNCING BULLETS `2200`

Golden Pistols' bullets bounce off walls.

GOLDEN YAMATO BLAST `3000`

Charge up your Golden Pistols even longer to do maximum damage. Prerequisite: Happiness is a Golden Gun

Golden Money Bags Path

Further develop Trigger Snappy's throwing skills.

JUST THROWING MONEY AWAY `1700`

Lob attack has longer range.

COINSPLOSION `2200`

Lob attacks explode in a shower of damaging coins.

HEADS OR TAILS `3000`

Toss a giant coin that deals extra damage. If it lands on heads, it turns into a mine, damaging enemies that touch it.

Bat Spin

No Rest for the Wicked!

Maximum Health	240
Speed	85
Armor	12
Critical Hit	50
Elemental Power	46

Bat Spin hailed from the underworld, where as a child she was separated from her people. After spending months searching for them, she eventually was welcomed by a colony of magical bats that raised her as one of their own. After many peaceful years living with the bats, the colony was invaded by an army of undead trolls, who were set on stealing their magic to build an ultimate sonar weapon. Bat Spin quickly took action and used powerful abilities that she had learned growing up with the bats and essentially becoming one of them. She heroically defeated the trolls and saved the colony. This caught the attention of Master Eon, who saw at once she would make a worthy Skylander.

Basic Attack Notes

▶ **Bat Attack**

Send out a bat minion that will continue to attack enemies for a short while.

▶ **Bat Swarm**

A 360-degree ring of bats that damages any foes in the vicinity. It is not available in Bat Form.

▶ **Go Batty!**

Turn into a Giant Bat to gain bite and screech attacks. Use Jump to return to normal.

Upgrade Paths

Pet Purveyor

All new bat buddies make up this path, and the first one to get is Mr. Bitey. This large bat is great for long-range attacks and does nearly three times the damage of his smaller cousins. Mr. Blocky and Mr. Dizzy stay close to Bat Spin and provide excellent defense by adding stun and deflective abilities. These three permanent bats work well with Bat Swarm, adding additional bats to the move. Note that these three special bats attack on their own and each of them can do significant damage.

Bat Betterment

Become a Giant Bat and use upgraded bat minions to deal with enemies. The first priority is Bat-tle Cry that boosts both the damage of the screech attack and the pet bats. Next, increase the amount of bats through Ultimate Bat Squad and Chiropteran Call. These combined upgrades work together to create lots of bats, but always use screech to power them up and do additional damage in melee range. Bat Spin can let the minions do a lot of the work on dangerous foes. However, its bite and screech can be used with the pets to overwhelm most foes up close.

⬤ SOUL GEM ABILITY

GREAT BALLS OF BATS! `4000`

Hold **Attack 1** to launch a giant ball of bats! Prerequisite: Find Bat Spin's Soul Gem in CH 8: Telescope Towers

This giant ball of batty goodness will pass through enemies doing damage to all in its path. This is an excellent choice to use with long range bat attacks to knock out foes before they can get close in.

Basic Attacks

BAT ATTACK

Press **Attack 1** to shoot bitey pet bats out at enemies.

BAT SWARM

Press **Attack 2** to summon a maelstrom of bat damage.

Upgrades

HEALING BITE `500`

Collect pet bats after they have bitten enemies to regain HP.

BRAWNY BATS `700`

Pet bats last longer, do more damage, and are more aggressive.

GO BATTY! `900`

Press **Attack 3** to transform into a Giant Bat! In Bat Form, press **Attack 1** to bite and **Attack 2** to screech.

A COLONY OF BATS `1200`

Increase the maximum number of pet bats.

Pet Purveyor

Improve abilities to summon bats.

MR. DIZZY `1700`

A new pet bat, Mr. Dizzy, stuns and confuses enemies.

MR. BLOCKY `2200`

A new pet bat, Mr. Blocky, protects you by deflecting projectiles.

MR. BITEY `3000`

A new pet bat, Mr. Bitey, does extra biting damage.

Bat Betterment

Improve Bat Form abilities.

BAT-TLE CRY `1700`

In Bat Form, the screech attack does extra damage and powers up pet bats.

ULTIMATE BAT SQUAD `2200`

More pet bats fly with you and have additional powers.

CHIROPTERAN CALL `3000`

In Bat Form, the bite attack shoots out three additional pet bats.

99

Eye Small

I've Got My Eye on You!

Maximum Health	430
Speed	50
Armor	30
Critical Hit	50
Elemental Power	53

Basic Attack Notes

▶ **Haymaker**

A straightforward heavy punching attack that can get upgraded damage.

▶ **Eye Fly**

Detach eyeball and fire while the headless body can upgrade to punch continuously.

▶ **An Eye in Team**

Summon numerous eyeballs that bounce and attack enemies. This is a great distraction move.

Upgrade Paths

Eye Brawler

Ultimate Pummeler adds extra damage while Beats an Eye Patch provides additional armor. Together these allow Eye Small to more easily go toe-to-toe with most enemies in melee range. To further enhance those close quarter combat skills he gets two new combos. Eye Ball Spin shoots an extra damaging eye straightforward and is great on tough foes. The 360 Spin does what it says hits any enemy is a relatively large radius. The Eye Ball Spin is best used for crowds of enemies or when surrounded.

Eye for an Eye

All three powers on this path upgrade Eye Fly. Eye-Crawlers and Bouncy Bouncy! add extra damage with auxiliary eyes and a direct attack. To make the most of Eye Fly abilities Asserting Independent is a must. It allows the eyeball to move faster as well as stay detached longer. Essentially it provides more time and mobility to take advantage of the new damaging upgrades. Keep in mind that using Eye Fly leaves Eye Small somewhat helpless. Don't leave his body in jeopardy when fighting large groups of enemies or really heavy damaging foes.

SOUL GEM ABILITY

YOU'LL SHOOT YOUR EYE OUT! 4000

Hold **Attack 1** to charge up Eye Small's eye, release to pop it off the body, smashing directly ahead.

This attack takes some practice; you must become good at releasing **Attack 1** at the right time. When you get it down, it's an effective high-damage attack, but should only be used against stationary objects.

Basic Attacks

HAYMAKER

Press **Attack 1** to throw some heavy punches. Press **Attack 1**, **Attack 1**, HOLD **Attack 1** for a special combo.

EYE FLY

Press the **Attack 2** button to detach the eyeball and fly around. While flying, press **Attack 1** to shoot eye lasers.

Upgrades

AN EYE IN TEAM 500

Press **Attack 3** to summon more eyeballs from the earth to attack enemies.

AWESOME OCCU-BLAST 700

Eye laser has a faster rate of fire.

THE PUMMELER 900

Punch attacks do increased damage.

HEADLESS, NOT HELPLESS 1200

While flying the eyeball, his headless body punches continuously.

Eye Brawler

Further develop Eye Small's melee combat skills.

EYE-BRAWL COMBOS 1700

Press **Attack 1**, **Attack 1**, HOLD **Attack 2** for Eye Ball Spin. Press **Attack 1**, **Attack 1**, HOLD **Attack 3** for 360 Spin.

ULTIMATE PUMMELER 2200

Melee attacks do additional damage.

BEATS AN EYE PATCH 3000

New armor provides additional protection.

Eye for an Eye

Further develop Flying Eyeball abilities.

ASSERTING INDEPENDENCE 1700

Eyeball can now fly faster and for a longer duration.

EYE-CRAWLERS 2200

When enemies are hit with eye lasers, eyes form around the point of impact.

BOUNCY BOUNCY! 3000

While flying the eyeball, press **Attack 3** to bounce the eye on the ground.

Funny Bone

I Have a Bone to Pick!

Maximum Health	270
Speed	70
Armor	24
Critical Hit	20
Elemental Power	46

Funny Bone once lived on Punch Line Island—the funniest place in the land of the Undead and home of the Eternal Chuckling Trees that magically make everyone laugh when the breeze tickles them. But after hearing stories of this, the evil Count Moneybone sent his minions to investigate if this magic could be used to make a "Funny Bomb" that would render Skylands helpless with laughter. Funny Bone was in the middle of burying his neighbors' birthday cake on a breezeless day when the invaders arrived. Seeing their large axes, Funny Bone instantly knew that the Chuckling Trees were in danger. Without hesitation, he sprang into action, fighting off the minions and driving them from his humorous home. Now as a Skylander, Funny Bone delivers his own punch line to evil!

Basic Attack Notes

▶ **Bone Saw**
Use the analog stick to control the motion of the saw as it rolls. Enemies are hurt while it is charging.

▶ **Flying Bone Disc**
Bone Disc passes through foes and can damage enemies in a straight line.

▶ **Bone Paws**
Can have three at a time that remain until a new one is created.

Upgrade Paths

Tail Wagger
For fans of up close combat, this path provides a massive boost in damage potential. The Bone Saw can damage foes while it charges and the longer the move is charged the more damage it does when released. The Supercharged Saw upgrade nearly doubles the damage of the Bone Saw! Head Case provides more damage versatility, creating a ghost skull to attack foes as you dash by them. Bone Paw Power can supercharge the Bone Saw while providing protection with the Bone Paws. This powerful combination allows foes to get into range while taking damage from the Bone Paws and then get shreaded by a supercharged Bone Saw.

Bone Zoner
Upgrade the Flying Bone Disc with an exploding effect from Flying Bone Boom that blows up at the end of the disc's path. This upgrade is essential for more effective long-range damage. Those that want to go face-to-face with foes should use Ultimate FBD to chase after the disc and deliver a fetching slam attack that covers a large area. However, it can be dangerous to chase the disc into some groups of enemies. Play Catch can create a deadly barrier by bouncing the disc back and forth between Bone Paws. It can also be used to ricochet the disc, adding more projectiles to cut through bad guys.

⬤ SOUL GEM ABILITY

HEALING PAWS — 4000
Bone Paws pet Funny Bone to heal him.
Prerequisite: Find Funny Bone's Soul Gem in CH 4: The Phoenix Psanctuary

The Bone Paws can create a defensive wall, keeping enemies at bay, and now slowly heal Funny Bone. This ability provides a way to retreat and recoup some health if a battle gets too hectic. This can also be used to rest between fights using three paws to pet Funny Bone.

Basic Attacks

BONE SAW
Press **Attack 1** to dash forward and slice enemies.

FLYING BONE DISC
Press **Attack 2** to shoot a Flying Bone Disc.

Upgrades

BONE PAWS — 500
Press **Attack 3** to raise Bone Paws from the ground which attack enemies.

DISC DEMON — 700
Flying Bone Disc does extra damage.

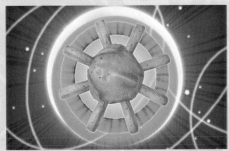

FEROCIOUS FETCH — 900
Press and hold **Attack 2** to chase after the Flying Bone Disc and release to fetch it.

BUMP UP THE BLADES — 1200
Press and hold **Attack 1** to charge the Bone Saw.

Tail Wagger
Improve Bone Saw attacks.

SUPERCHARGED SAW — 1700
Press and hold **Attack 3** to supercharge the Bone Saw.

BONE PAW POWER — 2200
Dash towards a Bone Paw to supercharge the Bone Saw.

HEAD CASE — 3000
Press and hold **Attack 3** to summon a ghostly skull to devour enemies during the Bone Saw attack.

Bone Zoner
Improve Flying Bone Disc attacks.

FLYING BONE BOOM — 1700
Flying Bone Discs now explode and do additonal damage.

ULTIMATE FBD — 2200
Flying Bone Disc Slam affects a larger area.

PLAY CATCH — 3000
Hit a Bone Paw with a Flying Bone Disc to play catch with other paws.

Hijinx

Fear the Dark!

Maximum Health	270
Speed	60
Armor	18
Critical Hit	30
Elemental Power	60

Basic Attack Notes

▶ **Conjure Phantom Orbs**
Magic Orbs that track foes and can be upgraded to shoot two at a time.

▶ **Rain of Skulls**
Can move slowly while the attack charges and it can be upgraded to use four skulls at once.

▶ **Wall of Bones**
A semi-circle barrier of bones that can be upgraded to larger and more durable protection.

Upgrade Paths

Shade Master

Long Distance Orbs may not seem that useful but these are tracking orbs and the extra range means they can hit foes anywhere on the screen. Caustic Phantom Orbs is a straightforward damage boost. Unstable Phantom Orbs also increase damage in the form of projectiles that explode on contact. The exploding orbs can damage nearby enemies, proving a wider effect for her long-range attack. This path is clearly geared towards boosting Conjure Phantom Orbs so stay back and use a Wall of Bones for protection while bombarding enemies with orb attacks.

Bone Crafter

Compound Fracture turns Wall of Bones into an offensive shield that hurts anything that touches it. This power can turn a shield into an attack by luring enemies into it. Troll Skull is a basic damage boost to Skull Rain, but it gets even better with another upgrade on this path. Master Caster reduces the time to cast both Wall of Bones and Skull Rain! This awesome upgrade helps deal with the long charge time for Skull Rain and is a must to use that attack effectively. The damage ability on Wall of Bones and quicker cast time means it can be created on the go and hurt any foes chasing you.

⬤ SOUL GEM ABILITY

SKULL SHIELD 4000

Skull Rain knocks away enemies and attacks.

This upgrade serves to make Skull Rain an even more vicious attack. One drawback to Skull Rain is that it can take a long time to fully charge. With this power, any enemy that tries to hit Hijinx while she is charging takes damage and gets knocked back.

Basic Attacks

CONJURE PHANTOM ORB

Press **Attack 1** to launch magic orbs of spectral energy that track Hijinx's foes.

RAIN OF SKULLS

Hold **Attack 2** to begin casting this spell. When fully charged, release and ghostly skulls rain down on Hijinx's enemies.

Upgrades

WALL OF BONES 500

Press **Attack 3** to create a Wall of Bones to protect Hijinx.

STORM OF SKULLS 700

Conjure up to four skulls with your Skull Rain attack.

BONE FORTRESS 900

The Wall of Bones is larger and takes more damage to destroy. Prerequisite: Wall of Bones

TWICE THE ORBAGE 1200

Press **Attack 1** to shoot two Phantom Orbs at once.

Shade Master

Further develop Hijinx's Phantom Orb attack.

LONG DISTANCE ORBS 1700

Hold **Attack 1** to increase the range of your Phantom Orbs.

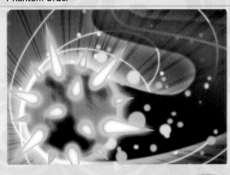

CAUSTIC PHANTOM ORBS 2200

Phantom Orbs do increased damage.

UNSTABLE PHANTOM ORBS 3000

Phantom Orbs explode, damaging nearby enemies.

Bone Crafter

Further develop Hijinx's Skull Rain and Wall of Bones abilities.

COMPOUND FRACTURE 1700

Wall of Bones damages any enemy that touches it.

MASTER CASTER 2200

Takes much less time to cast Skull Rain and Wall of Bones.

TROLL SKULLS 3000

Skull Rain does increased damage.

Krypt King

I've Got the Edge!

Maximum Health	300
Speed	60
Armor	24
Critical Hit	40
Elemental Power	32

The perfect blend of sword and sorcery, Krypt King wandered Skylands for years as the disembodied spirit of a knight—until he found his way into the depths of an ancient Arkeyan weapon vault. Upon finding an enormously powerful suit of armor, the spirit decided to make it his own. Unfortunately, this triggered a long dormant auto defense system. With alarms blaring, a massive sealed chamber was opened, revealing a huge army of war machines. Krypt King launched himself towards the attack force, swinging his newly found giant sword until every machine was utterly destroyed. Realizing the power he wielded could serve a broader purpose, Krypt King sought out the Skylanders and was made a member of the Trap Team, where he now uses his massive Traptanium blade to cut down evil!

Basic Attack Notes

▶ **Traptanium Broadsword**
If done mid-jump, Krypt King drives his sword into the ground.

▶ **The Swarm**
Krypt King stops moving while releasing homing insects.

▶ **Haunted Sword**
Attack 1 swings. Attack 3 recalls the sword. Attack 2 has no effect.

Upgrade Paths

Lord of the Sword

This path is ideal for those that want to take matters into their own hands and fight up-close. It is still possible to take advantage of the Haunted Sword abilities, but this path is more geared towards getting in close to rack up quick enemy victories. Each enemy defeat boosts both armor and damage, turning this Skylander into a "tank." Adding the Combo Attack upgrade provides even more ways to quickly cut down a single foe with the Saber Spin combo, or perform some crowd control using the Nether Blast Combo. Choose this path to play bold and brave, taking any enemy head on.

Swarm Summoner

The Swarm is an excellent form of passive attack that homes in on foes. This leaves Krypt King free to flee, gang up the same enemies, or challenge new foes. Adding the stun effect from Stunning Sting makes the Swarm a great tool for dealing with large groups of enemies. The increased damage from Stir Up The Swarm is a must if you rely on this ability as a main source of damage. The Swarm has excellent synergy with the Haunted Sword ability, especially after upgrading Spectral Slowdown. Release the Traptanium Broadsword and launch the swarm to wipe out most enemies from a safe distance before they can reach you.

⚫ SOUL GEM ABILITY

UNLIMITED TRAPTANIUM WORKS (4000)
Landing a critical hit causes swords to rain down upon Krypt King's enemies. Prerequisite: Find Krypt King's Soul Gem in CH 7: Monster Marsh

This benefits the bold who attack relentlessly and trigger critical hits. Each time a critical is scored not only does the attack do more damage, but the falling swords also add insult to injury to finish weaker foes.

Basic Attacks

TRAPTANIUM BROADSWORD
Press **Attack 1** to swing the Traptanium Broadsword.
Press **Attack 1**, **Attack 1**, **Attack 1** for a combo attack.

THE SWARM
Press **Attack 2** to release a swarm of Undead insects that seek out enemies.

Upgrades

HAUNTED SWORD (500)
Press **Attack 3** to release the Traptanium Broadsword and steer it towards enemies.

SPECTRAL SLOWDOWN (700)
Haunted Sword slows down all enemies it touches.

THE BROADER THE BROADSWORD (900)
Traptanium Broadsword attack does extra damage with greater reach.

SUPER SWARM (1200)
Hold **Attack 2** to charge up the Swarm attack to unleash a larger swarm.

Lord of the Sword Path
Improve Traptanium Broadsword attacks.

ENCHANTED ARMOR (1700)
Armor is increased upon defeating an enemy.

THE RICH GET RICHER (2200)
Attacks do increased damage after defeating an enemy.

COMBO ATTACKS (3000)
Press **Attack 1**, **Attack 1**, **Attack 2** for Sabre Spin Combo.
Press **Attack 1**, **Attack 1**, **Attack 3** for Nether Blast Combo.

Swarm Summoner Path
Improved Swarm Attacks.

STUNNING STING (1700)
Swarm attack now stuns enemies.

STIR UP THE SWARM (2200)
Hit the Swarm with your Traptanium Broadsword to power it up.

PARASITIC POWER (3000)
Get healed by the Swarm after it dies.

Short Cut

Cut to the Chase!

Maximum Health	280
Speed	70
Armor	18
Critical Hit	80
Elemental Power	39

Short Cut was renowned for making the finest clothing in all of Skylands. With his magic shears, no thread was too thick, no cloth was too bunchy, and no pattern was too hard to follow. But one day, a fleet of flying sailing ships appeared overhead, crewed by raucous Skeleton Pirates. Having plundered a cargo of golden yarn from fortunetelling soothsayers, their leader demanded that Short Cut stitch together a magic hat that would tell him the futures of everyone in Skylands—or suffer the consequences! Not wanting to see his work used for evil, he bravely snuck onto the ship that night and sewed the pants and shirts of the sleeping pirates together so they were unable to fight. Short Cut then used his magic shears to cut the sails and wrap them around the ship, preventing the pirates from escaping. His brave actions caught the attention of Master Eon, who quickly made Short Cut a member of the Trap Team, where he now uses powerful Traptanium Shears to cut evil's future short with every snip!

Basic Attack Notes

▷ **Traptanium Scissors**
A quick attack that becomes even quicker after Cutting Frenzy.

▷ **Phantom Puppets**
Summon minions to aid Short Cut; clip their rope to send them into action even sooner.

▷ **Nether Needle**
A ranged attack that brings enemies into melee distance and eventually immobilizes them.

Upgrade Paths

Scary Seamster

This path adds a lot of power and a new feature to the Nether Needle. The primary use of this technique is to draw enemies into melee range. Once they are up close Short Cut and his minions can slice them up with scissors attacks. However, the last two upgrades on this path add much needed additional damage. While Short Cut is really quick, his regular attacks do not dish out big damage. The increases these upgrades provide are critical. Treacherous Tangle is a great added feature that immobilizes foes to attack directly, temporarily takes them out of action, or lets your minions deal with them. However, this can't incapacitate all enemies.

Puppet Master

As the master of puppets make sure to create them constantly and cut them loose to free them quickly and do more damage. This path allows your minions to do more damage acting like bombs before they disappear. Also it is possible to create more Phantom Puppets to make a small army to assist in battle. Keep minions at all times and let them do a lot of the damage as this path does not directly increase Short Cut's scissor attacks. The final option on this path allows the minions to heal Short Cut giving him a chance to retreat and let his minions deal with most enemies.

⬤ SOUL GEM ABILITY

SCISSOR STILTS — 4000

Hold **Attack 1** and press **Attack 2** to walk on the Traptanium Scissors like stilts, damaging anything in your path. Prerequisite: Find Short Cut's Soul Gem in CH 17: Lair of the Golden Queen

Walk across foes, shredding them with the Traptanium Scissors. The added height from these stilts is a great boost to Short Cut's small stature and allows him to trample without much fear of retaliation.

Basic Attacks

TRAPTANIUM SCISSORS

Press **Attack 1** to snip away with Traptanium Scissors.

PHANTOM PUPPETS

Press **Attack 2** to summon puppet minions who attack enemies.

Upgrades

CUTTING FRENZY — 500

Rapidly press **Attack 1** to go into a cutting frenzy.

NETHER NEEDLE — 700

Press **Attack 3** to shoot a Nether Needle and pull enemies you hit in closer.

NO STRINGS ATTACHED — 900

Cut a Puppet's string with Traptanium Scissors to make it faster and more powerful.

CUT THROUGH WORLDS — 1200

Hold **Attack 1** and release to cut open a rift into another dimension.

Scary Seamster

Upgrade Traptanium Scissor attacks.

TREACHEROUS TANGLE — 1700

Enemies reeled in by the Nether Needle are tangled up in thread.

SUPER SNIPS — 2200

Enemies tangled up in thread take extra damage from Scissor attacks.

THREADSPLOSION — 3000

After an enemy becomes untangled, an explosion occurs doing extra damage.

Puppet Master

Upgrade Phantom Puppet attacks.

GO OUT WITH A BANG — 1700

Phantom Puppets explode before disappearing, damaging anything around them.

PUPPET POPULATION — 2200

Can summon more Phantom Puppets at a time and all do extra damage.

PAGING DR. PUPPETS — 3000

Phantom Puppets can heal you after damaging an enemy.

Echo

Let's Make Some Noise!

Maximum Health	270
Speed	50
Armor	42
Critical Hit	20
Elemental Power	46

Echo lived in an undersea kingdom that was built around an enormous oyster shell, and at its center was the Pearl of Wisdom. Every day water dragons from all around the kingdom would come to ask questions of the Pearl. Because this was a sacred ritual, anyone living near the Pearl was required to speak only in whispers. This was challenging for Echo, who lived directly next to it. She had a gift—and it was loud—that often got her in trouble. One day, a gang of sea horses known as the Aqua Jocks rode into town and claimed the Pearl for themselves. They cast an unbreakable bubble around it and began dragging it away with enormous chains. The nearby water dragons, who had been quiet for so long, were unable to even call for help. Then Echo appeared—and with her loudest sonar blast, she shattered the bubble and blew the sea horses out of the kingdom! Her heroic actions caught the attention of Gill Grunt, who recruited her as a Skylander. Now Echo sounds off against evil all throughout Skylands!

Basic Attack Notes

▶ Siren Scream
The attack button can be held to perform a continuous attack while moving slowly.

▶ Bubble Bombs
An explosive bubble that damages nearby enemies and bounces to the beat.

▶ Sonic Slam
An attack with a 360-degree area of effect that can create a shockwave when upgraded.

Upgrade Paths

Bubble Up!
Power Pop provides maximum damage and increased range, making bombs even more effective for reducing groups of enemies. Unlike other projectiles, Bubble Bombs float and linger instead of directly hitting foes. Use them at mid-range and also to create a minefield to lure enemies in. Echo's two bubble boosts create a Bubble Shield that can be turned into a bomb. Keep the shield for as long as possible and detonate it only when necessary. Echo can deal a lot damage with its other attacks and the shield's damage reduction is a great asset.

Singalong
Siren Scream gets infinite use ability from Ultimate Pitch Control making it very effective against smaller enemies at mid-range. Scream Out adds an extra shout attack, which should be used to end a Siren Scream. Sonic Slam also receives a new power form Ultrasound. This charge attack takes a while to build up and is best left for less crowded situations. While it may take a while to use it does hurt enemies that get close and it is one of the most damaging moves in the game.

⬤ SOUL GEM ABILITY

CALL OF THE SIREN — 4000
Use Siren Scream on a Bubble Bomb to put enemies in a painful trance. Prequisite: Find Echo's Soul Gem in CH 10:The Secret Sewers of Supreme Stink

Enemies can't help heeding the Call of the Siren from this enhanced Bubble Bomb. They become paralyzed and continue to take damage as they gaze into the bubble. This does fairly low damage but it continues to hurt enemies and it is a great method to distract foes.

Basic Attacks

SIREN SCREAM
Hold **Attack 1** for a Siren Scream, damaging enemies.

BUBBLE BOMBS
Press **Attack 2** to create explosive bubbles that move to the beat.

Upgrades

SONIC SLAM — 500
Press **Attack 3** to create a sonic slam, damaging enemies on the ground.

PITCH CONTROL — 700
Can hold the Siren Scream notes for longer, doing more damage.

4-BEAT — 900
Deploy up to 4 Bubble Bombs at any one time, which now do extra damage.

SUBSONIC — 1200
Sonic Slam now creates an aftershock that deals extra damage. Prerequisite: Sonic Slam

Bubble Up!
Improve Bubble Bomb attacks.

BUBBLE SHIELD — 1700
Hold **Attack 2** to protect yourself in a bubble that absorbs damage until it pops.

POWER POP — 2200
All Bubble Bombs do MAXIMUM damage at an increased range.

BURST MY BUBBLE — 3000
While in a Bubble Shield, press **Attack 3** to make it explode and damage nearby enemies. Prerequisite: Bubble Shield

Singalong
Improve Siren Scream attacks.

ULTIMATE PITCH CONTROL — 1700
Hold **Attack 1** indefinitely for an never-ending Siren Scream.

SCREAM OUT — 2200
Quickly press **Attack 1** again after a Siren Scream to deliver a powerful shout attack.

ULTRASOUND — 3000
Hold **Attack 3** to charge the Sonic Slam attack and unleash another, more powerful burst.

Flip Wreck
Making Waves!

Maximum Health	300
Speed	60
Armor	30
Critical Hit	30
Elemental Power	39

Most of the dolphins of Bottlenose Bay spent their days playing in the waves. However, Flip Wreck was different. Always the adventurous one, he took it upon himself to be a self-appointed protector of his undersea world. One day, while exploring an underwater graveyard of shipwrecks, he came across a massive Ice Viking ship that was still intact. Suddenly, a huge crew of Ice Vikings burst out from inside and began leading an attack on the unarmed dolphin residents. Flip Wreck took off at once and quickly fastened together armor, shield, and sword using pieces from the nearby wrecks. He then single-handedly defeated the Ice Vikings, who retreated never to be seen again. For his heroic actions, Flip Wreck was made a Skylander and now turns the tide against evil in Skylands!

Basic Attack Notes

▶ **Sea Saw**

Can be used three times for a combo and performs a downward slam in air.

▶ **Wheeling and Dealing**

Moves around enemies riding the wheel shield and can use the See Saw attack at the same time.

▶ **Wheel Shield Bash**

A bashing attack that can be upgraded via Shield Mode to grant invulnerability.

Upgrade Paths

Fish Commander

Fish?!? grants a powerful fish projectile attack while riding the Wheel Shield. Building on that power, Endless Fish allows unlimited fish to send out but it significantly reduces movement speed while being used. The fish projectiles are great at mid-range, covering a wide area and providing the most damage of all Flip Wreck's attacks. Homing Fish provides a longer-range attack that sends fish flopping towards enemies. It is not a high damage move but it does home in on foes.

Sword Specialist

Become a melee master on this path with several new combos. Sword Swells is a good option when enemies are in a tight group. The Whirlpool combo is excellent when you are surrounded as it damages bad guys in a circular radius for several seconds. Use the Undersea Ambush for a large burst of damage at the end of the combo that covers a wide area in the direction you are facing. Blowhole Blaster is a must for using Splash Damage as it provides the range and increased damage it really needs.

⬤ SOUL GEM ABILITY

SEA SLAMMER — 4000

While riding the wheel shield, press **Attack 1**, **Attack 1**, **Attack 1** to slam down on the ground. Prerequisite: Find Flip Wreck's Soul Gem in CH 9: Mystic Mill

Ride the Wheel Shield to gain some mobility, and in the middle of a horde of enemies, use the Sea Slammer to smash them for extra damage. This is especially useful on the Sword Specialist path, which does not upgrade Wheeling and Dealing.

Basic Attacks

SEA SAW

Press **Attack 1** to swing the saw sword.

WHEELING AND DEALING

Press **Attack 2** to hop on the wheel shield, damaging anything in your path.

Upgrades

WHEEL SHIELD BASH — 500

Press **Attack 3** to bash enemies with the wheel shield.

SPLASH DAMAGE — 700

Hold **Attack 1** to blast enemies with your blowhole.

SUPER SEA SAW — 900

Sea Saw does increased damage.

SHIELD MODE — 1200

Hold **Attack 3** to enter Shield Mode, invulnerable to enemy attacks.

Fish Commander

Improve Wheeling & Dealing attacks.

FISH?!? — 1700

Press **Attack 3** to release fish projectiles while riding the Wheel Shield.

HOMING FISH — 2200

Press **Attack 3** to release a fish projectile that hops towards enemies.

ENDLESS FISH — 3000

While riding the wheel shield, hold **Attack 3** to shoot unlimited fish projectiles.

Sword Specialist

Improve Sea Saw attacks.

SWORD SWELLS — 1700

Press **Attack 1**, **Attack 1**, **Attack 1** to gush forward a damaging water swell.

SEA SAW COMBOS — 2200

Press **Attack 1**, **Attack 1**, HOLD **Attack 2** for Whirlpool combo.

Press **Attack 1**, **Attack 1**, HOLD **Attack 3** for Undersea Ambush combo.

BLOWHOLE BLASTER — 3000

Splash Damage attack has more range and does increased damage.

Tidal Wave Gill Grunt

Fear the Fish!

Maximum Health	270
Speed	50
Armor	6
Critical Hit	50
Elemental Power	25

Gill Grunt was a brave soul who joined the Gillmen military in search of adventure. While journeying through a misty lagoon in the clouds, he met an enchanting mermaid. He vowed to return to her after his tour. Keeping his promise, he came back to the lagoon years later, only to learn a nasty band of pirates had kidnapped the mermaid. Heartbroken, Gill Grunt began searching all over Skylands. Though he had yet to find her, he joined the Skylanders to help protect others from such evil, while still keeping an ever-watchful eye for the beautiful mermaid and the pirates who took her.

Basic Attack Notes

▶ **Harpoon Gun**

Slight delay between blasts. Watch for new harpoon to appear to know when to fire.

▶ **Power Hose**

Significantly slows down Gill Grunt while active. Usable with Water Jetpack, but not while jumping.

▶ **Water Jetpack**

Must be on the ground to initiate Water Jetpack. Lasts for three seconds maximum, unless you choose Water Weaver Path.

Upgrade Paths

Harpooner

The Harpooner Path is more effective for battles against multiple enemies. Piercing Harpoons and Tripleshot Harpoon increase the number of enemies hit by each shot, both of which come in handy when you're working through Arenas and Kaos Doom Challenges.

Water Weaver

Power Hose and Jetpack get big boosts from the Water Weaver Path. Use Power Hose to punish melee-focused characters and keep them at bay even longer (never running out of water is an incredible perk). Power Hose doesn't have the range of Harpoon Gun, so work on steering with Water Jetpack activated to quickly close the distance on ranged enemies.

SOUL GEM ABILITY

ANCHOR CANNON — 4000

Hold **Attack 1** to charge Anchor Cannon.

Prepare Anchor Cannon when you see enemies stacked up and waiting in the distance. Its charge up time (plus the fact that it doesn't track enemies and slows down Gill Grunt) makes it difficult to use effectively when you're already engaged with enemies.

Basic Attacks

HARPOON GUN

Press **Attack 1** to shoot high-velocity harpoons at your enemies.

POWER HOSE

Press and hold **Attack 2** to spray water at your enemies to knock them back.

Upgrades

BARBED HARPOONS — 500

Harpoons do increased damage.

HIGH PRESSURE HOSE — 700

Power Hose attack does extra damage and knocks enemies back further.

HARPOON REPEATER — 900

Harpoons reload faster.

WATER JETPACK — 1200

Press **Attack 3** to fly until the water jetpack runs out. Increased speed and armor while flying.

Harpooner Path

Further Develop Gill Grunt's Harpoon Attacks

QUADENT HARPOONS — 1700

Harpoons do even MORE increased damage.

PIERCING HARPOONS — 2200

Harpoons travel straight through enemies and hit new targets.

TRIPLESHOT HARPOON — 3000

Shoot three Harpoons at once.

Water Weaver Path

Further Develop Gill Grunt's Power Hose and Jetpack skills

RESERVE WATER TANK — 1700

The Power Hose and Water Jetpack never run out of water.

BOILING WATER HOSE — 2200

Power Hose attack does even MORE increased damage.

NEPTUNE GUN — 3000

When using the Power Hose, press **Attack 1** to launch exploding creatures.

WOW POW!

RIDE THE LEVIATHAN! — 5000

In Jet Pack Mode, press **Attack 2** to ride a giant Leviathan, taking out anything in its path. Prerequisite: Water Jetpack

The Leviathan remains under your control over its duration (don't expect to make sharp turns) and ends with a big splash. It deals damage to everything it touches, destroying objects and enemies alike. Keep in mind that Gill Grunt remains vulnerable to any attack that can reach him on the aquatic beast's back.

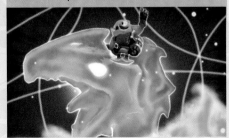

Gill Runt

Fear the Fish!

Maximum Health	270
Speed	50
Armor	6
Critical Hit	50
Elemental Power	25

Basic Attack Notes

▶ **Harpoon Gun**

Slight delay between blasts. Watch for new harpoon to appear to know when to fire.

▶ **Power Hose**

Significantly slows down Gill Runt while active. Usable with Water Jetpack, but not while jumping.

▶ **Water Jetpack**

Must be on the ground to initiate Water Jetpack. Lasts for three seconds maximum, unless you choose Water Weaver Path.

Upgrade Paths

Harpooner

The Harpooner Path is more effective for battles against multiple enemies. Piercing Harpoons and Tripleshot Harpoon increase the number of enemies hit by each shot, both of which come in handy when you're working through Arenas and Kaos Doom Challenges.

Water Weaver

Power Hose and Jetpack get big boosts from the Water Weaver Path. Use Power Hose to punish melee-focused characters and keep them at bay even longer (never running out of water is an incredible perk). Power Hose doesn't have the range of Harpoon Gun, so work on steering with Water Jetpack activated to close the distance to ranged enemies quickly.

○ SOUL GEM ABILITY

ANCHOR CANNON — 4000

Hold **Attack 1** to charge Anchor Cannon.

Prepare Anchor Cannon when you see enemies stacked up and waiting in the distance. Its charge up time (plus the fact that it doesn't track enemies and slows down Gill Runt) makes it difficult to use effectively when you're already engaged with enemies.

Basic Attacks

HARPOON GUN

Press **Attack 1** to shoot high-velocity harpoons at your enemies.

POWER HOSE

Press and hold **Attack 2** to spray water at your enemies to knock them back.

Upgrades

BARBED HARPOONS — 500

Harpoons do increased damage.

HIGH PRESSURE HOSE — 700

Power Hose attack does extra damage and knocks enemies back further.

HARPOON REPEATER — 900

Harpoons reload faster.

WATER JETPACK — 1200

Hold **Attack 3** to fly until the water jetpack runs out. Gain increased speed and resistance while flying.

Harpooner Path

QUADENT HARPOONS — 1700

Harpoons deal even MORE increased damage.

PIERCING HARPOONS — 2200

Harpoons travel straight through enemies and hit new targets.

TRIPLESHOT HARPOON — 3000

Shoot three Harpoons at once.

Water Weaver Path

RESERVE WATER TANK — 1700

The Power Hose and Water Jetpack never run out of water.

BOILING WATER HOSE — 2200

Power Hose attack deals even MORE increased damage.

NEPTUNE GUN — 3000

When using the Power Hose, press **Attack 1** to launch exploding creatures.

Lob-Star

Star Bright, Star Fight!

Maximum Health • • • • • •	**240**
Speed • • • • • • • • • • •	**60**
Armor • • • • • • • • • •	**30**
Critical Hit • • • • • • • •	**40**
Elemental Power • • • • •	**46**

Hailing from the depths of the undersea kingdom of Star City, Lob-Star was the head chef of his own five-star restaurant, often cooking for the King Fish himself. However, few knew that Lob-Star had secretly been training in a mysterious art of fighting known only to a few crustaceans. For a while, Lob-Star was able to keep the peace while still keeping his hidden identity. But when a giant Leviathan threatened to swallow up Lob-Star's guests and capture the King Fish himself, he had no choice but to swim into action. Calling on every trick his mysterious training had taught him, Lob-Star defeated the Leviathan and drove it out of Star City. For risking everything, Lob-Star was recruited by Master Eon to join the Skylanders. Now, as part of the Trap Team, he uses his powerful Traptanium Throwing Stars to serve up defeat to anyone who threatens Skylands!

Basic Attack Notes

▶ Starshooter
Long-range projectile attack that is faster when Boiled.

▶ Boiling Temper
Generate a steam blast and when held (boiling) increases speed and power, however using steam reduces duration.

▶ Lob-Star Roll
A dashing roll the plows through enemies and becomes Lob-Star Express that knocks enemies away.

Upgrade Paths

Shooting Star
Charge to become Boiled and Super Stars becomes a devastating long-range attack. The added speed and damage are great on their own but the slicing effect can cut up entire groups of enemies in no time. The other two upgrades require charging and make it effective to use both at the same time. Twice the Starpower releases a single massive attack while Star Defense provides a protective shield of stars. The circling stars from Star Defense can also be very effective using the Lob-Star Roll to add extra damage when dashing into enemies.

Hard Boiled
Try to always stay in the Boiled state to take advantage the two new steam upgrades. Getting Steamed! is a passive form of retaliation to damage foes that land a blow. Self E-Steam is an absolute must because it increases all steam abilities as well as consuming less Boiling Power while doing so. These combined powers allow Lob-Star to become a tank and attack at melee range using more powerful steam attacks for a lot longer. Full Steam ahead adds a burning trail of steam, making this charge attack an effective way to retreat or dash into enemies while burning them up.

⬤ SOUL GEM ABILITY

THE BOILER — 4000
Improve Boiling Temper attacks. Prerequisite: Find Lob-Star's Soul Gem in CH 6: Rainfish Riviera

Continue charging Boiling Temper to its limits to perform a jumping slam attack that does massive damage to any foes nearby. Lob-Star remains Boiled after the assault and is ready to deal with any foes that can withstand the initial assault.

Basic Attacks

STARSHOOTER
Press **Attack 1** to shoot Traptanium Stars. Shoot faster when Boiled.

BOILING TEMPER
Press **Attack 2** to release a steam blast. Hold **Attack 2** to boil up with rage, increasing speed and power.

Upgrades

LOB-STAR ROLL — 500
Press **Attack 3** to dash and evade attacks. Go faster and further while Boiled.

SHARP SHOT — 700
New Traptanium Stars do increased damage.

BOILING OVER — 900
Release steam while boiling to repel enemies. Tap **Attack 2** to let off more steam.

LOB-STAR EXPRESS — 1200
Lob-Star Roll is faster and knocks away enemies. If Boiled, releases a steam blast afterwards. Prerequisite: Lob-Star Roll

Shooting Star
Improve Starshooter attacks.

SUPER STARS — 1700
While Boiled, Traptanium Stars do increased damage and cut through enemies.

TWICE THE STARPOWER — 2200
Hold **Attack 1** and release to shoot two Traptanium Stars at once.

STAR DEFENSE — 3000
Hold **Attack 1** longer to create more Traptanium Stars for protection. Prerequisite: Twice the Starpower

Hard Boiled
Fully charge up the Boiling Temper attack to release the ultimate steam blast.

GETTING STEAMED! — 1700
After getting hit by enemies, automatically release steam to damage them right back.

SELF E-STEAM — 2200
All steam abilities get stronger and consume less Boiling Power.

FULL STEAM AHEAD — 3000
Leave a trail of damaging steam behind. Prerequisite: Self E-Steam

Snap Shot

Croc and Roll!

Maximum Health	290
Speed	70
Armor	24
Critical Hit	30
Elemental Power	46

Snap Shot came from a long line of Crocagators that lived in the remote Swamplands, where he hunted chompies for sport. After rounding up every evil critter in his homeland, Snap Shot ventured out into the world to learn new techniques that he could use to track down more challenging monsters. He journeyed far and wide, perfecting his archery skills with the Elves and his hunting skills with the wolves. Soon he was the most revered monster hunter in Skylands—a reputation that caught the attention of Master Eon. It then wasn't long before Snap Shot became the leader of the Trap Masters, a fearless team of Skylanders that mastered legendary weapons made of pure Traptanium. It was this elite team that tracked down and captured the most notorious villains Skylands had ever known!

Basic Attack Notes

▶ **Traptanium Arrow**
When upgraded to Sure Shot Croc it gains a charge ability that allows arrows to pass through enemies.

▶ **Crystal Slam**
Performs a downward slam while in the air and can be upgraded with a charge ability to do nearly twice the damage.

▶ **Torrential Tidepool**
A controllable water attack that continues to hurt enemies it touches, but Snap Shot can't move while it's used.

Upgrade Paths

Crackshot Croc

Each additional power further enhances Snap Shot's Traptanium Arrows making him one of the most effective Skylanders at long-range. Arrowsplosion is a great upgrade for normal arrows due to its explosive effect that hurts surrounding foes. Traptanium Flechette also increases basic arrow attacks with splintered shards that cover even more area instead of adding a lot of damage. Hydro Arrow is an incredible attack that has a short charge time. If you immediately charge after letting an arrow lose it is almost possible to continually shoot these Water-Element infused arrows for big damage.

Tide Turner

The additional damage and size from Big Wave Torrent is a significant enhancement and should be the first priority. What's Kraken? uses a fearsome sea creature to do extra damage and it extremely cool to behold. Water Trap provides the added effect of trapping enemies so they continue to suffer the damage boosts from the other two upgrades. After acquiring all of these upgrades Torrential Tidepool becomes a lot more powerful and can dominate enemies at mid-range. However, Snap Shot is unable to move while performing this attack so don't let enemies surrounded him or extend the attacks so far it can't protect him.

⚪ SOUL GEM ABILITY

A SHARD ACT TO FOLLOW `4000`

Crystal Slam in the air creates a new Traptanium attack. Prerequisite: Find Snap Shot's Soul Gem in CH4: Phoenix Psanctuary

A jumping attack from Crystal Slam hits enemies in melee range but it also sends a series of Traptanium crystals straight ahead to damage any enemies in its path. This ability provides some extended range for Crystal Slam and is best utilized when a group of enemies is closing in on Snap Shot.

Basic Attacks

TRAPTANIUM ARROW
Press **Attack 1** to fire Traptanium arrows.

CRYSTAL SLAM
Press **Attack 2** to perform a Crystal Slam.

Upgrades

SURE SHOT CROC `500`
Hold **Attack 1** to charge up a Traptanium Arrow attack.

TORRENTIAL TIDEPOOL `700`
Hold **Attack 3** to create a controllable Torrential Tidepool.

SUPER SLAM `900`
Hold **Attack 2** to charge up an extra powerful Crystal Slam.

AMAZING ARROW `1200`
Improved Traptanium Arrow does extra damage.

Crackshot Croc
Improve Traptanium Arrow attacks.

ARROWSPLOSION `1700`
Traptanium Arrows now explode on impact.

TRAPTANIUM FLECHETTE `2200`
Shards of Traptanium splinter off arrows doing additional damage.

HYDRO ARROW `3000`
Hold **Attack 1** to charge up a Water Element-infused Traptanium Arrow.

Tide Turner
Improve Tide Turner attacks.

BIG WAVE TORRENT `1700`
Torrential Tidepool is bigger and does more damage.

WATER TRAP `2200`
Enemies caught in Torrential Tidepool become trapped.

WHAT'S KRAKEN? `3000`
Torrential Tidepool now calls forth the power of the Kraken!

Thumpling

Hail to the Whale!

Maximum Health	460
Speed	40
Armor	30
Critical Hit	50
Elemental Power	25

Basic Attack Notes

▶ **Anchor Assault**
A swinging attack that hits enemies when sent out and when it returns.

▶ **Belly Flop**
A fast sliding attack that can plow through large groups of enemies.

▶ **A Whale of a Chomp**
A high damage attack that is effective up close but can open him up to counter attacks.

Upgrade Paths

Anchor's A-Yay!!

Thumpling's primary attack Anchor Assault receives damage and combo upgrades on this path. The attack is slow, but its extended range and extra damage are tremendous benefits. Memorize Thumpling's Combos and practice them to deal with enemies up close or at mid range. The Power Swing combo ends with a 360-degree spin to deal with enemies that surround you. Whirlpool Ripper is the best choice at mid range due to its power upgrade from Bermuda Triangle and the lingering whirlpool that damages any enemies unfortunate enough to be nearby.

Up Close and Personal

Thumpling's trademark Belly Slide lets him power through large groups of enemies. His speed while sliding makes him hard to hit and the Belly Flop doubles as an excellent evasive maneuver, even if you don't focus on upgrading it. Breakfast in Bed provides the ability to chop at enemies while sliding to add extra damage. Be careful though, all that sliding makes it very easy to go over the edge! Bad Sushi is a mid-range attack that adds variety but it's not as effective as Anchor Assault. Armor of the Sea is a great passive ability that increases armor, allowing Thumpling to take more damage up close or during a slide.

◯ SOUL GEM ABILITY

BLOWHARD — 4000

While belly sliding, press **Attack 1** to spray water and starfish.

This is a great add-on for the Belly Flop attack. When you hit **Attack 1** Thumpling blows a starfish and water out of his blowhole, which blasts any enemies he is sliding near. This can be done once per slide, but is very effective, especially if you miss with the belly Flop attack directly.

Basic Attacks

ANCHOR ASSAULT

Press **Attack 1** to swing Thumpling's anchor at enemies. Press **Attack 1**, **Attack 1**, HOLD **Attack 1** for a special combo!

BELLY FLOP

Press **Attack 2** to dive into a belly flop, damaging enemies.

Upgrades

A WHALE OF A CHOMP — 500

Press **Attack 3** for a big, whalesized chomp.

SLIPPERY BELLY — 700

Slide longer after a belly flop and do increased damage.

THE WHALEST CHOMP — 900

Bigger, most powerful Whale Chomp attack.

NOW THERE'S AN ANCHOR! — 1200

Increases Anchor Assault's damage.

Anchor's A-Yay!!

Provides more upgrades for the Anchor attacks.

THUMPLING COMBOS — 1700

Press **Attack 1**, **Attack 1**, and HOLD **Attack 2** for Power Swing. Press **Attack 1**, **Attack 1**, and HOLD **Attack 3** for Whirlpool Ripper.

BERMUDA TRIANGLE — 2200

Increase the power of the Whirlpool Ripper combo attack. Prerequisite: Thumpling Combos

ULTIMATE ANCHOR — 3000

Best anchor you can find! Does maximum damage.

Up Close and Personal

Provides more upgrades for the Belly Flop and Chomp attacks.

BREAKFAST IN BED — 1700

While Belly sliding, press **Attack 3** to chomp enemies.

ARMOR OF THE SEA — 2200

Seashells make for better armor.

BAD SUSHI — 3000

Hold the **Attack 3** button to release a stream of projectile water vomit, damaging enemies.

Improving Your Skylanders

		Armor	6
Max Health	540	Speed	50
Level	10	Critical Hit	50
Playtime	7:19.0	Elemental Power	39

As a Portal Master, one of your primary tasks is improving your Skylanders so they can stand up to their enemies throughout the Skylands. This chapter covers the many facets and methods of improving and customizing your Skylanders.

Leveling

Whenever you defeat an enemy, they leave behind tiny XP orbs. There are other means of acquiring XP orbs, such as finding **Story Scrolls**, but enemies are your Skylander's primary source. When your Skylanders absorb these orbs, they gain experience and get closer to leveling up. You can see how close your Skylander is to leveling up by examining the XP Bar just below their health.

Stats

Each Skylander has five Stats: Max Health, Speed, Armor, Critical Hit, and Elemental Power. Max Health is the only stat that increases when your Skylander gains a level. Elemental Power increases when you add Skylanders of the same Elemental type to your collection.

Max Health

This is your Skylander's most important statistic. Whenever their health reaches zero, they are knocked out and you must place another Skylander on the portal.

Speed

This is how fast your Skylander can move around.

Armor

Whenever a Skylander is hit by an enemy attack, it has a chance to be completely deflected by their armor. This stat reflects that chance. For every six points of armor your Skylander has, they have a 1% chance of deflecting an enemy attack. So, a Skylander with 90 Armor has a 15% chance to deflect an attack.

Critical Hit

This stat determines the chance a Skylander will score a Critical Hit or "crit." A crit scores 150% regular damage of an attack. For every five points in Critical Hit, the chance to score a crit increases by 1%. So a Skylander with 50 Critical Hit has a 10% chance of scoring a crit.

Elemental Power

Throughout the Skylands, certain zones have favored elements. If you are using a Skylander of that element in one of these zones, they get bonus damage based on how high their Elemental Power is. Each point adds 1% to the bonus damage, so a Skylander with 100 Elemental Power will get 100% bonus damage in their favored zone.

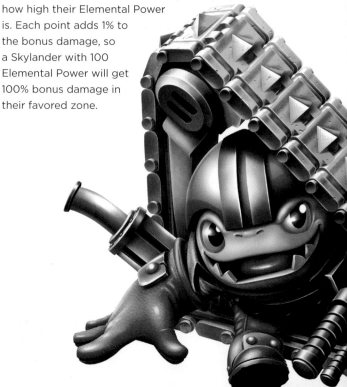

Powers & Upgrades

Each Skylander starts out with two Powers. For more details on what powers your Skylanders start out with, check out the chapter entitled "Meet The Skylanders." In addition to these starting powers, each Skylander can also unlock additional abilities, but you must purchase them from Persephone. Power Upgrades are also purchased from Persephone, who appears at Skylanders Academy and at one location during each adventure chapter.

Upgrade Paths

Skylanders must also choose a Path. This Path is a specialty the Skylander takes in choosing to develop one power or ability over another. Most Skylanders must permanently commit to one path once they have unlocked their first four power upgrades.

The exceptions to this rule are the Series 2, 3, and 4 figures. These Skylanders may switch paths by speaking with Persephone.

Soul Gem Ability

All the characters introduced in *Skylanders Trap Team* must find their Soul Gem before they can purchase their Soul Gem Ability. The walkthrough contains more information on where to find each Soul Gem, or check out The Skylanders section of the guide.

Skylanders from the previous games purchase their Soul Gem Power without the need to find a Soul Gem.

Wow-Pow Powers

Series 2, 3, and 4 Skylanders have new Wow-Pow powers that are expensive, but significantly improve an existing power. For more details on Wow Pow powers, check out the Skylanders' individual chapters.

Hats & Trinkets

Each Skylander can wear one magic Hat, and one Trinket at a time. Hats and Trinkets are available for purchase from Auric, and found throughout the adventure. Hats provide bonuses to stats, while Trinkets are purely cosmetic. You can change your Skylander's Hat at any time via the Skylanders Outfit menu.

Once you find a Hat or Trinket, you can put it on as many Skylanders as you like. There are 99 Hats available in *Skylanders Trap Team,* and the game tracks Hats you bring in from other Skylanders games in slots 100-245 of your Hats inventory screen. There are 33 trinkets in *Skylanders Trap Team.*

Trapped Villains

What could be more satisfying than showing a misguided being the error of their ways and giving them a chance to do good after being bad? With the elemental traps in Skylanders Trap Team, you have the opportunity to do that many times over!

When you defeat certain Villains during your adventure, place a trap of the proper element into the *Traptanium* Portal to capture the Villain and convince them to become good. They lend their abilities to your cause and often get a chance to perform good deeds in the form of quests.

Putting Villains to Good Use

Unless you're completing their quest or at Skylanders Academy, when you tag Villains, a timer appears instead of a health bar. Unlike Skylanders, who need to rest when their health is depleted, Villains only need to return to their Elemental Trap to build up additional playing time. They are available to return to action as soon as the meter fills past the line on the left side of their timer. Villains are also a chatty bunch. They'll provide audio clues when they're ready to rejoin the fight.

Tips for Using Villains

Always have a Villain in the Traptanium Portal

There's never a good reason not to have one ready. There are Treasure Chests, called Villain Stashes, only they can open. There are areas in the adventure where Villains are strong. And remember, they can't steal from your Skylander because...

XP Bubbles and Gold collected by the Villain go to your Skylander

If your Skylander is low on health but just needs a little more XP to level up, tag in your Villain and your Skylander still levels up while off-screen. However, you do need to switch to eat the food that appears. Villains ignore food.

For Arena Challenges and fights against Doom Raiders, save your Villain for stages where you can't attack

You know those times when the big, bad boss jumps out of reach, rains down destruction, and there's nothing you can do but avoid the beams or blades or floor made of lava? Save your Villain timers for those times. If you mistime a jump or don't quite reach cover, all you lose is a bit of time that regenerates after you tag in your Skylander.

Build Villain/Skylander teams that have complementary abilities.

For example, use Chill Bill to freeze enemies in place, then tag in Fling Kong who can charge up Make It Rain! without the worry of taking damage. There's almost no limit to what different combinations of Villains and Skylanders can do. Play around and have fun!

Dreamcatcher

CAPTURED
Last seen in the final tower of Telescope Towers

QUEST DATA

NAME
Sweet Dreams

LOCATION
Bring her to Rochester at the Wilikin Workshop
to help him sleep

Cloudcracker is not the first prison from which
Dreamcatcher has escaped. She had actually
escaped from Lucid Lockdown within the
Realm of Dreams—before escaping from the
dream realm itself! Not only can she read
your mind while you're sleeping but she can
bring your worst nightmares to life. Using
her mischievous powers of dream-stealing,
she has driven entire villages to the point
of madness—all for the sheer thrill of it. Her
playfully evil nature is what got her noticed
by the Golden Queen, who needed a good
psychic for her evil schemes...and also for
relationship advice. Loving both cunning
plans and gossip, Dreamcatcher was happy
to oblige and promptly joined the Doom
Raiders. Although due to her aforementioned
mischievous nature, the Golden Queen has
found the relationship advice questionable.

Abilities

▶ Press **Attack 1** to summon a sheep-filled dream
tornado.
   UPGRADE: Tornado does more damage and can hit
   multiple targets.

▶ Press **Attack 2** to summon dream devices that
attack enemies they land on.
   UPGRADE: Can summon more at a time.

▶ Press **Attack 3** to create a dreamquake.
   UPGRADE: Dreamquake lasts longer.

*You don't want this head
in your head.*

Bad Juju

She'll take you for a spin.

She'll summon a tornado that sucks enemies in and plant a lightning rod to shock them. Will they weather the storm? No.

Abilities

▶ Press **Attack 1** to call a lightning strike.
UPGRADE: Lightning strike hits multiple enemies.

▶ Press **Attack 2** to summon a whirlwind.
UPGRADE: Summon larger whirlwind that does more damage.

CAPTURED
Last seen by a double-key gate in the Lair of the Golden Queen

QUEST DATA

NAME
Remote Location

LOCATION
Bring her to Glumshanks in the Lair of the Golden Queen to find his remote

Buzzer Beak

See what the buzz is all about.

What he lacks in size, Buzzer Beak more than makes up for in courage, helicopter blades, and a good dive bomb attack.

Abilities

▶ Press **Attack 1** to grow and spin the blades on Buzzer Beak's hat, damaging nearby enemies.
UPGRADE: Blades increase in size.

▶ Press **Attack 2** to lift Buzzer Beak off the ground, creating a vortex that draws in enemies.
UPGRADE: Buzzer Beak dive bombs the ground to damage enemies at end of attack.

CAPTURED
Last seen across a Traptanium bridge at Know-It-All Island

QUEST DATA

NAME
Family Reunion

LOCATION
Bring him to Buzz at the Phoenix Psanctuary for a family reunion

Krankenstein

So strong, he fears nothing...except termites.

Named after his creator, Dr. Krankcase, Krankenstein can both suck enemies up and shoot them back out.

Abilities

▶ Press **Attack 1** to spin arm blades and damage enemies.
UPGRADE: Hold Attack 1 to keep blades spinning.

▶ Press **Attack 2** to snap arm at enemies.
UPGRADE: Attack deals more damage.

CAPTURED
Last seen at the very top of the Mill in Mystic Mill

QUEST DATA

NAME
Onward Wilikin Soldiers

LOCATION
Bring him to Wooster at Operation: Troll Rocket Steal to make Wilikin

Golden Queen

CAPTURED
Last seen in her own temple in the Lair of the Golden Queen

QUEST DATA

NAME
Bank on This!

LOCATION
Bring her to Dr. Noobry at The Ultimate Weapon to make his treasure device

A wicked queen made entirely of gold and rich beyond her wildest imagination, the aptly named Golden Queen would gladly trade her entire fortune for just a little more. But why trade when you can steal? And that's what she did. She stole, and stole, and stole! But no matter how much she took, it was never enough. Through evil sorcery, she even learned how to turn people and objects into solid gold. However, that STILL wasn't enough. The idea that any amount of treasure in Skylands did not belong to her was infuriating, so she embarked on a quest to take every last cent of it. But she couldn't do it alone. It was then that she formed the Doom Raiders— the most notorious group of villains ever assembled. As the leader, the Golden Queen promised riches, world domination, and even all-you-can-eat shrimp in order to recruit special criminals to serve her cause. Together, the Doom Raiders terrorized Skylands until Master Eon and the Trap Masters put a stop to them, locking up all of them inside Cloudcracker Prison!

Abilities

▶ Press **Attack 1** for a spinning staff strike.
UPGRADE: Staff attack does more damage.

▶ Press **Attack 2** to fire golden rays from Golden Queen's staff.
UPGRADE: Attack lasts longer and does more damage.

▶ Press **Attack 3** to summon golden wings, which attack enemies.
UPGRADE: Summon more powerful golden wings.

As good as gold and a lot more evil.

Chomp Chest

Who better to find treasure than a chest...with teeth!

If you open a treasure chest and it immediately comes to life and bites you, you might be opening a Chomp Chest. But at least he'll help you find hidden treasure.

Abilities

▶ Press **Attack 1** for a dashing bite attack that propels Chomp Chest forward.

UPGRADE: Bite has more range and does greater damage.

▶ Press **Attack 2** to search for buried treasure.

UPGRADE: Greater search area.

CAPTURED
Last seen in the graveyard area of Monster Marsh

QUEST DATA

NAME
Hot Diggity Dash!

LOCATION
Bring him to Flam Bam at the Secret Sewers of Supreme Stink for some hot dog eating

Grave Clobber

A face only a mummy could love.

The Grave Clobber will clobber you with one serious punch as well as his telekinetic powers. Who knew mummies were so diverse?

Abilities

▶ Press **Attack 1** for a crouching arm sweep.

UPGRADE: Attack deals more damage.

▶ Press **Attack 2** to smash the ground with both hands and summon bones from the ground. Hit bones with arm sweep to scatter damaging fragments.

UPGRADE: Attack has greater range and summons more bones.

CAPTURED
Last seen guarding the Golden Queen at the Golden Desert

QUEST DATA

NAME
Where is Flynn?

LOCATION
Bring him to Cali in the Lair of the Golden Queen to save Flynn

Tussle Sprout

Even more dangerous than a Brussels sprout.

More dangerous and harder to eat than a Brussels sprout, the Tussle Sprout releases both poison gas and poison spores.

Abilities

▶ Press **Attack 1** to create a gas cloud that poisons enemies. Hold Attack 1 to continue attack, but Tussle Sprout can't move.

UPGRADE: Range and damage are increased.

▶ Press **Attack 2** to lob a spore that falls under Tussle Sprout. Spore creates a puddle on the ground. Enemies that touch it are poisoned.

UPGRADE: Puddle is larger and damage is greater.

CAPTURED
Last seen in a pit accessed by breaking a Traptanium shard at Know-It-All island

QUEST DATA

NAME
Sproutin' Up!

LOCATION
Bring him to Arbo at the Phoenix Psanctuary to grow some new vines

Chef Pepperjack

Chef Pepper Jack was once the most renowned celebrity chef in all of Skylands—until he discovered ancient recipes for evil delicacies. That's when he turned his thriving restaurant business into a formidable criminal empire. The scam was simple. He would fly his zeppelin fortress over a village and order the townsfolk to surrender all of their money. If they didn't, he would promptly serve up a main course of spicy pepper bombs that would blow everything to smithereens! The Golden Queen valued both his explosive and non-explosive culinary skills and recruited him into the Doom Raiders at once. Now, when he's not serving time in Cloudcraker Prison, he's serving up atomic omelets of doom!

Abilities

▶ Press **Attack 1** to toss out explosive peppers.
  UPGRADE: Adds more peppers to the pot to bring up the heat.

▶ Press **Attack 2** to dash and attack with giant egg beaters.
  UPGRADE: Faster dash and more damaging egg beaters.

▶ Press **Attack 3** for a fiery breath attack. That's spicy cooking!
  UPGRADE: Spicier breath means more pain for enemies.

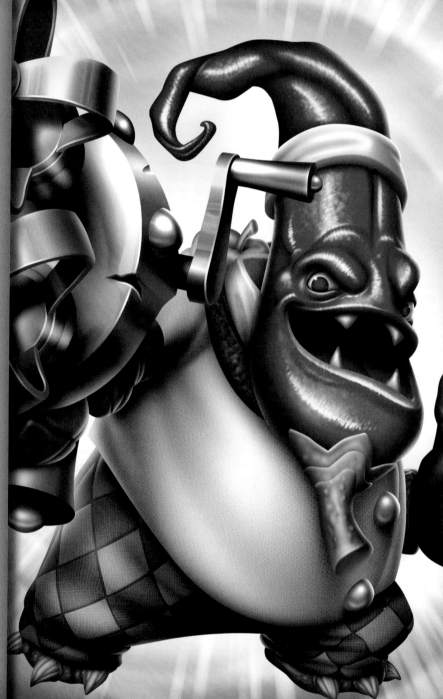

For those who like their bad guys extra spicy.

Grinnade

A walking time bomb. Literally!

Not surprisingly, this guy explodes. And if that's not enough for you, he creates mini versions of himself, which also explode.

Abilities

▶ Press **Attack 1** to start the self-destruct sequence. Don't worry, Grinnade always pulls himself back together.
UPGRADE: Explodes for additional damage.

▶ Press **Attack 2** to spawn mini-Grinnades that explode on contact with enemies.
UPGRADE: Mini-Grinnades explode for more damage.

CAPTURED
Last seen inside a Troll weapons lab at Operation: Troll Rocket Steal

QUEST DATA

NAME
Miner Troubles II

LOCATION
Bring him to Diggs at the Skyhighlands to blow through some ore

Scrap Shooter

One creature's trash is another one's treasure.

One creature's trash is another creature's treasure. Or in this case, ammo, as the Scrap Shooter loves to shoot trash at his foes.

Abilities

▶ Press **Attack 1** to lean forward and launch a barrel.
UPGRADE: Fires two barrels with each attack.

▶ Press **Attack 2** to fling four barrels along the ground.
UPGRADE: Barrels come out faster and do more damage.

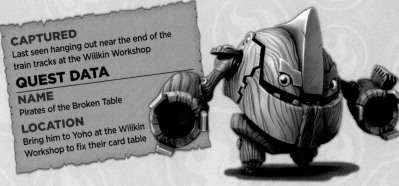

CAPTURED
Last seen hanging out near the end of the train tracks at the Wilikin Workshop

QUEST DATA

NAME
Pirates of the Broken Table

LOCATION
Bring him to Yoho at the Wilikin Workshop to fix their card table

Smoke Scream

No one ever told him not to play with fire.

Score another victory for Troll technology! Smoke Scream's mech is outfitted with a powerful plasma beam and an array of smoky missiles to keep his enemies' heads in the clouds.

Abilities

▶ Press **Attack 1** to burn enemies with a flame thrower.
UPGRADE: Flame thrower does more damage.

▶ Press **Attack 2** to fire a bouncing barrel.
UPGRADE: Barrel attack hits harder.

CAPTURED
Last seen near the base of the big machine at The Ultimate Weapon

QUEST DATA

NAME
Fight Doom with Boom

LOCATION
Bring him to Buzz at the Ultimate Weapon to help set up explosives

Chompy Mage

CAPTURED
Last seen cooking up a storm in his own kitchen inside Chef Zeppelin

QUEST DATA

NAME
Head of the Cheese

LOCATION
Bring him to Galley at Rainfish Riviera to recover some fancy cheese

Believe it or not, the Chompy Mage actually hatched from inside a Chompy Pod. At least that is how his Chompy hand puppet tells the story. Having been raised by Chompies, it is no surprise that the old magician is a little strange. He simply grew up embracing the Chompy way—believing that Skylands would be a better place if everyone was a Chompy—an illegal enchantment which he has actually tried to perform on several occasions. It was this kind of magic that led to him being locked up inside Cloudcracker Prison, where he met the other Doom Raiders. Of course, they all thought he was completely crazy, but the Chompy Mage can see through the eyes of any Chompy in Skylands—and having a few billion little spies can come in handy when trying to enact revenge on the Skylanders. Plus, he could secure the Chompy vote for any sort of political elections that followed.

Abilities

▷ Press **Attack 1** for a two-handed staff strike. In Giant Chompy Form, create fiery rings that ripple along the ground.
UPGRADE: Staff swing hits harder. Rings deal more damage.

▷ Press **Attack 2** to switch forms between giant Chompy and Chompy Mage.
UPGRADE: N/A

▷ Press **Attack 3** to summon Chompies (up to four active at a time). In Giant Chompy form, create fiery rings that ripple along the ground.
UPGRADE: Chompies are more powerful. Rings deal more damage.

The champ of chomp!

Broccoli Guy
Heals his friends, hurts his enemies.

Besides healing your Skylander and harming bad guys with his powerful magic, Broccoli Guy is perhaps best known for his charm, wit, and sparkling personality.

Abilities

▶ Press **Attack 1** to fire projectiles that damage nearby enemies.
UPGRADE: Projectiles do more damage.

▶ Press **Attack 2** to create a healing zone on the ground for Skylanders to use (must stand in it).
UPGRADE: Food appears inside healing zone.

CAPTURED: Last seen inside Chompy Mountain, near the 2nd cannon
QUEST DATA
NAME: Broccoli Guy En Fuego
LOCATION: Bring him to Bernie on board the Chef Zeppelin to create a signature dish

Chompy
The classic Skylands Chompy.

The classic Chompy can chomp like no other but did you know he can also create his own spear wall? Me neither!

Abilities

▶ Press **Attack 1** to chomp. What did you expect?
UPGRADE: Travels farther and does more damage.

▶ Press **Attack 2** to summon three smaller Chompies. Press Attack 2 again and they keep coming!
UPGRADE: Chompies do more damage with each bite.

CAPTURED: Last seen in the back yard of Uncle Ziggy's Garage at Mirror of Mystery
QUEST DATA
NAME: Workers' Chompensation
LOCATION: Bring him to Butterfly at Mirror of Mystery to wake up a lazy Troll

Cuckoo Clocker
He's cuckoo for clobbering.

Many fear this big, brutish bird and for good reason. He has a powerful roar and an even more powerful smash attack. Plus he really is quite cuckoo.

Abilities

▶ Press **Attack 1** for a two-handed overhead smash.
UPGRADE: Overhand smash does more damage and affects a small area.

▶ Press **Attack 2** for a sonic shriek that damages enemies in front of Cuckoo Clocker.
UPGRADE: Shriek does more damage.

CAPTURED: Last seen around the Phoenix Chicken's nest at Phoenix Psanctuary
QUEST DATA
NAME: Song Bird
LOCATION: Bring him to Da Pinchy at Phoenix Psanctuary to sing baritone

Sheep Creep
He's baaaaad news!

After years of being pestered, it was inevitable that a sheep would finally go bad. And this one has a big gun.

Abilities

▶ Press **Attack 1** to fire a round of missiles.
UPGRADE: Missiles deal more damage.

▶ Press **Attack 2** to cover up and send out wooly projectiles.
UPGRADE: Wooly projectiles travel farther and deal more damage.

CAPTURED: Last seen in Soda Springs, near a very strange, glowing crystal
QUEST DATA
NAME: Mildly Irritated Sheep
LOCATION: Bring him to Gumbus outside of Chompy Mountain to lead his kin to freedom

Shield Shredder
The best defense is a good offense.

While one might normally expect a shield to be used defensively instead of as a spinning saw blade, such is not the case with Shield Shredder.

Abilities

▶ Press **Attack 1** to dash forward behind a spinning shield. Hitting enemies with the shield charges it up for a longer dash.
UPGRADE: Shield does more damage and charges up faster.

▶ Press **Attack 2** to toss up two shields. Enemies under shields take damage when they land. Shields act as defensive barriers.
UPGRADE: Shields are larger and last longer.

CAPTURED: Last seen inside one of the mill offices just past the first cannon at Mystic Mill
QUEST DATA
NAME: Wood-Be Band
LOCATION: Bring him to Gilmour at the Wilikin Workshop to make SPECIAL NOISE

Bomb Shell

Pain-Yatta

Rage Mage

Bomb Shell

Did you hear the one about the tortoise and the bomb?

Bomb Shell can both throw bombs and use his shell to repel enemies. Makes you wonder why he is called "Bomb Shell," huh?

Abilities

▶ Press **Attack 1** to drop some bombs.
  UPGRADE: Toss rate increases and bombs cause extra damage.

▶ Press **Attack 2** to spin and dash. Any enemies that get hit are knocked back.
  UPGRADE: Bombs surround spinning Bomb Shell. Enemies receive more damage from explosions.

CAPTURED
Last seen near the first shishkabob trap on the Chef Zeppelin

QUEST DATA

NAME
Mission: Demolition

LOCATION
Bring him to Rizzo at the Mystic Mill to destroy an evil Troll fortress

Pain-Yatta

Filled with candy. And evil.

If you've ever wanted to be a big piñata who barfs candy and swings a giant lollipop, this is probably as close as you're going to get.

Abilities

▶ Press **Attack 1** to smack the ground ahead of Pain-Yatta with a lollipop.
  UPGRADE: Lollipop has more pop.

▶ Press **Attack 2** to fill the air with candy that damages enemies.
  UPGRADE: More candy. More Pain. And piñatas?

CAPTURED
Last seen just outside the Dreamcatcher's chamber at Telescope Towers

QUEST DATA

NAME
I'm With the Band

LOCATION
Bring him to Bag 'O Bones at the Secret Sewers of Supreme Stink to deliver a new song

Rage Mage

He's all the rage!

The Rage Mage summons a magical ball. Big deal, right? Well this magical ball makes your Skylanders faster and stronger than ever.

Abilities

▶ Press **Attack 1** to swing a staff, with a small forward movement.
  UPGRADE: Staff has greater range and does more damage.

▶ Press **Attack 2** to create an orb. Skylanders who pick up the orb enjoy a temporary boost to speed and damage.
  UPGRADE: Effects of Orb last longer and are more powerful.

CAPTURED
Last seen at the bottom of a giant pipe in the Secret Sewers of Supreme Stink

QUEST DATA

NAME
Ice Cream in the Future?

LOCATION
Bring him to Noobman at The Future of Skylands to help sell ice cream

Dr. Krankcase

No one is really quite sure exactly what Dr. Krankcase is a doctor of...but his technical engineering achievements are legendary. The secret to his success lies in his modified concoction of glowing green goo, which causes wooden objects to come to life and turn evil. His unique skillset makes him a valuable asset to the Doom Raiders, who have plenty of nefarious uses for evil wooden creatures. It is also commonly known that Dr. Krankcase served as an evil inspiration to Kaos once upon a time, who had figured out how to make his own wooden creatures, the Wilikin, come to life after reading about the doctor's exploits in the Minion Monthly Catalog. Kaos also respected Dr. K's interest in world domination and doom engineering, not to mention his well-documented love of pickles.

Abilities

▶ Press **Attack 1** to spin Dr. Krankcase's legs and slide forward.
UPGRADE: Increased damage and distance traveled.

▶ Press **Attack 2** to fire a goo blast.
UPGRADE: Each blast hits more often.

▶ Press **Attack 3** to generate lightning from Dr. Krancase's fingertips.
UPGRADE: Increased damage and number of hits.

Not the healing kind of doctor.

Brawlrus

Brawl + Walrus = Brawlrus

Harnessing the awesome power of the starfish, Brawlrus fires a cannon and drops mines, which hurt and slow down whomever they touch.

Abilities

▶ Press **Attack 1** to fire a burst of tiny starfish.
UPGRADE: Increased damage.

▶ Press **Attack 2** to fire a giant starfish that spins and damages enemies.
UPGRADE: Starfish does more damage and lasts longer.

CAPTURED: Last seen hanging out with pirates just outside of Rainfish Riviera

QUEST DATA

NAME: Submarine Bros 4 Life

LOCATION: Bring him to Argle Bargle at Rainfish Riviera to deal with some trust issues

Mab Lobs

A Mabu gone bad? No way!

Mab Lobs throws, drops, and even kicks his fire bombs. He also calls them "blombs" for reasons known only to him.

Abilities

▶ Press **Attack 1** to throw three large bombs.
UPGRADE: Bigger bombs mean bigger booms.

▶ Press **Attack 2** to throw out many smaller bombs that explode after a delay.
UPGRADE: More bombs covering a larger area.

CAPTURED: Last seen about to invade a peaceful Troll Village at Mirror of Mystery

QUEST DATA

NAME: Fishness Protection Program

LOCATION: Bring him to Kaos at Mirror of Mystery to help save some fish

Shrednaught

2 Trolls, 1 giant chainsaw, unlimited possibilities.

Picture two Trolls inside the biggest chainsaw mech ever built—now add a large, spinning blade. Boo-yah!

Abilities

▶ Press **Attack 1** to start up the giant chainsaw.
UPGRADE: Hold Attack 1 to charge up the chainsaw to run longer and do more damage.

▶ Press **Attack 2** for a backseat driver blast.
UPGRADE: Blast does more damage.

CAPTURED: Last seen on a ledge past the first bounce pad at Phoenix Psanctuary

QUEST DATA

NAME: Sure Beats Keys

LOCATION: Bring him to Loggins at the Mystic Mill to get him back into his office

Trolling Thunder

Wears a tank for pants!

It's bad enough to be hit by Trolling Thunder's mortar shells but being smashed by the tank itself is another thing entirely.

Abilities

▶ Press **Attack 1** to fire a shell from the turret.
UPGRADE: Shell travels faster and does more damage.

▶ Press **Attack 2** for a backfire that damages nearby enemies.
UPGRADE: Backfire does more damage.

CAPTURED: Last seen outside the Temple of Boom in the Nightmare Express

QUEST DATA

NAME: Statue of Limitations

LOCATION: Look for Da Pinchy in Temple Ruins Approach in the Nightmare Express

Wolfgang

CAPTURED
"Last" seen building a big, bad woofer 10,000 years in the future at the Future of Skylands.

QUEST DATA

NAME
An Inconvenience of Imps

LOCATION
Bring him to Q.U.I.G.L.E.Y. in The Future of Skylands to clear out some imps.

Wolfgang wasn't always a werewolf. He was once a handsome, brilliant musician set to marry a beautiful princess. Before the wedding, he planned to unveil his ultimate symphony to the greatest music aficionados in Skylands, convinced they would love it and instantly hail him as the best composer of all time. But they didn't. They hated it—and even worse, it actually physically hurt when heard. Turns out Wolfgang had unintentionally discovered the musical note for pain. Being shunned like this drove Wolfgang utterly and completely mad, physically transforming him into the werewolf he is today. With the princess no longer wanting to marry him, he turned to a life of crime, terrorizing the royal subjects and using his evil music as a weapon. The Golden Queen took note of this and realized that Wolfgang could make a powerful ally, if she could control his rage and keep him in line. And that's a pretty big "if!"

Abilities

▶ Press **Attack 1** for a musical slash. Jump for an overhead smash.
  UPGRADE: Slash has greater range and hits harder.

▶ Press **Attack 2** to slide along the ground and bask in adulation.
  UPGRADE: More distance, damage, and rocking.

▶ Press **Attack 3** for a killer lick that produces damaging musical notes.
  UPGRADE: Notes come out faster and do more damage.

His music is edgy—
sharp steel edgy.

Bone Chompy

Even skeleton Chompies gotta eat!

Chompies bite, we all know that, but the Bone Chompy can actually leave
a trap of his own on the ground. Which also bites.

Abilities

▶ Press **Attack 1** for a dashing chompy bite.
   UPGRADE: Faster dash that travels farther.

▶ Press **Attack 2** to leave a chompy trap on the ground,
   which bites enemies when they walk over it.
   UPGRADE: Biting traps bite harder, or latch onto
   victim, inflicting damage over time.

CAPTURED
Last seen in a pit accessed by breaking a
Traptanium shard at the Golden Desert

QUEST DATA

NAME
Paging Dr. Bone Chompy

LOCATION
Bring him to Buzz at Operation: Troll Rocket
Steal to heal some soldiers

Hood Sickle

Blink and you'll miss him. But he won't miss you!

The only thing scarier than a big, scythe-wielding executioner is one who can
teleport anywhere he wants. Especially right behind you.

Abilities

▶ Press **Attack 1** to teleport a short distance in any
   direction.
   UPGRADE: Targets in the path of teleport take additional
   damage.

▶ Press **Attack 2** for a slow swing that hits a wide arc in
   front of Hood Sickle.
   UPGRADE: Attack causes special state (jaded) and does
   more damage.

CAPTURED
Last seen in front of the first locked door at
Telescope Towers.

QUEST DATA

NAME
Hatastrophe!

LOCATION
Bring him to Hatterson at Skylands Academy
to break up a hat forgery ring

Masker Mind

Everyone's entitled to HIS opinion.

Through dark sorcery, Masker Mind can take control of an enemy's mind for a
spell. He also has a telekinetic push that comes in handy during combat.

Abilities

▶ Press **Attack 1** for a moderate speed projectile that turns
   enemies into allies for a short time.
   UPGRADE: Affected enemies remain allies for an
   extended period of time.

▶ Press **Attack 2** to push back enemies. Nice area of effect,
   but deals no damage.
   UPGRADE: Now deals a small amount of damage and has
   a larger area of effect.

CAPTURED
Last seen inside the control room of Rainfish
Riviera.

QUEST DATA

NAME
Hypnosis Schnipnosis

LOCATION
Bring him to Arthur at Telescope Towers to
prove that hypnosis is real

The Gulper

CAPTURED
Last seen completely ruining a perfectly good
soda festival in Soda Springs

QUEST DATA

NAME
Balloon Redemption

LOCATION
Bring him over to Mags at the beginning of Know-
It-All Island to make amends for his bad deeds

From the moment he oozed from the ceiling
of the Gelatinous Caverns, the Gulper
had possessed an enormous appetite and
insatiable thirst for anything and everything
he could stuff in his mouth. At a young age,
he won first place in the annual Deep-Fried
Triple-Cheeseburger eating contest—and has
proudly worn the Crown of Gluttony ever
since. But it was his particular affinity for
soda, which caused him to grow to colossal
proportions and go on rampages, that first
caught the eye of the Golden Queen. She
was looking for special types of people—or
creatures—to join her Doom Raider gang that
was bent on unleashing total mayhem. It was
also her desire to recruit someone who was
incredibly dim-witted, so that if they were
ever captured, the Skylanders would not be
able to extract any useful information. The
Gulper fit these requirements to a tee!

Abilities

▶ Press **Attack 1** to thrust trident. Trident Picks up
smaller targets and tosses them over The
Gulper's head.
   UPGRADE: Attack does more damage.

▶ Press **Attack 2** for a bite attack that hits multiple
enemies.
   UPGRADE: Bite does more damage and swallows
   smaller enemies.

▶ Press **Attack 3** to slide and leave a slime trail in
The Gulper's wake. Hold Attack 3 to charge up the
attack and increase distance traveled.
   UPGRADE: Slide goes farther and does more
   damage.

His gulp is worse than his bite.

Brawl & Chain
No chains, no pain!

Another angry walrus pirate, this time with chains for arms and sharp hooks for hands. This is probably why he doesn't get a lot of hugs.

Abilities

▶ Press **Attack 1** for a spin attack with both hook hands.
  UPGRADE: Spin lasts longer and hits harder.

▶ Press **Attack 2** to fire a hook hand. Smaller enemies are pulled closer when hit.
  UPGRADE: Attack does more damage.

CAPTURED: Last seen on a big tanker at Rainfish Riviera

QUEST DATA

NAME: Fairy Night Lights

LOCATION: Bring him to Hawk at Telescope Towers to restore light to a village

Chill Bill
Was evil BEFORE it was cool.

Chill Bill is a radio DJ by day, and crazy Troll who freezes people with his ice gun by night. Of course, he also does that last part in the daytime too.

Abilities

▶ Press **Attack 1** to fire a freeze beam. Enemies caught in beam are frozen in place.
  UPGRADE: Beam does more damage and enemies are frozen longer.

▶ Press **Attack 2** to activate Chill Bill's jetpack. Enemies caught in wash take damage.
  UPGRADE: Flight time is longer. Enemies take more damage.

CAPTURED: Last seen hiding out near a bird cage at Phoenix Psanctuary

QUEST DATA

NAME: The Cold Front

LOCATION: Bring him to Rocky at Chompy Mountain to make Troll Radio awesome again

Cross Crow
Don't cross Cross Crow!

Cross Crow would prefer to shoot you with his crossbow but if need be, he's happy to call in a swarm of angry crows too. Who wouldn't be?

Abilities

▶ Press **Attack 1** to fire a crossbow. Hold Attack 1 to kneel and fire continually. Can't move while firing.
  UPGRADE: Bolts fire faster and hit harder.

▶ Press **Attack 2** to summon a swarm of crows to attack a single target.
  UPGRADE: Swarm lasts longer and can hit multiple targets.

CAPTURED: Last seen harassing Da Pinchy near the steam locks of Time Town

QUEST DATA

NAME: Skylands' Biggest Fans

LOCATION: Bring him to Tessa in Time Town to save Skylands' biggest fans

Slobber Trap
Just your average plant monster dog.

If you like dogs, you'll love Slobber Trap. Especially if you like big, plant monster dogs who can do belly flops and burrow underground.

Abilities

▶ Press **Attack 1** for a belly flop that damages nearby enemies.
  UPGRADE: Belly flop deals more damage over more area.

▶ Press **Attack 2** to leave a slobber trail on the ground that slows enemies.
  UPGRADE: Trail lasts longer and slowing effect is greater.

CAPTURED: Last seen near the cannon at Know-It-All Island

QUEST DATA

NAME: Gumbus' Fortune

LOCATION: Bring him to Gumbus at Know-It-All Island to push over a statue

Threatpack
A Troll in a jetpack. Now THAT'S a threat!

A former scientist, Threatpack now applies his knowledge of aerodynamics to homing missiles and rocket-powered jet packs.

Abilities

▶ Press **Attack 1** to fire rockets that seek enemies.
  UPGRADE: Rockets deal more damage.

▶ Press **Attack 2** to blast off and damage enemies caught in the wash.
  UPGRADE: Deals more damage and extends flight time.

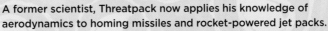

CAPTURED: Last seen guarding the rocket at Operation: Troll Rocket Steal

QUEST DATA

NAME: You Break It, You Fix It

LOCATION: Bring him to Tessa at the Skyhighlands to fix a cannon

KAOS

CAPTURED
Last seen...come on, we're not going to give this away!

QUEST DATA
NAME
Who Wants Kaos Kake?

LOCATION
Bring him to Blobbers at the Skylands Academy to make Kaos Kake

Before becoming the archenemy of the Skylanders, Kaos always demonstrated an insatiable hunger for absolute power. Even as an infant, Kaos seized control of his nursery with his "evil baby army of evil drool" which threatened to crawl across the face of all Skylands. Fortunately, this uprising was crushed at naptime. Kaos was then sent to the finest evil school of magical villainy, as were many in his long and twisted family history. It was here that Kaos met Glumshanks, who was persuaded by Kaos to become his evil servant with the promise of career growth. But soon after, they were expelled when Kaos appeared as a giant floating head at a school assembly and ate the gymnasium. With the long suffering and still unpromoted Glumshanks at his side, Kaos continues to come up with plan after plan to take over Skylands; some say to fulfill his ambition to become Skylands' "ultimate evil overlord," though others think that he's still trying to impress his immensely powerful and overbearing mother—herself a Dark Portal Master. All agree, however, that Kaos should never be underestimated.

Needs no introduction.

Abilities

▷ Press **Attack 1** to place a random element icon on the ground. Each icon produces a different attack. Attack 1 becomes eye beams in Kaos head form.

UPGRADE: Icon attacks do more damage.

▷ **Attack 2** for Doom Sharks! **Attack 2** becomes a sonic attack in Kaos head form.

UPGRADE: More sharks are summoned.

▷ Press **Attack 3** to assume giant Kaos head form.

UPGRADE: Attacks do more damage.

Other Enemies

Not every creature you fight wants to get a chance to change their evil path. The following minions can't be captured and do their best to keep you from accomplishing your goals.

Chompies

En Fuego Chompy

The Chompy Mage summons these incendiary menaces while you battle him at Chompy Mountain. They like to get close to your Skylander and explode.

Goo Chompy

Exposure to the waste of the Secret Sewers of Supreme Stink gave these Chompies the ability to change their shape into a pile of goo and blend in with the rest of the goo oozing from the Sewers.

Mega Chompy

A small silver Chompy that borrows other Chompies to grow to massive size. It has a powerful belly flop attack that sends out a shockwave as well as several Chompies.

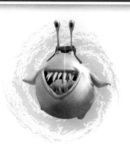

Pirate Chompy

Some Chompies enjoy the pirate life. They're not any more powerful than other Chompies, but they do have a slightly better fashion sense with their bandanas and curved swords.

Cyclopes

Cyclops Dragon

These powerful undead beasts unleash rings of deadly eyeballs. Avoid the eyeballs and focus on the dragon when you encounter one. They have an enormous amount of health to get through.

Cyclops Spinner

Watch out when these Cyclopes slash with their knives. That's the sign that they're about to begin a spin that renders them invulnerable. All you can do is stay clear and wait for the spin to end. There isn't a big break before they start spinning again, so get your shots in quickly.

Evilikins

Evilikin Cannon

Evilikin Cannons set up and lob cannonballs at spots on the ground marked by a red ring. Avoid the spot when it appears and take down the cannon while it's reloading.

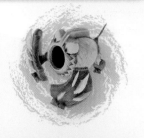

Evilikin Spinner

Evilikin Spinners look like narrow pins until they extend wooden wings and turn into a wooden whirlwind. Stay away while they spin, and wait for them to come to a complete stop before you retaliate.

Woodenstein

Woodenstein assists Dr. Krankcase during the final battle at the Wilikin Workshop. He's a big bruiser with blades on both forearms. He moves at a lumbering pace and would be easy to avoid, except you fight him in a hazard-filled arena.

Feathered Fiends

Raven Lobber

When you see ravens in green carrying shoulder-mounted mortars, watch out for the red rings on the ground that indicate their targets. They fire three shells at a time, and like to stay on the move between launches.

BirdBrain

Birdbrains wield wicked scimitars taller than they are. They shriek just before spinning with their blade held at their waist. If you manage to dodge the spinning swing, they are briefly off-balance and vulnerable.

Mabu

Mabu Warrior

Only in an opposite world like Mirror of Mystery would the peace loving Mabu turn into vicious warriors. These heavily armored foes can absorb a lot of damage and they usually travel in packs.

Mabu Tank

The Mabu may not have as many destructive toys as the Trolls but they were able to piece together a tank with a powerful turret. Luckily the big gun moves slowly, allowing you to slip behind it.

The Reanimated

Shield Skeleton

Strike these shield-wielding skeletons from behind, or goad them into an attack you can avoid. When their swords are extended, they're vulnerable. If you're the patient type, you can destroy the shields slowly.

Transformed Barrel

These torch-headed stone creatures try to stay out of combat and lob Bombs at your Skylander. When you see the red circle with a green center, you must make a decision. You can either get away from the red circle to avoid the Bomb, or stand in the green part and catch it before it lands.

Stitched Enemies

Cuddles

Don't be fooled by its squat look and seemingly short appendages. Cuddles can extend its arms and legs (and fingers!) to give it a surprisingly long reach when it attacks with a two-handed clap.

Snozzler

Flies above the reach of most attacks and spits out stitched balls that roll around and damage your Skylander. Wait for Snozzler to land and take it out before it can take to the air again.

Oogler

These bright-eyed pests fire two charged orbs from their eyes that maintain a current between them as they sweep across the area. Watch the top of their heads to see their hairs appear.

Trolls

Eggsecutioner

Eggsecutioners are Troll Warriors with an extra layer of protection. Somehow they've encased themselves in an eggshell that requires a few hits to clear away. Then an Eggsecutioner becomes a regular Troll Warrior.

Troll Warrior

The majority of the Troll forces wield maces. Wait for them to swing their heavy maces and attack while they pull their weapons out of the ground after a miss.

Extending Shield Troll

Trolls are generally very aggressive but this variation sets up a shield with extended coverage to block the way and protect their buddies. Don't fight these foes head on, go around their shield and let them have it.

Troll Welder

These busy Trolls take time out of their day welding mechanical weapons to cause you trouble. They have a heavy-duty welder's mask and a blowtorch that provides a mid-range attack.

Other Enemies

Plant Warrior

These creatures don't have an actual name, but they stab with their 'arms', which are really hardened leaves and shoots. These plants must be at least part weed. They seem to be everywhere!

Pirate Henchmen

These pink menaces of the sea first appear alongside Brawlrus, but they work for other evil-doers as well. They wield clubs with wicked curved blades at the end.

Soda Springs

OBJECTIVES

STORY GOALS	DARES	COLLECTIONS

STORY GOALS

▶ Find and defeat Sheep Creep

▶ Save Soda Springs from disaster

Buzz

here. Now how's about we go investigate all this

DARES

No Lives Lost

All Areas Found (17)

Enemy Goal (30)

Villains Defeated

Traptanium Gates

DIFFICULT DARES

Time to Beat: 11:30

Don't Switch

COLLECTIONS

 1 Story Scrolls

 4 Treasure Chests

 3 Soul Gems

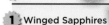 1 Winged Sapphires

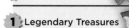 1 Legendary Treasures

 4 Hats

MAP KEY

(A)	Connector Point
	Hat
	Legendary Treasure
	Quest
	Skystones Smash Player
	Soul Gem
	Story Scroll
	Treasure Chest
	Villain Stash
	Winged Sapphire

Sugar Plateau, Cola Stream & Backwash Spillway

Speak with Buzz to learn how to use your Skylander's Primary attack, and how to jump. There are many destructible items in the area to destroy, so don't be shy. Smash away!

When you discover a large cannon in an open area, Buzz appears again to explain how it works. Interact with the cannon to blast the gate and open the path ahead. Before you pass through the gate, jump up on the ledge to the right. Open the **Treasure Chest** and collect the coins that pop out of it.

Walk past the gate and push the turtle with the arrow floating over its shell into the gap to form a bridge. Whenever you see arrows like these, you can push the object (or creature) they float over in the direction indicated. Long-time Portal Masters are familiar with these objects, but if this is your first adventure in Skylands, keep a sharp eye out for them.

START

Hop off the right side of the turtle bridge to fall into the Cola Stream. Follow the coins over the soda falls to Backwash Spillway. Collect the piles of valuables, then use the blue Bounce Pad to return to the starting area. Retrace your steps back to the turtles.

There's a Troll Radio between the first turtle and the stacked turtles. These radios allow you to change channels, and you should continue to switch things up until you are awarded a cash prize. Repeat this with every Troll Radio you find for easy money. Push the stacked turtles into the flowing soda and cross the newly-formed bridge.

Defeating Sheep Creep also opens up a Bounce Pad near Buzz. Hop over the gap and follow the dirt path past the turtle. There's a doorway hidden on the other side of the stone ledge that leads to the Hidden Flavor Grotto.

Collect the coins and **Winged Sapphire** from the middle of the room, then return outside. Push the turtle into the gap between ledges. Use the Bounce Pad to reach the Natural Ingredients Tree.

Soda Flats & Hidden Flavor Grotto

Buzz pops up again and explains how to trap certain villains after you defeat them in battle. The first such enemy, Sheep Creep, is just ahead. The nearby red button with crossed swords is a Battle Gate, and indicates an object that remains locked until certain enemies are defeated. In this instance, it's Sheep Creep.

personally assure you that Sheep Creep here is bad news.

Buzz

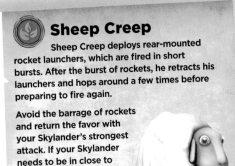

Sheep Creep

Sheep Creep deploys rear-mounted rocket launchers, which are fired in short bursts. After the burst of rockets, he retracts his launchers and hops around a few times before preparing to fire again.

Avoid the barrage of rockets and return the favor with your Skylander's strongest attack. If your Skylander needs to be in close to attack, the best time to move in is immediately after Sheep Creep fires his rocket barrage.

When Sheep Creep's health is depleted, you are prompted to capture him with a Life Trap. Whether you capture him or not, you are rewarded with gold and a new Skystone. The Skystone is part of a game that will be introduced in a few chapters. Every chapter has villains like Sheep Creep, so have your traps nearby as you continue the adventure.

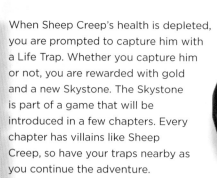

Put a Life Trap in the portal to trap this Villain.

Natural Ingredients Tree & Seltzer Pit

Buzz points out the *Traptanium* nearby and notes the need for a Trap Master's crystal weapon to break it. Defeat the waves of Chompies and other enemies to open the nearby Battle Gate.

Place a Trap Master on your *Traptanium Portal* and destroy the *Traptanium* crystal to break the floor and reveal the Seltzer Pit. Grab the coins and open the **Treasure Chest**. Use both Bounce Pads to reach your first *Traptanium* Gate. You must use a Trap Master of the indicated Element to open it. Use the nearby purple Super Bounce Pad after your trip inside the gate.

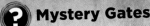

CARBONATED PLANT

Use the Bounce Pads to collect the coins floating in the area. Push the turtle nearest the edge over it to set it spinning around. Hop on its back and ride it over to the ledge with the Hat Box. Open the Hat Box for the **Turtle Hat**. Use the Bounce Pad near the Hat Box to return to the ledge with the turtles, then leave the area.

Twisting Top

The Super Bounce Pad trip ends at Twisting Top. Step off the edge and collect the floating coins on the way down. Claim the **Story Scroll** here and note the gate with a mystery element. You can't enter it yet, but remember its location for a return trip in the future. Because the gate is locked for now, you can't earn the Dare Star (Areas Found and *Traptanium* Gates), or the Collections Star (missing **Soul Gem** and Hat) for this Chapter, yet.

Hint: You need an unknown Trap Master to open this gate

? Mystery Gates

As you journey through Skylands you occasionally come across Mystery Gates which require an unknown element. The required element is not yet available for your Skylanders. Because you cannot access these areas right now, you are not always able to collect every Soul Gem, Hat, or Treasure Chest for a Chapter. Our maps show you every collectible location outside of these Mystery Gates.

Be patient, Portal Master, you will be able to explore these mysterious areas in the future!

Jump on the Bounce Pad to reach the raised center of Twisting Top. Grab Blades' **Soul Gem (Instant Swirl Shards).** There's another Super Bounce Pad nearby, but don't use it until after a trip through the Life Gate.

MELON FLAVOR FARM

Push the large pumpkins onto the wooden platform to raise another platform filled with Chompies. Roll one pumpkin onto the scale and take down the attacking enemies. Push the second pumpkin onto the wooden platform. Jump up to the higher platform and open the box containing the **Melon Hat**.

ZERO CALORIE CAVERN

Go to the left and hop from platform to platform to reach the right bank. Jump up to the higher ledge and hop across back to the left. There are no enemies to worry about, so take your time and claim your reward, the **Bucket Hat**.

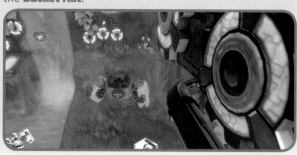

Sugar Free Landing & Really Secret Spot

A Battle Gate appears and blocks your progress. There's a Tech Gate down the ramp to the left, as are the enemies you need to defeat to open the Battle Gate. With the enemies out of the way, jump off the left side of the ramp to reach the aptly named Really Secret Spot. Grab the coins and use the Bounce Pads to return to the Tech Gate.

Grape Flavored Vista, Bottleneck Balcony & Fizzlewort's Rooftop

With the Battle Gate out of the way, go up the ramp to reach Grape Flavored Vista. You know you're in the right spot when you see Mabu running from The Gulper.

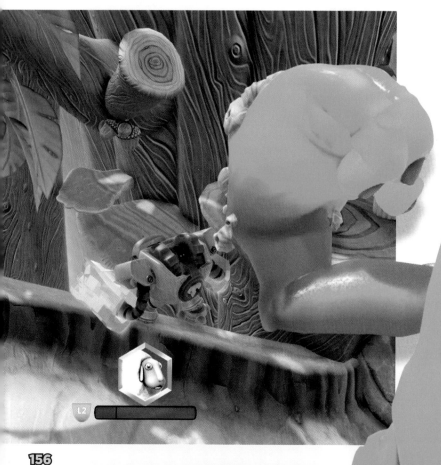

The Gulper

Go up the left ramp and smash the *Traptanium* crystal to reveal a **Treasure Chest**. The right ramp leads to Buzz and a purple Bounce Pad. Don't use the pad until you check in with Pibb and grab the coins just beyond him.

Pibb is a Skystones Smash Player, but you can't take him until after you learn Skystones Smash later in the adventure. Step on the purple Bounce Pad to reach Bottleneck Balcony and another Troll Radio.

Bounce up to the rooftop and destroy the vat of soda. Walk off the roof and veer right. There is a **Villain Stash** nearby. If you trapped Sheep Creep earlier, tag him in and claim the treasure.

Walk down the ramp until The Gulper's belch causes the corks of the soda vats to rise and fall. Buzz appears again at Fizzlewort's Rooftop. The Gulper's giant hand blocks the path ahead, but there's a convenient canon nearby. Use the cannon to move The Gulper's hand.

Destroy the vat and jump up to the ledge with a Bounce Pad. Jump to the right and drop down to a ledge with another Bounce Pad and Jaw Breaker's **Soul Gem (Hypercharged Haymaker)**. Use the Bounce Pads to reach the rooftop with Buzz.

Push the vat filled with the orange soda over the edge. Slide the noxious green vat up to where The Gulper can reach it. After he downs the nasty concoction, use a Water Trap to claim your rewards.

After your victory over The Gulper, the next stop is Skylanders Academy, where you meet up with many old friends, including Cali, Flynn, Buzz, and Persephone.

Villain Stash

A Villain Stash is a special Treasure Chest that can only be open by a Captured Villain. It counts as a Treasure Chest when listed in the Collectibles available for each Chapter.

Skylanders Academy - First Visit

Persephone re-introduces herself and summons her home. She sells upgrades nearby, between the three aquatic creatures on springs you can use for target practice. Go inside her treehouse to collect a few coins and the **Elemental Diamond** trinket.

Cali stands near a statue of Kaos. Talk to her to learn about Kaos Doom Challenges. The locked area in the center of the courtyard is the Villain Vault. The Vault tracks villains defeated and captured, and also allows you to switch which villain is active in your traps. Most of the Academy remains blocked for now, so speak to Flynn to head off to the next stop in the adventure.

OBJECTIVES

STORY GOALS

▶ Gather info about Doom Raiders

▶ Clear out trolls from the island

DARES

No Lives Lost	
All Areas Found (11)	
Enemy Goal (45)	
Villains Defeated	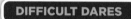
Traptanium Gates	

DIFFICULT DARES

Time to Beat: 9:20	
Don't Switch	
Complete all Villain Quests (2)	

COLLECTIONS

1	Story Scrolls	
4	Treasure Chests	
2	Soul Gems	
1	Winged Sapphires	
1	Legendary Treasures	
3	Hats	

MAP KEY

(A)	Connector Point
	Hat
	Legendary Treasure
	Quest
	Skystones Smash Player
	Soul Gem
	Story Scroll
	Treasure Chest
	Villain Stash
	Winged Sapphire

Quest Preparation

Know-It-All Island introduces Villain Quests. Completing a Villain Quest upgrades their look and abilities. Unless you capture Villains during the same level where their quests occur, you must place the proper Villains in a trap at Skylanders Academy before you depart for the level.

If he's not already there, put The Gulper in a Water trap. Slobber Trap's quest appears later in the level, but you'll be able to backtrack to it after capturing him.

SLOBBER TRAP

🌿 Pompous Point & Told You So Terrace

The bridge to the right leads to a Troll Radio and Mags, who has a quest for The Gulper. Cross back to Buzz and use the key from the higher ledge to open the locked gate.

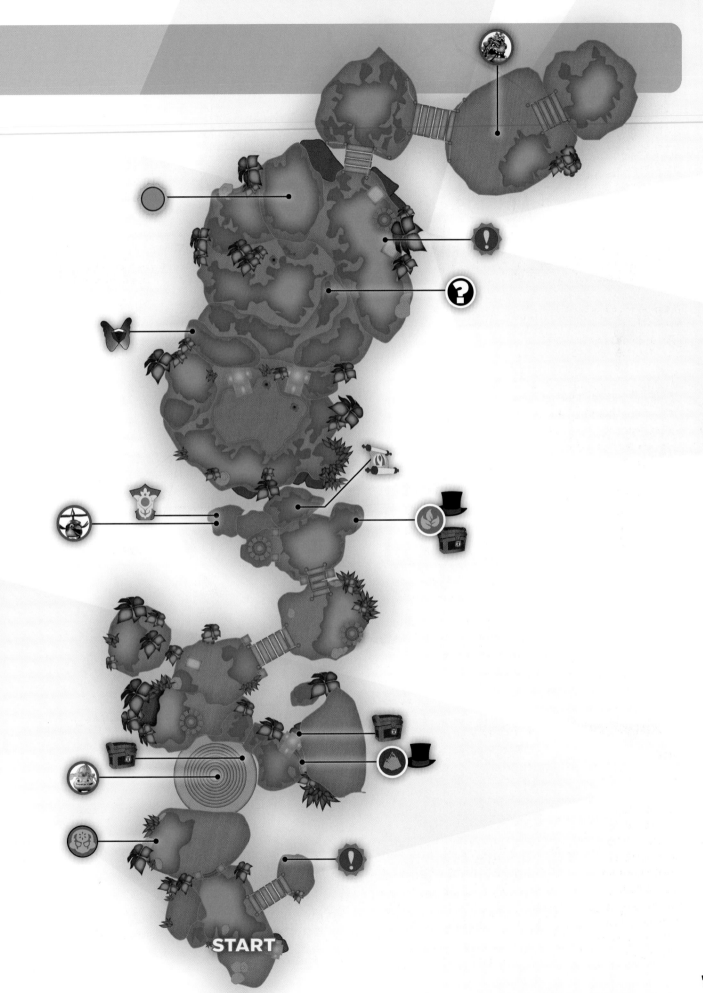

START

BALLOON REDEMPTION

Mags wants to give The Gulper the opportunity to redeem himself by delivering balloons to ten Mabu children in ten minutes or less. The Gulper can carry up to four balloons at a time while delivering them to children.

The children are being tormented by Tussle Sprouts and Slobber Traps, so be ready for a few fights along the way. Destroy hay carts to reveal Teleport Pads that lead back to the balloon hub. Using them saves you considerable time.

If you take too long to deliver a balloon, Mags helps by providing the location of a Mabu child.

There's a **Villain Stash** to the left beyond the gate. Drop down into the pit with the *Traptanium* crystal and take out the Buzzer Beaks before you destroy the crystal. Destroying the crystal opens up the floor and begins a battle against Tussle Sprout.

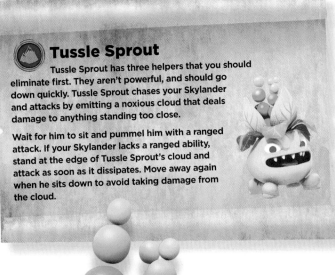

Tussle Sprout

Tussle Sprout has three helpers that you should eliminate first. They aren't powerful, and should go down quickly. Tussle Sprout chases your Skylander and attacks by emitting a noxious cloud that deals damage to anything standing too close.

Wait for him to sit and pummel him with a ranged attack. If your Skylander lacks a ranged ability, stand at the edge of Tussle Sprout's cloud and attack as soon as it dissipates. Move away again when he sits down to avoid taking damage from the cloud.

With Tussle Sprout safely out of the way, open the **Treasure Chest** and use the Bounce Pads to bound up to the Knucklehead Buzz pointed out earlier.

Stuck-Up Steppes

Speak with the Knucklehead, then go back to the right for an Earth Gate. The Bounce Pad beyond the Knucklehead goes up to a ledge with a doubly locked gate.

 THE WEIGHTING ROOM

Two stone platforms are linked together. Push the two loose stone blocks onto the left platform to lower it and raise the platform on the right. Jump up to the now higher platform (stand on one of the stone blocks if necessary). Jump up to the ledge with the **Treasure Chest**.

Push the last stone block to join the other two on the lowered platform. Jump up to the ledge with the hat box and open it to reveal the **Sleuth Hat**. The blue disc on the ground beyond the hat box is a teleport pad. Use it to return to the front of the cave.

Push the stacked stone blocks toward the ledge with a key and Persephone. If any Skylanders have enough gold for upgrades, you can buy them here. Push the single stone to build a bridge to the ledge with another Knucklehead and the second key.

⟳ Windbag Woods

The short bridge beyond the locked gate ends in a quick fight against a group of enemies that are primarily Buzzer Beaks. Defeating the enemies reveals Buzz and a Bomb. Use the Bomb to destroy the gate.

A tank appears and only another Bomb can harm it. Grab Buzz's next Bomb and throw it at the tank. A small group of trolls supports the tank, but wait to take them out until after the tank is destroyed.

A **Story Scroll** appears in the cave where the tank originated, and there is a Life Gate to the right.

 ENCHANTED FOREST

Take out the Trolls, and use the Bombs to blow up their chainsaw tanks. There's a **Treasure Chest** past the first tank, with two Troll guards.

Avoid the spinning arms and use the Bounce Pad to reach an encounter with a second chainsaw tank. Avoid the sawblade and follow the trail of coins to the Bounce Pads that lead up to another Bomb. Toss the Bomb from its high perch toward the tank to destroy it and create the path up to the **Hedgehog Hat**. The Teleport Pad behind the hat box is a quick trip back to Windbag Woods.

Blobbers demonstrates how the steam vents work, but don't follow him yet. Destroy the nearby *Traptanium* crystal to create a path to the **Legendary Tribal Statue** being guarded by Buzzer Beak and some friends.

Buzzer Beak

There are a few Buzzer Beaks in the fight, but the one you can capture lets a few waves of his allies soften you up first.

Buzzer Beak's primary attack is flying with his head down, with the spinner atop his head damaging anything it touches. Avoid the attack by moving out of its path, launch attacks of your own, and this battle should end quickly.

Steam Vent Junction

Follow Blobbers up the steam jet to reach Steam Vent Junction. He points out a boulder on the left that you need to roll over the steam vent. Go to the right first. Gather up the loose coins and speak with the Knucklehead. Push the boulder over the steam vent and follow Blobbers up to the next ledge.

Boulder Falls Circle

Before meeting up with Blobbers, hop up the ledge on the left for a **Winged Sapphire**. There's another mystery gate on a lower ledge in the right side of the area. Because the gate is locked for now, you can't earn the Dare Star (Areas Found and *Traptanium* Gates), or the Collections Star (missing **Soul Gem** and **Hat**) for this Chapter, yet.

Blobbers is stuck again, needing another boulder to continue. Ride the steam vent up on the left. Take out the Chill Bill and Buzzer Beaks (hitting them with the boulder is effective) and push the boulder down to the area below and cap off the steam vent. Follow Blobbers up to the next area.

Patronizing Plateau

Check in with the Knucklehead and with Gumbus, who has a quest for Slobber Trap. Clear off the Bounce Pad near the bridge, then bounce up to Food Fight's **Soul Gem (That's How I Roll)**.

Blobbers and Buzz appear on the other side of the bridge, next to a Battle Gate. Buzz explains how to use the nearby turret. Shoot down the flying Trolls to open the Battle Gate.

GUMBUS' FORTUNE

Gumbus asks Slobber Trap to push over a stone. The toppled stone creates a bridge to a floating island filled with treasure you can collect.

Embellesher's Retreat

There's a second Battle Gate across the bridge, with Slobber Trap waiting behind it. Before Slobber Trap joins the battle, you must take out the initial enemies and a few waves of airborne reinforcements. It's possible to take out the wooden gunships before their cargo disembarks.

🔥 Slobber Trap

The first round of enemies is made up of Tussle Sprouts and other plant-based baddies. A mix of ranged and melee Trolls appear next. When the Trolls are gone, Slobber Trap leaps over the Battle Gate.

Slobber Trap has a single, lunging bite attack. His jaws are powerful, so try to stay to one side of his mouth. Attack when Slobber Trap is on the ground, shaking his head to recover from a missed lunge. He has a good deal of health to get through, so it may not be a quick battle.

The Battle Gate drops and reveals another turret. Run back to complete Slobber Trap's quest before meeting up with Buzz.

Buzz asks you to shoot down more Troll ships, to drive them from the island. When that's done, you return to Skylanders Academy.

Back at Skylanders Academy

Mags opens up new areas at Skylanders Academy. If your Portal Master Ranking increased, Eon appears and explains the special

rewards you earn with each rank. The first gift box contains a gem worth 1000 gold.

If you picked up the Legendary Tribal Statue from Know-It-All Island, step to the right and interact with the question mark to place it on a floating island.

Use the mysterious gate platform to jump across to the red carpet. Run up to the carpet and interact with the switch on the wall to enter the Courtyard Tower. It's a room filled with coins, and contains the **Iris' Iris Trinket**.

The Main Hall is locked with a speical puzzle. Guide the Lock Master around the Lock Puzzle to open it. Send him up, down, up, and down to collect all the coins and open the lock. Most of the Main Hall is blocked off, but Auric has opened his store near the fireplace.

Interact with the switch next to the fireplace to enter the Grand Fireplace. It's another coin-filled area to explore. In fact, you can return to both locations after each trip to a new Chapter of this adventure.

AURIC'S INVENTORY

Cheats	Price
Lock Puzzle Key	200
Trinkets	**Price**
Vote for Cyclops	100
Lizard Lilly	100
Bubble Blower	100
Medal of Heroism	100
Hats	**Price**
Flight Attendant Hat	50
Bellhop Hat	50
Storm Hat	25000

When you're done shopping and exploring, interact with the hot air ballon to return to the Courtyard and speak with Flynn to head off to Chompy Mountain.

Chompy Mountain

3

OBJECTIVES

STORY GOALS

▶ Gather Mabu Workers

▶ Unlock Chompy Mountain Entrance

▶ Find and Defeat the Chompy Mage

DARES

No Lives Lost

All Areas Found (20)

Enemy Goal (110)

Villains Defeated

Traptanium Gates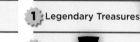

DIFFICULT DARES

Time to Beat: 20:30

Don't Switch

Complete all Villain Quests (3)

Mabu Landing Pier & Old Mabu Town

The path to Old Mabu Town is blocked by a wooden gate. Ignore the gate for now. Head to the right and grab the **Winged Sapphire** floating above the wooden planks. Next, continue straight ahead from the starting point for Sheep Creep's quest.

COLLECTIONS

1 Story Scrolls

4 Treasure Chests

3 Soul Gems

1 Winged Sapphires

1 Legendary Treasures

3 Hats

MAP KEY

(A)	Connector Point
	Hat
	Legendary Treasure
	Quest
	Skystones Smash Player
	Soul Gem
	Story Scroll
	Treasure Chest
	Villain Stash
	Winged Sapphire

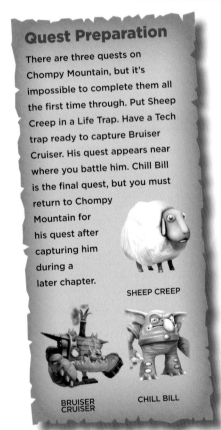

Quest Preparation

There are three quests on Chompy Mountain, but it's impossible to complete them all the first time through. Put Sheep Creep in a Life Trap. Have a Tech trap ready to capture Bruiser Cruiser. His quest appears near where you battle him. Chill Bill is the final quest, but you must return to Chompy Mountain for his quest after capturing him during a later chapter.

SHEEP CREEP

BRUISER CRUISER

CHILL BILL

164

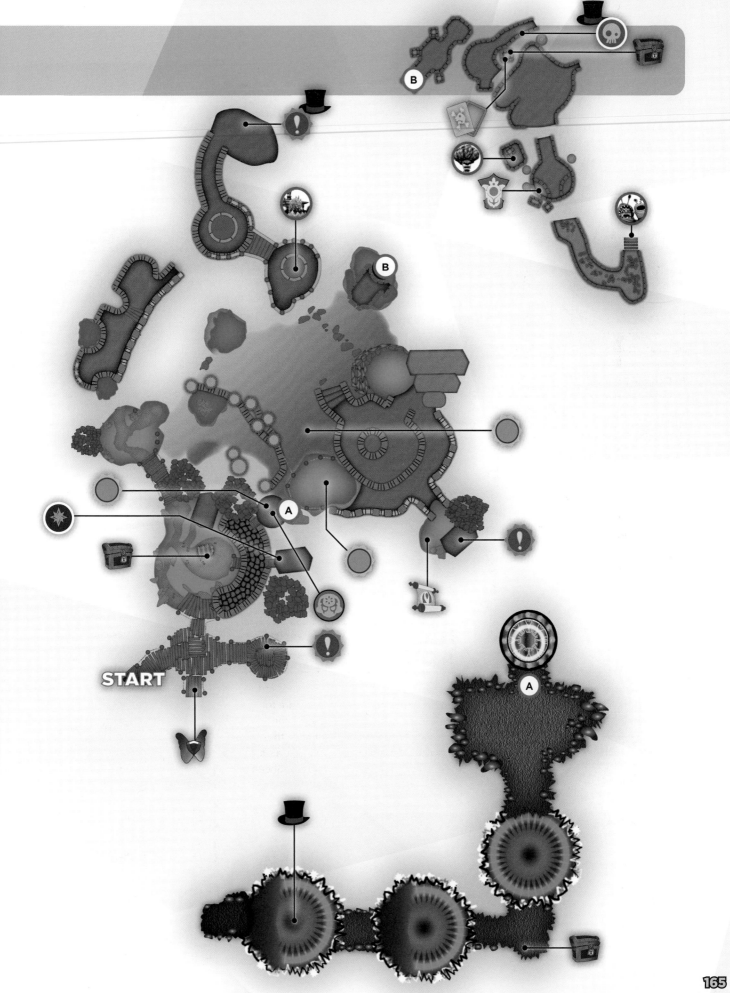

START

MILDLY IRRITATED SHEEP

Gumbus wants Sheep Creep to act as catapult ammunition to take out the buffalo terrorizing the sheep. You have just less than nine minutes to complete the task.

First, aim at the structures the buffalo use as cover. Hold the jump button to build up power, then let go to fire Sheep Creep. There are 15 total buffalo to take out, though they aren't all in the same spot. Aim for weak spots in the structures to take out the buffalos faster.

Go up the ramp and destroy the wooden gate at the end of the docks. Buzz asks you to talk to three Mabu and gain their assistance.

They're on the timid side, so approaching them causes them to flee inside their houses. The Mabu closest to Buzz is Snuckles. Follow him inside his home.

Snuckles' House & Rizzo's House

Approaching Snuckles restores his confidence. Don't follow him until after you interact with the Troll Radio and get its loot.

Rizzo is the next Mabu to recruit. Use the Bomb inside the house to gain his help. Destroy the wooden barricade in his home to reveal stairs that end at a Magic Gate.

Stepping onto the round platform causes gates to appear and block the way forward and back. You must collect all the coins that appear to open the gate.

Stop for the **Treasure Chest** before moving to the next platform. There are more coins to collect here, and slow-moving orbs are an added hazard. You can either destroy the orbs (they split twice into smaller orbs before being destroyed completely) or avoid them while collecting the coins.

The orbs on the final platform are faster and more plentiful, but the goal is the same. When the gate drops at the end of the platform, the **Horns Be With You Hat** is yours.

Wishing Well & Nort's House

Grab the Bomb from Rizzo's house and carry it outside. Use it to blast open the covering on the town's Wishing Well. Jump down the well, collect the piles of valuables, and smash the *Traptanium* crystal to reveal a **Treasure Chest**. Return to the surface to talk with the final Mabu, Nort.

Follow Nort into his house. Open the **Villain Stash** on the right, then go to the back of the room and jump on the flashing button. When the platform reaches the top level, Nort rides it back down. Jump to the right to get Gusto's **Soul Gem (Boomerangs 4 Breakfast)**.

Spinner's Landing

The three Mabu work together to open the gate. A Battle Gate blocks the path ahead, and you must defeat a small group of Trolls to take it down. Interact with the Chompy-topped coil to open one of the locks to a large gate in the distance. Cross the newly-constructed bridge to reach Overgrown Ramparts.

Spin the Chompy-topped spire beyond where you fought Bruiser Cruiser. Backtrack to the quest, or head down the wooden path away from gate.

Overgrown Ramparts

The Chompy Mage introduces himself by destroying the bridge. Avoid the Chompy Mage's attacks (stay clear of the yellow crosshairs on the ground) and return fire with the cannons in the area. You must move the cannons to get a clear shot, but two hits are enough to convince the Chompy Mage to leave.

The Mabu build another bridge, but the path ends at a wooden gate. Follow the stone path to the left (away from the wooden gate) for Bruiser Cruiser's quest. To complete the quest, you must first capture Bruiser Cruiser. He just happens to be waiting for you on the other side of the wooden gate.

NEED MORE THAN SINGING

Brady's singing isn't enough to free the miners trapped by a rockslide. Take Bruiser Cruiser to help clear the rocks, then get the Paperboy Hat from inside the cave.

Bruiser Cruiser

Bruiser Cruiser runs in a straight line, pummeling everything in his path. Move off the bridge as quickly as possible. You don't want your Skylander trapped in a narrow passage!

Avoid his charge by moving to the side. Hit him with your best attack while he recovers from his charge. Sometimes he will fly backward and start a charge again quickly, so be ready to dodge again.

Mountain Falls Lagoon

The wooden path leads to Mountain Falls Lagoon. Drop into the water, walk to the right, and look for a *Traptanium* crystal. Destroy the crystal to reveal Wallop's **Soul Gem (Now That's A Hammer!)**. Wade past the Mabu Defense Force and solve the Lock Puzzle.

This puzzle has a new element, a cracked block. The block cracks each time it is hit until it is destroyed. Go left, up, right, down, then left, up, right to collect all the coins. Go left, down, right, and up to reach the exit.

The second stage of the lock has fire. Touching fire returns the Lock Master back to the starting point. Go down and left to collect the coin. Go right, up, left, down, and down again to clear the stage.

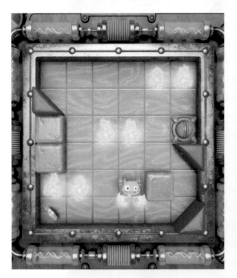

Troll Fortress

As soon as the lock falls away, get ready for a fight against a horde of Chompies supported by two types of Trolls and a Broccoli Guy. Broccoli Guys are the primary targets when they appear since they have the ability to heal their allies. Villains are stronger here, so it's a good time to try out the recently-upgraded Bruiser Cruiser, but any Villain will enjoy the same benefits.

With the enemies defeated, spin the Chompy-topped coil but don't follow Mabu just yet. Follow the stone path away from the Mabu Defense Force. Jump up to speak with Persephone if any Skylanders have enough gold for upgrades. Use the buttons to collect the coins floating over their platforms.

Follow the stone path around to a small house and a **Story Scroll**. The house is home to K-Troll Troll Radio. Bushwack's **Soul Gem (Timber)** is at the end of the path.

Chompy Mountain

Cross the bridge built by the Mabu Defense Force and enter Chompy Mountain. Your first task is to rescue the Mabu Defense Force. Destroy the wooden gate near Buzz. Use the cannon at the bottom of the ramp to destroy the two Chompy Head statues and knock down the wooden gate.

Rizzo's Rescue

Chompies and a Slobber Trap rush out to attack. Either move ahead to meet them or backtrack to the cannon and blast them when they try to squeeze through the gate. Defeating the enemies opens Rizzo's gate, but don't join him immediately. Destroy the *Traptanium* crystal to open the path to Artillery Storage. An Undead gate is nearby as well. Join Rizzo on the elevator after exploring both areas.

K-TROLL Troll Radio

Rocky wants Chill Bill's help with his radio station. There are also a few Troll Radios in the room that you can't reach without Chill Bill's assistance.

THE COLD FRONT

Rocky runs a radio station, but none of the current DJs are any good. He wants Chill Bill to take over and make the station better.

Chill Bill, my main man! You ready to hop back into the booth and show these other

Artillery Storage

Destroy the objects in the room to reveal a **Treasure Chest**. The lone Mabu in the room, Bungo, is a Skystones Smash player.

Come to challenge me to a game of Skystones Smash?

Bungo

Note his location for a return trip after you learn how to play Skystones Smash.

☠ UNDEAD VISTA

Defeat Chompies guarding the Lock Puzzle. The fires are back, but this time you have a way to deal with them. Touch the shimmering drop to coat the Lock Master in water. When he touches a flame afterward, it will be extinguished.

Go left, down, down, and down to collect the coins. Go left and left again to get to the drop of water. Go right, left, down, right, and up to collect additional coins. Go left, right, and right again to get the final coins. Go left, up, down, left, up, right, and right to reach the exit. Your reward for completing the puzzle is the **Hunting Hat**.

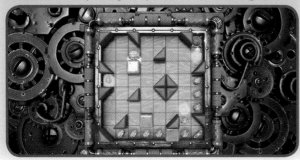

Broccoli Guy

While Broccoli Guy is the enemy you can capture, he's not exactly the enemy you fight here. He remains safely above the fight and allows the pair of Slobber Traps to handle the battle. Focus on one Slobber Trap at a time because Broccoli Guy heals them.

If you're having a hard time keeping up with the healing, attack the logs Broccoli Guy is standing on to bring him into range. He doesn't have any offensive abilities, so once the Slobber Traps are gone, it's a matter of tracking him down and depleting his health.

Snuckles' Rescue

Push the blocks to open the path. Push the center block over the edge to smash a Chompy Head statue. If you destroyed the other three previously, you earn the Statue Smasher Achievement.

Drop down on the left side and take out the Troll below. Collect the valuables and use the Bounce Pad to get to the enemies above. To free Snuckles, defeat the enemies near his cage, then defeat the reinforcements that come up the underground path.

Nort's Rescue & Chompy Hatchery

Destroy the wooden fence on the left to reveal the **Legendary Chompy Statue**. Use the nearby cannon to blast the Chompy Head statue. You can also use the cannon to take out the Trolls guarding Nort if you don't want to fight them directly.

Walk around the short wall the cannon rests against and step on the button to drop the wall into the ground. Push the cannon over until you have a clear shot at the gate marked with the Bomb icon. The newly opened path leads to Chompy Hatchery and a fight against Broccoli Guy. Walk over to Nort afterward to move on and rescue Snuckles.

Chompy Head Spire

Stand next to Snuckles to ride up to Chompy Head Spire. Run up the stone steps where you fight against the Chompy Mage.

Chompy Mage

The Chompy Mage sends out swarms of Chompies to start the battle. Avoid the red rings on the ground, but be ready to fight the various types of Chompies that appear. Destroy the red Chompies before they pause and explode.

After clearing out the Chompies, the Chompy Mage joins the battle. He changes into his Mega Chompy form and jumps around the area. Avoid the fiery rings that he creates each time he lands on the ground. Hit him with attacks when possible (it won't be often, he moves quickly) to begin whittling down his health.

The Chompy Mage jumps to his pedestal and changes into a giant magma Chompy. He continues to summon other Chompies (watch out for the red rings) and sends out fiery rings from where he lands. Use a flying Skylander to fly over the fiery rings to more easily avoid them.

Skylanders with ranged attacks have an easier time with this battle, but even they must stay on the move to avoid the fiery rings and hordes of Chompies. If you're limited to melee attacks, don't try to do too much at one time. Your Skylander will lose health much faster than the Chompy Mage will!

Back at Skylanders Academy

Talk to Mags in the Main Hall. She opens an area of the Main Hall that has a slot machine. Give it a spin to claim your reward. If you found the Legendary Chompy Statue, interact with the yellow "?" in the middle of the red carpet nearby. Talk to Flynn to fly to your next destination, The Phoenix Psanctuary.

OBJECTIVES

STORY GOALS

▶ Gain entrance to the Aviary

▶ Save the Phoenix Chicken

Quest Preparation

Put Buzzer Beak in an Air Trap and Tussle Sprout in an Earth Trap. Have a Life Trap ready to capture Cuckoo Clocker, but you must take a second trip through The Phoenix Psanctuary to complete his quest.

BUZZER BEAK

TUSSLE SPROUT

CUCKOO CLOCKER

DARES

No Lives Lost

All Areas Found (18)

Enemy Goal (50)

Villains Defeated

Traptanium Gates

DIFFICULT DARES

Time to Beat: 19:55

Don't Switch

Complete all Villain Quests (3)

COLLECTIONS

1 Story Scrolls

4 Treasure Chests

2 Soul Gems

1 Winged Sapphires

1 Legendary Treasures

3 Hats

MAP KEY

(A)	Connector Point
	Hat
	Legendary Treasure
	Quest
	Skystones Smash Player
	Soul Gem
	Story Scroll
	Treasure Chest
	Villain Stash
	Winged Sapphire

Outer Plumage

Destroy the *Traptanium* crystal near Tessa to open the way to a **Treasure Chest**. Tessa explains how to use nuts to grow bridges. Use the Boingo Nut to grow the first vine bridge. Cross the bridge, and be ready to fight a group of Eggsecutioners. Get the nut from the cage. Use it to grow a vine bridge, and cross it.

START

You can't use the Bounce Pad here yet, so pick up the nut and toss it into the ground to grow a forked vine bridge. The left fork goes to Buzz, who offers a quest for Buzzer Beak.

Take out the Trolls that appear after defeating Shrednaught to clear the Bounce Pad. Step on the blue platform (it's the top of a cage) on the area's right side and ride it down. Drop off the side and get the **Legendary Egg** from inside the cage. The **Treasure Chest** is out of reach for now, but remember its location.

Bounce back up to Rump Feather Roost and use the Bounce Pad there to reach a bridge blocked by Blocker Birds. Plant the nut to draw them out and clear the path ahead. Jump over the railing near where you first saw the birds to reach Down Feather Wash.

Down Feather Wash

Use the Bounce Pads in the grassy area to collect the coins. Drop down into the water and follow the trail of coins over the edge to reach a Water Gate and Arbo, who has a quest for Tussle Sprout.

FAMILY REUNION

Bring Buzzer Beak to his family for a happy reunion. Beyond upgraded abilities for Buzzer Beak, you also get a hat, **Parrot Nest**.

The right fork ends at the switch needed to open the cage with the Bounce Pad. Return to the Bounce Pad and jump up to Rump Feather Roost, which has a Battle Gate-locked Bounce Pad and a battle with Shrednaught.

SPROUTIN' UP

Tussle Sprout plants himself and creates a bridge to an island with a Villain Stash.

Shrednaught

Shrednaught advances slowly with its huge chainsaw blade rotating around its chassis. Get to a safe distance and pelt it with ranged attacks if your Skylander has them. When Shrednaught shudders to a stop, jump in and pound on it with melee attacks. Get away before it starts up again and repeat the process until Shrednaught is defeated.

No hidden tricks or enemies here. Jump up to the ledge with the hat box and get the **Daisy Crown**.

Hooked Bill Ascent

The bridge formerly blocked by the Blocker Birds goes to Hooked Bill Ascent. Defeat the Trolls guarding the nut, then plant the nut to create a bridge. More Trolls appear and you must defeat them to clear the Battle Gate from the Bounce Pad ahead.

Aviary Gate

Bounce up to meet Flynn and Tessa outside a locked door. They tell you where to get the key, but first drop off the ledge near Flynn. A worn, dirt spot marks the place to do it.

Rare Species Walk

Go through the doorway ready for a fight. A small group of Trolls, featuring a Shrednaught, guard a Battle Gate. Take them out and get Snap Shot's **Soul Gem (A Shard Act to Follow)** on the bridge. Continue through the exit. The path leads back to Aviary Gate. Step on the round platform and ride it down. It's the cage with the **Treasure Chest** from earlier, but now it's yours to claim.

Return to Flynn and Tessa outside the Aviary Gate. To open the gate, you must clear out Clockwork Nest, the nearby, Troll-infested area.

Clockwork Nest & Hatchling Hall

Settle in for an extended battle. After you defeat the initial Troll forces, reinforcements arrive by dropship and grappling hook. The Troll forces include Lob Goblins, Chill Bills, and Shrednaughts appearing in groups. Whenever you see a grappling hook appear, attack it before too many Trolls climb up to join the fight. If you manage to destroy one of the dropships, you earn the Preemptive Power Achievement.

Tessa and Flynn appear when the fight is over. Go through the now opened door to reach Hatchling Hall. Speak with Persephone in the back to purchase upgrades if necessary. Push the bird cages to create a path to the Key from the corner of the room. When you return to Clockwork Nest with the Key, Chill Bill appears.

Chill Bill

Chill Bill has only a ranged attack, so stay on top of him during the fight. Stay on the move until Chill Bill discharges his icy blast. Attack while he's waiting for his weapon to recharge. If your Skylander is hit, press Attack 1 rapidly to break free. Two Lob Goblins assist Chill Bill during the fight, but they can wait until after you take care of him.

Use the nut that appears to open the cage with the Bounce Pad. Bounce back up to the Aviary Gate and use the nut there to open the cage with another Bounce Pad. Ride up to the top of the cage and collect the piles of loot and the **Story Scroll**.

Carry the nut across the way and plant it to grow a bridge to the ledge above the locked gate. Collect the coins and Funny Bone's **Soul Gem (Healing Paws)**.

Feather Bed Hatchery, Songbird Perch & Little Chicken Landing

The Feather Bed Hatchery is the first area beyond the Aviary Gate. Da Pinchy is off to the right in Songbird Perch with a quest for Cuckoo Clocker. An Air Gate is to the left. Explore both areas before moving up to talk with Tessa.

SONG BIRD

Da Pinchy needs Cuckoo Clocker to round out his singing group. With Cuckoo Clocker as baritone, his quartet is complete.

⊙ FAN WING THERMALS

Step into the tube for a wild ride down to an area filled with fans. Jump over the updrafts created by the fans to be carried higher. There are some coins to collect, and a switch in a cage. Flip the switch to turn the higher cage and gain access to a Bounce Pad. Bounce up to the higher ledge and follow the path to the **Ceiling Fan Hat**. Drop off the side and collect the line of coins on the way down. Step back into the tube to return to Feather Bed Hatchery.

Talk to Tessa to learn more about your mission. Avoid or destroy the eggs tumbling down the ramp. When the suction tube is clear, drop

into it to reach Little Chicken Landing. Destroy the *Traptanium* crystal to reveal a **Winged Sapphire**. Mess with the Troll Radio before jumping into the tube to return to the ramp.

⊙ Free Range Rollers

Continue upward on the ramp. Use the rounded areas to step aside when an egg passes if you can't destroy them quickly enough. A handful of Trolls waits just ahead to slow you down. Head away from the steps where they fight you and step off the ledge.

Wish Bone Balcony

Use the Bounce Pad up to the short ledge and collect the valuables. Destroy the *Traptanium* crystal at the other end of the Balcony to clear the way to a **Treasure Chest**. Use the Bounce Pad to return to Free Range Rollers. Ascend the steps where you fight the Trolls, then continue up the rollers to reach Aviary Heights. Use the suction tube to reach Chef Pepper Jack.

Aviary Heights

The Arena Battle kicks off with waves of Trolls, primarily Lob Goblins and Eggsecutioners. Watch out for Phoenix Chicks popping up from under the nest. Their heads push up the three circular areas in the nest and nip at anything in their reach.

The second wave's enemies include Chill Bills and a Shrednaught. The third wave seems to be more of the same, but then Pepper Jack sends in Cuckoo Clocker.

Cuckoo Clocker

Cuckoo Clocker is slow and incredibly strong. His attack is an overhand two-hand smash that sends out little shockwaves to damage anything too close. Avoid the smash and retaliate immediately afterward. Don't think Pepper Jack is content to let Cuckoo Clocker fight alone. Additional Trolls continue to join the fight.

Back at Skylander Academy

Heed Mags' advice and walk to the Main Hall (don't use the shortcut). Brock appears after the door opens, and makes the Rumble Challenge Arenas available. Place the Legendary Egg above the fireplace's mantle, then check out Auric's updated selection.

AURIC'S NEW INVENTORY

Trinkets	Price
Blobbers' Medal of Courage	100
Medal of Gallantry	100
Snuckles' Sunflower	100
Goo Factory Gear	100

Talk to Crossbones who opens a new wing of the Main Hall and introduces Skaletone Showdown. For more information about Skaletone Showdown, check out the Skylanders Academy section of this guide. When you're done with your tour of the Main Hall, speak with Flynn.

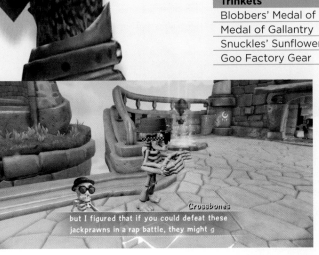

Crossbones
but I figured that if you could defeat these
jackprawns in a rap battle, they might g

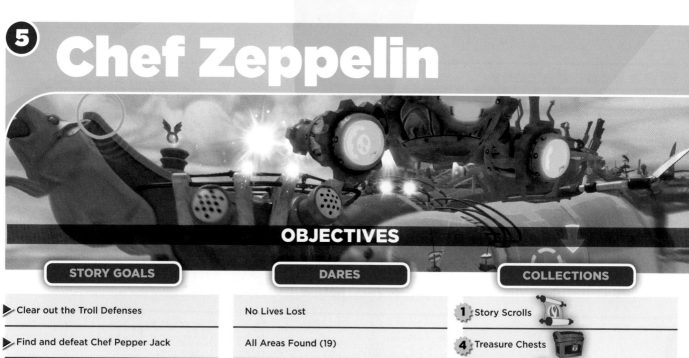

OBJECTIVES

STORY GOALS

▶ Clear out the Troll Defenses

▶ Find and defeat Chef Pepper Jack

Quest Preparation

The quests during this level are both for Life Villains, Chompy Mage and Broccoli Guy. Unless you own more than one Life Trap, you need two trips through the level to earn the Difficult Dares star.

CHOMPY MAGE   BROCCOLI GUY

DARES

No Lives Lost

All Areas Found (19)

Enemy Goal (50)

Villains Defeated

Traptanium Gates

DIFFICULT DARES

Time to Beat: 19:55

Don't Switch

Complete all Villain Quests (2)

COLLECTIONS

1	Story Scrolls
4	Treasure Chests
1	Soul Gems
1	Winged Sapphires
1	Legendary Treasures
3	Hats

MAP KEY

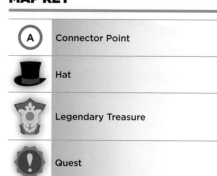

Ⓐ	Connector Point
🎩	Hat
	Legendary Treasure
	Quest
	Skystones Smash Player
	Soul Gem
	Story Scroll
	Treasure Chest
	Villain Stash
	Winged Sapphire

Landing Pan

The level opens with your Skylander in control of a defense turret on Flynn's ship. It functions the same as the turrets used previously, but it has an extra attack that charges with each enemy taken down. The extra attack changes based on the Element of your Skylander (and Villain, if you have one).

There are four winged gems that appear around the ship. If you manage to hit all four with blasts from the turret, you earn a x2 Bonus to your score. Don't worry about taking a few hits if it means getting a winged gem; Flynn's ship is tough! You earn the Cannon Completist achievement for shooting down eight Troll transports

(they're the first targets you shoot down). You don't need to get all eight in one run. After clearing out the defenses, your Skylander appears on the Landing Pan.

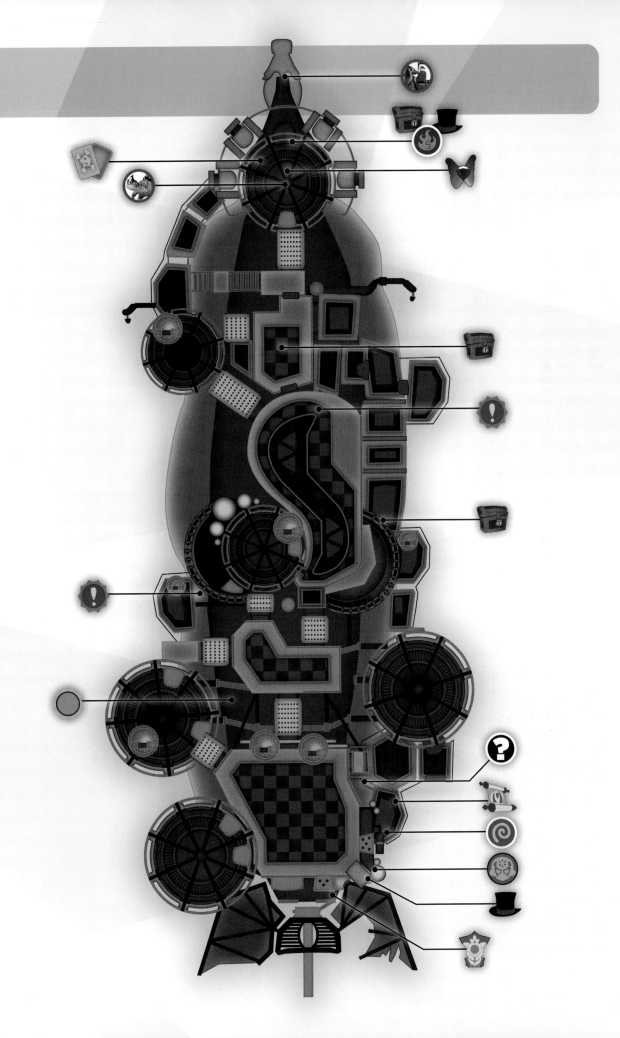

Main Counter Top

Take out the Trolls and Grinnades that jump on the deck. Use the deck gun, then the handle that turns the gun. Fire the gun two more times to knock down two more doors, one after each turn of the crank.

Walk toward the gun on the right, but jump over the low spot in the loaf of bread railing. Collect the coins and the **Legendary Pepper**, then use the Teleport Pad to return to the upper deck. Turn the crank near the second deck gun and fire it to knock down a wooden barricade.

Side Spinner & Bottom Shelf

Dropping off the ledge past the second deck gun leads to two different places. The side with the flaming kabobs and coins is Side Spinner. The opposite side is Bottom Shelf. There's an Air Gate at one end of Bottom Shelf. The other side has a mystery element gate and a **Story Scroll**. Use the Super Bounce Pad to return to Main Counter Top when you're done exploring.

TAIL WINDS

Use the Bounce Pad to hop on the floating balloon. Ride the balloon to the ledge with the **Villain Stash**. Ride the other floating balloon through the line of coins to reach the **Scooter Hat**.

Main Kabobs

Main Kabobs is the area to the left of Main Counter Top. Avoid the flaming arms and jump over the railing above where a **Soul Gem** is visible. Claim Chopper's **Soul Gem (Ultimate Dino Destruction)**, then use the Teleport Pad to return to Main Counter Top. There's a small landing beyond the flaming kabob arms. Going up the cheese grater ramp leads to Topside Burners. Follow the hovering coins down one level to reach Chopping Block.

Topside Burners & Chopping Block

Persephone is the only attraction in Topside Burners. Hold off on visiting her until after you go down to the Chopping Block. The doorway in Chopping Block is locked with a Lock Puzzle. To solve the puzzle, send the Lock Master left, up, right, and down to douse him in water. Go left, up, right, and down to complete the puzzle and open the path to the Kitchen of Shame.

Kitchen of Shame

The chef in the Kitchen of Shame is culinarily challenged, and asks for help from Broccoli Guy.

BROCCOLI GUY EN FUEGO

Bernie wants Broccoli Guy's help in restoring his reputation. Unfortunately, he's so inept even Broccoli Guy can't keep him from destroying his last pot! At least the concoction was potent enough to upgrade Broccoli Guy.

Return to Main Kabobs and walk up the cheese grater ramp. Bomb Shell introduces himself here, but the fight against him doesn't start yet. The ramp on the right leads back to the Main Counter Top, but it's a one-way trip (it's too high to jump back up to the ramp). The second left ramp goes to Smorgasboard, which you can also reach from Persephone's perch in Topside Burners.

Smorgasboard

The way through Smorgasboard is locked with a Battle Gate. You must defeat waves of Trolls to open it. Expect to see at least one of each Troll type encountered up to this point. Grinnades join the fight as well. Take them out before they drop to the ground and detonate. When the coast is clear, Cookie has a quest for the Chompy Mage.

FREE THE CHOMPIES

Cookie is tired of being chomped on by Chompies. The Chompy Mage puts things right by turning the Chompies friendly. As an added bonus, completing this quest opens a few new areas of the zeppelin.

Top Shelf

The Chompies of Top Shelf don't bother you. Ignore them on your way to the Lock Puzzle. The puzzle is full of breakable boxes, which require backing up and smashing into a few times to break them completely. Go down, up, down, right, up, down, up, right, left, right, down, left, up, down, up, down, left, right, left, right, left, right, left, right, and finally down. Gather the piles of valuables and the **Treasure Chest**. Drop down to Bottom Shelf (silver coins mark the spot) and use the Super Bounce Pad to return to Smorgasboard.

Cooling Rack

The warm-up act consists of a few Trolls and Grinnades. A gate blocks the exit, so the fight takes place in tight quarters. After you take down a Shrednaught, Bomb Shell joins the battle. Defeating him opens the way to the key needed to open the door in Port Gangway.

Cheese Graters & Auxiliary Kitchen

Descend the ramps that look like cheese graters until Tessa appears and points out a key. The Bomb needed to blast the wooden fence is down a long flight of stairs in Port Gangway. The Trolls guarding the locked door in Port Gangway won't bother you if you grab the Bomb and use the Super Bounce Pad quickly.

Bomb the way clear. Go into Auxiliary Kitchen and defeat the Trolls and Grinnades to drop the Battle Gate. Claim your **Treasure Chest** and other valuables. Head back outside. To open the Battle Gate with the key, go down to Cooling Rack.

Bomb Shell

Bomb Shell does not come alone. A pair of Chill Bills supports him at the start of the fight. Watch for the large red circles to appear on the ground. They mark Bomb Shell's target zone. Don't think they're safe after his bombs detonate. Purple fire clings to the area briefly and it's just as dangerous as being hit by a bomb.

Bomb Shell is not mobile and takes a few seconds between bomb tosses. Bait throws away from his position if you need to keep the area clear for melee attacks.

Port Gangway

Grab the key and return to Port Gangway. Eliminate the Trolls and Grinnades. Unlock the door and step inside Command Kitchen.

Command Kitchen & Garbage Disposal

Batterson introduces Skystones Smash and explains how the game works. You must defeat Pot Roast to earn his trust and gain access to Chef Pepper Jack.

Don't hurry off for the final battle until after you tune the Troll Radio, slide down the sink across from Pot Roast, and visit the Fire Gate. Slide down to Garbage Disposal, where the **Winged Sapphire** waits. Use the Bounce Pad to return to Command Kitchen.

OVEN

The flames of this oven are so hot they even burn Fire Skylanders! Push the pans of dough over the flame jets on the ground. The dough turns to bread and cuts off the flame. There are three pans to move against the back wall.

Bake a path to the left, then go to the corner for a **Treasure Chest** guarded by a pair of flame jets. Follow the metal path up, then push the final pan of dough down to complete the path to the **Colander Hat.**

So here it is, Skystones Smash!

Chef Pepper Jack

Chef Pepper Jack drops peppers that turn into expanding fiery orbs. He charges behind the fiery attack with an egg beater. Dodge the charge, and attack while he's recovering from the pots and pans falling on him. If your Skylander needs some health, look for food in the piles of cookware.

After losing some health, Chef Pepper Jack jumps back up to his perch and uses laser wires that make the floor hazardous. Jump over the beams, or use a flying Skylander, and aim for wider spots when the lasers change angles and directions.

Chef Pepper Jack drops down to the floor again and repeats his charging attack behind pepper bombs. He throws down more peppers this time, so less of the floor is safe when avoiding his charge. After another round of charging and lasers, Chef Pepper Jack tosses out giant steaks. Jump on the steaks to avoid the lasers, but watch for them to flash white. That flash means Chef Pepper Jack is about to destroy the steak with one of his peppers.

Be ready for one more round of pepper-tossing and egg beater-charging, but the battle ends with your Skylander hopping between steaks until Chef Pepper Jack is well-done.

Back at Skylander Academy

The kitchen opens in the Main Hall. Put the Legendary Pepper in its place. Hit the floating dodecahedrons in the cauldron with an attack from a Skylander of the proper element to destroy them. Destroy all the dodecahedrons to earn rewards. Talk to Cali when you're ready for a squid hunt.

6 Rainfish Riviera

OBJECTIVES

STORY GOALS

▶ Retrieve Mags' "Information Squid"

Quest Preparation

For the villain quests you can complete at this time, keep the recently captured Pepper Jack in a Fire trap. Have a Tech trap ready for Brawlrus, then keep him handy for his quest later in Rainfish Riviera.

PEPPER JACK   BRAWLRUS

DARES

No Lives Lost

All Areas Found (20)

Enemy Goal (75)

Villains Defeated

Traptanium Gates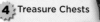

DIFFICULT DARES

Time to Beat: 19:30

Don't Switch

Complete all Villain Quests (3)

COLLECTIONS

1 Story Scrolls

4 Treasure Chests

2 Soul Gems

1 Winged Sapphires

1 Legendary Treasures

3 Hats

MAP KEY

(A)	Connector Point
	Hat
	Legendary Treasure
	Quest
	Skystones Smash Player
	Soul Gem
	Story Scroll
	Treasure Chest
	Villain Stash
	Winged Sapphire

Monsoon Point & Waste Water Cove

Walk down to Mags and talk with her to learn more about what happened. Before destroying the wooden fence, look for a gap in the stones directly behind Mags. Lob-Star's **Soul Gem (The Boiler)** is the prime attraction in Waste Water Cove, but there are other valuables in the sand. When you're done exploring, use the Bounce Pad to get back up and destroy the wooden gate.

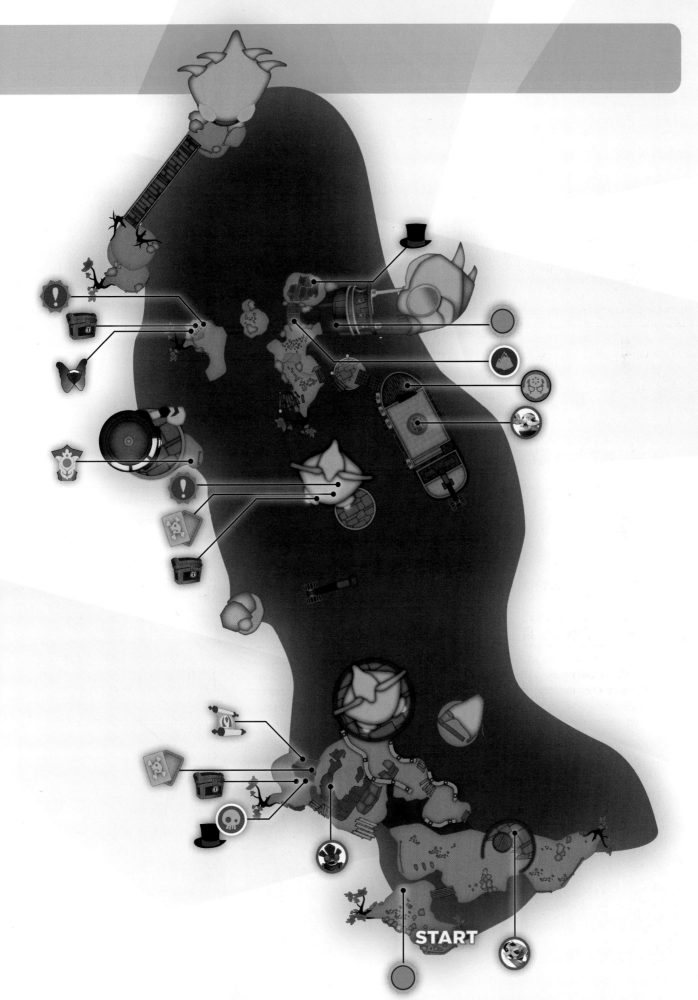

START

Blowhole Beach

The Chompies are dressed like Pirates, but they're not much different than the other Chompies you've faced up to this point. Shortly after the fight begins, Brawlrus and his pirate henchmen join in. After you defeat Brawlrus, Mags points out spare wood that could be used to build a bridge.

Brawlrus

Brawlrus uses a short-range starfish gun that's more annoying than dangerous. It coats its target in starfish (up to three at a time) that slow movement speed until they're shaken off, or they fall off a few seconds later. It deals minor damage, but it won't do as much harm as the henchmen.

Steel Fin Balcony

The gate has two locks on it. Reuse your bridge to reach the first key. To get the second key, talk to Bucko in the nearby shack.

Fish Bone's Card Shack & Brackwater Falls

The shack near the locked gate is Fish Bone's Card Shack. Bucko is inside and offers his key, but only if you beat him at Skystones Smash. After winning a game, get the key and the **Story Scroll**. Head outside, but be ready for a fight.

Masker Mind

The fight begins against Chompies (including one clumsy Chompy, who trips) and a Bomb Shell. Masker Mind soon joins the battle by taking control of the Bomb Shell. Take out the Chompies, then the Bomb Shell. When Masker Mind has no other bodies to possess, all it can do is run away. Chase it down and finish it off to add an Undead Villain to your collection.

Follow the line of coins at the end of the steel plate down to Brackwater Falls. Doublooney has a quest for Eye Five, an enemy who can't be captured yet. Go to the other side of the bridge for an Undead Gate. Use the Bounce Pad to return to Steel Fin Balcony when you're done.

FISH BONE'S RETREAT

The floor here is covered in squares that fire different cannons when they're stepped on. Run diagonally across the squares to the square with the skull on it. Don't hesitate, or the cannonballs will hit your Skylander.

There's a **Treasure Chest** in the far corner of the area. To get to the **Metal Fin Hat**, return to the Skull square and look toward the back row of cannons. The cannons one row to the left are set back from the rest. Run straight toward the cannons in the same line as the Skull square. When the square in front of the cannons erupts from the sand, jump to the sand-covered square in front of the gap to avoid triggering the square from blocking your path. After you get the hat, use the raised block to exit the boat.

Fish Eyed Walk

Go through the unlocked gate and follow Fish Eyed Walk to Mags, who explains the way ahead is blocked by raised posts. Go up to the door to find the controls to lower them.

Fish Eyed Control

The controls are behind a Battle Gate guarded by waves of pirate henchmen and Bomb Shells. The Bomb Shells like to hide on the walkway, so you may need to go up there to eliminate them.

Step on the button behind the Battle Gate to drop the posts outside. Mess with the Troll Radio, then head out to catch up with Mags.

classic case of gate-in-the-way. There's a switch inside that opens it but also a lot of

Mags

Brawlrus

The next bridge has been retracted and the only way to restore it is to move Mags with a crane. Interact with the controls to clear out the Brawl

and Chain guards. When they're gone, carry Mags over and drop her in the indicated spot.

Clam Tower

Cross the bridge to meet up with Mags again. Extend the bridge over to the yacht. Drop off the side of the platform and collect the floating coins. The doorway here leads to the Submarine Pen. Before going through it, use the Bounce Pad to grab the Bomb from atop the tower. When you finish with the Submarine Pen, use the Bounce Pad to reach the top of the tower again and use the Bomb to blow up the wooden gate blocking the path to the yacht.

⬣ Submarine Pen

Blow up the gate and open the **Treasure Chest**. Take a minute to mess with the Troll Radio afterward. Cross the wooden walkway. Bucko wants a Skystones Smash rematch. Brawlrus' quest is nearby, but you must fight through a small group of pirates backed by a Bomb Shell to reach it.

Starfish's Sub

The Submarine hatch opens after Brawlrus completes his quest. Look for the **Steampunk Hat** inside.

⬣ Dredger's Yacht

Mags points out another crane control station. There are five Brawl and Chain guards roaming the yacht and they must be eliminated before the raised posts will fall. These guards are more alert than the earlier guards, but you have two ways of dealing with them. You can pick them up and drop them over the side, or you can pick up the stacks of pipes and drop them on their heads. Either way, destroy the four stacks of pipes before taking out the final Brawl and Chain to earn the Pipe Down achievement.

Go down to the lower deck. A trio of Bomb Shells appears, ready for a fight. They're just a warm-up act; the real fight begins when they are eliminated.

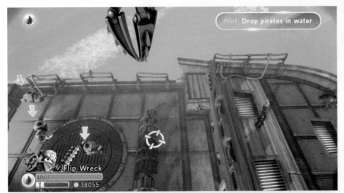

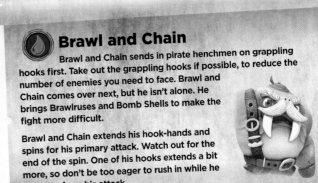

Brawl and Chain

Brawl and Chain sends in pirate henchmen on grappling hooks first. Take out the grappling hooks if possible, to reduce the number of enemies you need to face. Brawl and Chain comes over next, but he isn't alone. He brings Brawlruses and Bomb Shells to make the fight more difficult.

Brawl and Chain extends his hook-hands and spins for his primary attack. Watch out for the end of the spin. One of his hooks extends a bit more, so don't be too eager to rush in while he recovers from his attack.

When the Battle Gate drops, walk around to the wooden crate. Push it aside to reveal a Bounce Pad. Bounce to the *Traptanium* crystal and destroy it to reveal a passage that leads to Below Deck.

Below Deck

A Battle Gate pops up and a group of Chompies, Bomb Shells, and Brawlruses attack. After you dispatch them, open the **Villain Stash** and return to the upper deck.

Dire Sands

Walk down the yacht's gangway and break down the wooden fence. Mags appears again and tells you what must be done next. Hop down to the sand. An Earth Gate is next to a group of large snails. Push the snails into the water to build a path to Déjà Vu's **Soul Gem (Black Hole Bedlam)**.

BARNACLE SHOAL

More giant snails are beyond the Earth Gate entrance. Push them around and down into the water to build a bridge of shells to the **Imperial Hat**. Despite most of the snails starting stacked atop each other, no snails should be stacked when you're done.

Bluster Squall Island

Cross the wooden bridge near the Earth Gate and take out the Chompies on the small island. Pick up the bridge and move it to the other bridge spot. Defeat the small group of evil minions on the other side, then pick up the bridge and move it again. Before crossing the bridge, go into Cheddar House, the small hut on the island.

Cross the bridge to the larger island. Destroy the *Traptanium* crystal to reveal the **Legendary Bubble Fish**. Continue up the metal walkway to reach Big Hook.

Cheddar House

Get the **Winged Sapphire** from the corner of the house. Speak with Galley to learn more about Chef Pepper Jack's quest. Completing the quest opens the way to a **Treasure Chest**.

HEAD OF THE CHEESE

Galley needs the finest cheeses and only Chef Pepper Jack can get them. Pick up cheeses and carry them back to the starting point. To help things along, Chef Pepper Jack can carry more than one cheese at a time.

Watch out for the haunted head that appears after picking up some cheese. If the head touches Chef Pepper Jack, it removes five seconds from the timer. Use Chef Pepper Jack's dashing attack to move faster.

them the ideal place to store amazing cheese but the angry, evil head who haunts

Galley

Big Hook & Fish Mouth

The winding metal walkway ends at a claw control panel. Interact with the panel and get ready for some odd fishing. Pick up a bucket of bait and drop it into the water. When the Rainfish swims under the bait, grab it with the crane. Jump down and walk into the beast's mouth and retrieve the Information Squid.

Back at Skylander Academy

When you have control of your Skylander, step to the left and place Legendary Bubble Fish near the quick travel portals. Follow the coins that lead to the Main Hall. Crossbones has another challenger for Skaletones Showdown. Auric has new items for sale.

AURIC'S INVENTORY

Cheats	Price
Skystone Key	200
Hats	**Price**
Palm Hat	200
Rude Boy Hat	200
Pork Pie Hat	200
Miniature Skylands Hat	200

The Upper Hallway of the Main Hall is now open. Visit the Hat Store, where Hatterson has a quest for Hoodsickle.

The Game Room is also open. Dreadbeard offers to play Skystones Smash inside. Jump on the Element-based platforms with a matching Skylander to move up higher. Reach the top and claim your prize.

7

Monster Marsh

OBJECTIVES

STORY GOALS

▶ Free Hedwick

▶ Find Sleepy Village

▶ Rescue the Sleepy Villagers

Quest Preparation

You are unable to complete the quests for this level at this time.

DARES

No Lives Lost

All Areas Found (20)

Enemy Goal (120)

Villains Defeated

Traptanium Gates

DIFFICULT DARES

Time to Beat: 23:45

Don't Switch

Complete all Villain Quests (2)

COLLECTIONS

1 Story Scrolls

4 Treasure Chests

2 Soul Gems

1 Winged Sapphires

1 Legendary Treasures

3 Hats

MAP KEY

(A)	Connector Point	
	Hat	
	Legendary Treasure	
	Quest	
	Skystones Smash Player	
	Soul Gem	
	Story Scroll	
	Treasure Chest	
	Villain Stash	
	Winged Sapphire	

Haunted Wreck & Haunted Approach

Destroy the *Traptanium* crystal near the starting point to reveal a **Winged Sapphire**. Look for a Troll Radio near Gomper, who offers help about where to go next. There's a **Soul Gem** just out of reach, but you'll get it soon.

Krypt King
567
9 6834

START

Move the wooden blocks out of the path and destroy the wooden gate beyond them. The first wooden ramp leads to Cali and a quest for Eye Scream, an enemy who can't be captured yet.

The iron gate is locked, but Hedwick speaks up to help out. Go past the destructible wooden gate (it leads to Spirestone Mausoleum). Push the boxes to clear the path to the Undead Gate and expose a low spot in the ground. Push a box into the hole and move the other boxes in place to make a ramp back up to the Haunted Wreck. Gather the coins and pick up Krypt King's **Soul Gem (Healing Hack)**.

Spirestone Cliffs & Spirestone Grotto

Look for a gap in the stones along the side of the cliff and step over the edge. Go inside the doorway and destroy the fence. Smash the fence in the back to reveal a **Treasure Chest**. Use the Bounce Pad outside to return to the top.

Spirestone Graveyard

The way ahead splits. One way goes to an Undead Gate, the other to a **Soul Gem**. Fist Bump's **Soul Gem (Riding the Rails)** is behind a Lock Puzzle. To open the gate, go left, left, up, left, up, right, and down to douse the Lock Master in water. Go up, left, left, up, left, up, and left to get to the exit. The Super Bounce Pad goes to Hungry Isle.

Hungry Isle

Hungry Isle is Chomp Chest's home turf. After defeating him, use the Super Bounce Pad to return to Spirestone Graveyard.

Chomp Chest

The fight takes place in a confined area, which is a big advantage for Chomp Chest. He dances around and rushes forward while chomping anything in his path. Move out of his path and attack quickly. There is one bonus to this fight: every time you hit Chomp Chest, he drops loot for you to scoop up.

☠ SPIRESTONE CRYPT

Tiny eye enemies appear immediately, and they continue popping up as you push the blocks to build the path to the hat box. Push the blocks to the right to reach the ledge above. Push the block from that ledge to the left to fill in the channel. Jump to the highest ledge and cross over to the box, which contains the **Dragon Skull Hat**.

☠ Spirestone Mausoleum

Destroy the wooden gate in Haunted Approach and walk over the bridge. Hedwick is locked behind a Battle Gate. Defeat the tiny eyeballs and other stitched-together enemies to free him.

Windmill Hill & Supply Room

Join Hedwick at the now opened iron gates. You must cross the bridge, but two enemies across the way make the journey hazardous. Avoid or destroy the barrels, then take out the barrel-rolling Eye Screams. Go through the opened door to reach the Supply Room, where you must defeat Millington in Skystones Smash to remove the wooden stakes blocking the path.

Follow the winding path upward and avoid the windmill blades. Look for a **Story Scroll** behind the windmill at the top. Drop carefully to the ledge below. The doorway leads to Secret Basement.

Secret Basement & The Little House on the Misty Marshes

Use the Troll Radio and get upgrades from Persephone if you can afford them. Return to the top of the hill and pull the lever to lower the platform. Jump on the platform and ride it down to The Little House on the Misty Marshes.

The path ahead is blocked by a Battle Gate. The guardians of the Battle Gate are an odd mix of bizarre creatures, including tiny eyeballs and an Eye Scream. Clear out the enemies and the Battle Gate falls away.

The Misty Marshes

Cross the bridge and talk with Hedwick. Complete the Lock Puzzle to free Marsha. Start by going right and up to get the coin. Next, go down, right, and up to hit the drop of water. Finally, go down, left, up, and left to clear the first board. For the second puzzle, go left, right, down, and up to get the coins. Go down, right, left, right, down, right, left, down, up, and down to break the lock.

Marsha's field protects Skylanders who stay within it. If you manage to collect 20 coins while following Marsha here, you earn the No Coins Left Behind achievement.

When Marsha pauses on dry land, walk away from the direction she faces. Push the stone blocks to form a safe path above the water. Collect the coins and **Legendary Golden Frog** here. Return to Marsha and continue the trip. Her next stop is at a mystery gate. The trip ends at a *Traptanium* crystal. Destroy it to reveal a Super Bounce Pad that sends you to Empty Isle.

 ## Empty Isle & Village Approach

Empty Isle is a fight against the mysterious Eye Scream. It spawns the tiny eyeball enemies and stays moving most of the time. Despite being

unable to trap Eye Scream, defeating it still awards you with a bounty and a Skystone. Use the Super Bounce Pad to return to the Village Approach.

Push the stones to clear the way to the enemies guarding a Battle Gate. The early enemies are a warm-up act for Eye Five, another enemy of an unknown element. Eye Five pummels the ground directly in front of him, so step to the side when he starts swinging. Take down Eye Five to end the battle and earn another Skystone. Destroy the *Traptanium* crystal to open the way to Smuggler's Hideout.

Smuggler's Hideout

The smugglers trusted a Lock Puzzle to keep their **Treasure Chest** safe. Bad idea! Go down, left, up, right, left, down, right, up, right, up, left, and down to get all the coins and hit the water. Go up, left, down, left, up, down, left, and up to reach the exit.

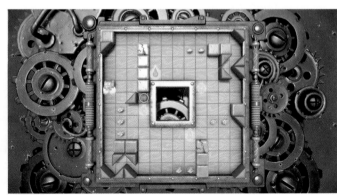

Return to Village Approach and go up the ramp. Two sets of barrel-rolling enemies try to stop your progress to Sleepy Village. Avoid or destroy the barrels, then take out the Eye Screams doing the rolling. Wake up Winkle outside the gates to gain access to Sleepy Village.

Sleepy Village, Grocer Jack's & "Boots" the Cobbler

Smeekens has a quest for Fisticuffs, an enemy who can't be captured yet. Wake up Rip and destroy the gate behind him. The house next to him is Grocer Jack's, where you can play Skystones Smash against Bing. Destroy the *Traptanium* crystal to reveal the **Villain Stash**. Head up the wooden ramp and enter the first building on the left.

Check on the Troll Radio before waking Boots. Head back outside and start waking up the Mabu. Follow the trail of coins to find them. Dreamcatcher makes the task more difficult with her taunts and random destruction of the area. Don't forget to grab the nearby **Treasure Chest**.

Arena Battle Against Dreamcatcher

This is a long battle against many waves of enemies. If you have any magic items, keep them near your *Traptanium Portal* so you can put them to use quickly! Consider putting Broccoli Guy in your Villain slot for his healing ability. It won't be easy to switch to him and set down a healing circle, but it could keep your Skylander healthy enough to finish the fight without switching.

None of the enemies you're facing here are new, but Dreamcatcher keeps things lively by ripping apart the ground and putting it back together. She also continues her taunts.

After you defeat all the enemies, everyone regroups back at Skylanders Academy.

Back at Skylanders Academy

Go to the Main Hall and talk to Brock, who has a new Arena for you to try out. Go past Mags and the slot machine to reach Academy Defense Tower, which has coins to collect and Troll Radio.

Talk to Cali to head out for the next destination, Telescope Towers.

8

Telescope Towers

OBJECTIVES

STORY GOALS

▶ Find and defeat Dreamcatcher

Quest Preparation

Put Brawl and Chain in a Water Trap, and put Masker Mind in an Undead Trap. You're ready to go!

BRAWL AND CHAIN   MASKER MIND

DARES

No Lives Lost

All Areas Found (24)

Enemy Goal (60)

Villains Defeated

Traptanium Gates

DIFFICULT DARES

Time to Beat: 17:55

Don't Switch

Complete all Villain Quests (2)

COLLECTIONS

1 Story Scrolls

4 Treasure Chests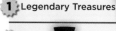

2 Soul Gems

1 Winged Sapphires

1 Legendary Treasures

3 Hats

MAP KEY

(A)	Connector Point
	Hat
	Legendary Treasure
	Quest
	Skystones Smash Player
	Soul Gem
	Story Scroll
	Treasure Chest
	Villain Stash
	Winged Sapphire

Galactic Bubble Center & Pulseblock Plains

The slumbering Hawk has a quest for Brawl and Chain not far from where the level opens. Red felt-topped platforms surround the area around the starting point. Jump on the platforms near Newt for Wildfire's **Soul Gem (Lion Form)**.

Flip Wreck
334
2 ▬▬▬▬▬ 29382

START

FAIRY NIGHT LIGHTS

Hawk wants Brawl and Chain to deliver lights to Mabu homes. Get a total of 7 lanterns from Tree of Light and take them to huts in under 10 minutes. Pick up a lantern from the tree in the courtyard and head out to the nearby Mabu homes. Avoid being too destructive while delivering the lights. Look for Super Bounce Pads; they are a big help in getting Brawl and Chain where he needs to go.

Destroy only what's necessary to open a path to a new house. This helps you keep track of where you've been. Trees are another good indicator of where you need to go. When you deliver a light to a home, enemies erupt from the trees. If a home still has trees, you haven't been there yet.

Headwick pops up and points out a pump button for you to jump on. Jumping on pump buttons until they turn red brings pulseblocks to the surface. Move the block nearest the pump button to bring them into alignment. Jump on the now unlocked pump button to reach a higher ledge. Jump on the ledge's pump button to open the bridge.

Embroidered Bridge, Chamber Entrance & Back-to-Back Stack-N-Jack

Move across the bridge while avoiding the jack-in-the-boxes. They wobble just before springing. Headwick pops up again at the Chamber Entrance, which is just a locked door, and points out a key and how to acquire it.

There are more jack-in-the-boxes to avoid on the bridge through Back-to-Back Stack-N-Jack. Floating platforms are on the right, halfway across the bridge, where Persephone is available for upgrades. The bridge ends at Watering Hole Encounter.

Watering Hole Encounter

Dreamcatcher appears and blocks your path with Battle Gates. Defeat Eye Scream and the tiny eye enemies that appear to clear the Battle Gates. Go to the platform on the right and bounce on the button. Grab the **Story Scroll** from the highest ledge. The shimmering doorway goes to Hypnosis Pocus; you should visit it before using the nearby pump button.

Hypnosis Pocus

Destructible items and the quest for Masker Mind are here.

HYPNOSIS SCHNIPNOSIS

Arthur and Stanley have a wager about hypnosis. Only Masker Mind can settle the wager. It doesn't go well for Stanley.

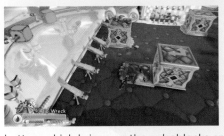

Jump on the pump button in Watering Hole Encounter to reach more platforms. Collect the loot and ascend to the highest pump button, which brings up the pulseblocks around the Chamber Entrance. Drop down to the blocks and move the two necessary to align them. Bounce on the unlocked pump button to reach the key. Unlock the door and enter.

Cosmic Chamber

Phantom platforms materialize and dematerialize slowly. Wait for them to appear and hurry across them before they vanish. Explore the area and collect the valuables before moving close to the bed and waking the scientist. Bounce on the pump button to reach the portal to Pulseblock Pillow Pit.

Pulseblock Pillow Pit

Dreamcatcher appears again and sets up a Battle Gate that blocks the pump button you need to conjure the pulseblocks from underground. Take out the enemies (you can attack them in their bubbles!), then use the pump button to bring up the blocks from underground. Move the three indicated boxes to clear the pump buttons on the nearby platforms.

Bounce on the pump button to raise the platform. Grab Bat Spin's **Soul Gem (Great Balls of Bats!)** on the way up. Use the pump button on the highest platform to build a bridge to a Super Bounce Pad.

Observation Terrace

The wild ride ends at Observation Terrace. A Battle Gate pops up, and one of its guardians is the colorful Pain-Yatta. Watch out for its powerful overhand attack. When the Battle Gate is gone, destroy the *Traptanium* crystal to create a bridge that extends to Observation Loggia.

Talk to Galli in the cage for a game of Skystones Smash. When you defeat him, he hands over the key needed to unlock the nearby door. Go through the door to reach Impossible Gravity Collider.

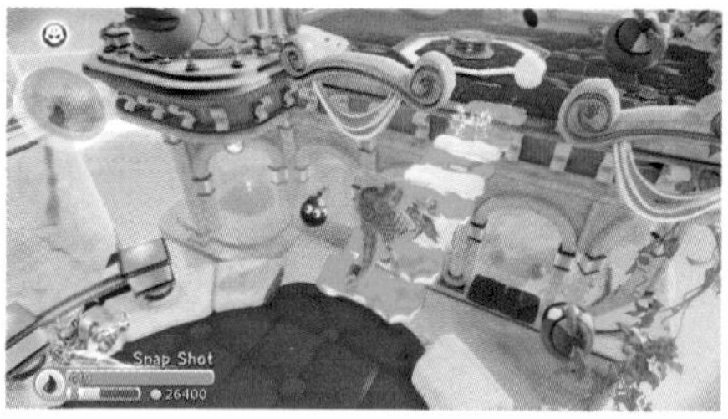

THE MAGIC FRAME GAME

Talk to the scientist to learn about the flying paintings. Attack the paintings until the missing stone platform appears and opens the way to the **Rugby Hat**.

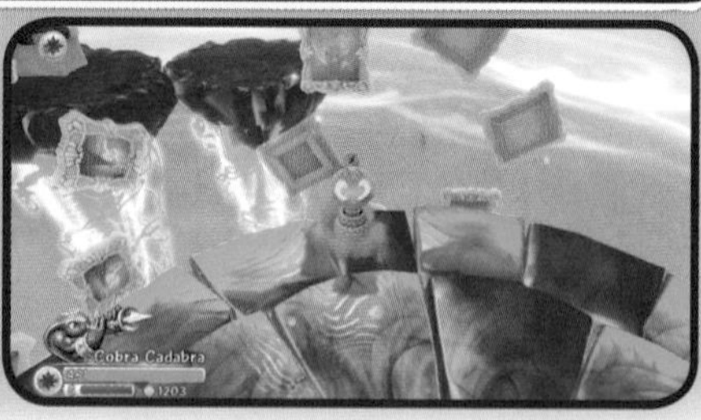

Observation Loggia & Meditation Pool

The Observation Loggia has not one, but two *Traptanium* gates. Step on the pump button to drop down to the Meditation Pool. Grab the **Winged Sapphire** in the corner, next to the scientist. Carefully push the golden balls to the waterfall flowing over the area's end to make coins rain. If you can push 12 over the waterfall, you earn the Ball Sprawler achievement.

GRINDING GEARS

Jump on one of the large gears on the left or right side of the area. Follow the gears and avoid the hazards to reach a pump button. Jump on it to set the gear in front of the initial platform in motion. Drop down and repeat the process on the other side to get the central gear floating up and down.

Return to the starting point and walk up the central path and jump on the floating gear. Ride it across the gap and up to another hazard-filled area. Your destination is the gear with the **Old-Time Movie Hat**.

Impossible Gravity Collider

Wake the scientist, then run across the phantom platforms. They end at a steam spout. Jump up to collect the coins. Dreamcatcher appears and sends another horde of enemies to stop you, including Hood Sickle.

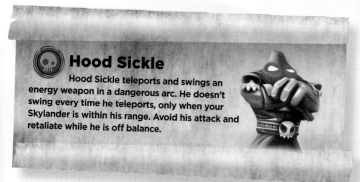

Hood Sickle

Hood Sickle teleports and swings an energy weapon in a dangerous arc. He doesn't swing every time he teleports, only when your Skylander is within his range. Avoid his attack and retaliate while he is off balance.

Unfortunately, capturing Hood Sickle doesn't end the fight. There's one last wave of enemies to take out. After they fall, stay on the green stones (avoid the red ones!) to reach more sleeping scientists. Avoid the pump button for now. Go across the phantom platforms to reach the **Villain Stash**.

Return to the pump button and go up to the next area with the sleeping scientists. Wake both scientists to unlock the pump button. The phantom platforms to the right lead to another sleeping scientist and valuables. Use the pump button to go up another level. Exit through the archway to reach the Roof Observation Deck.

Roof Observation Deck

Battle Gates block all the exits. Defeat the enemies that appear to remove the Battle Gates. Jump on the floating platforms on the right to play Skystones Smash against Ptol.

The portal at the area's end goes to Framing an Art Attack. Walk down the steps past the telescope and use the Super Bounce Pad to fly across a short gap and land in The Great Spiral Observatory.

Framing an Art Attack

Talk to Pern; he encourages you to attack the paintings. Take his advice and attack the paintings until a stone platform appears. It fills in a gap in the path to a steam vent that flings your Skylander to a **Treasure Chest**.

The Great Spiral Observatory

Barely two steps into The Great Spiral Observatory, Pain-Yatta attacks!

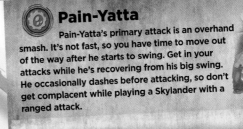

Pain-Yatta

Pain-Yatta's primary attack is an overhand smash. It's not fast, so you have time to move out of the way after he starts to swing. Get in your attacks while he's recovering from his big swing. He occasionally dashes before attacking, so don't get complacent while playing a Skylander with a ranged attack.

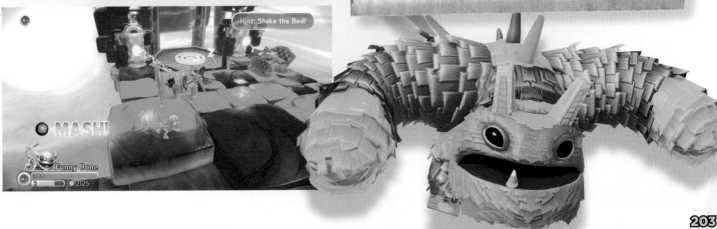

Dream a Little Dream Beds

The Lock Puzzle in the Great Spiral Observatory blocks the way to Dream a Little Dream Beds. Go down, left, down, right, left, up, left, down, left, down, left, down, and right to destroy all the pots. Go up, right, down, left, up, left, down, right, and down to pick up the moveable block. Go up, left, and down to drop off the block. Go right, up, left, up, left, down, left, down, left, down, right, up, right, and down to open the lock.

Wake both scientists to clear the lock from the pump button. Jump on the button to raise the platform to reach a **Treasure Chest**.

Feng Shui Shove

Use the pump button near the entrance to Dream a Little Dream Beds to drop down one level. The entrance there goes to Feng Shui Shove.

Talk to Tyche, then hit each piece of furniture in the area to summon a stone platform. Jump to the platform with the steam vent. Ride the steam vent to a higher platform with a **Treasure Chest**.

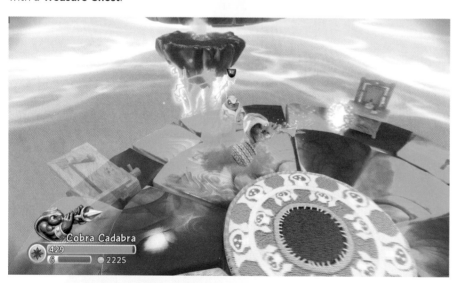

Stairway to the Stars & Spiral Balcony

Use the pump buttons and steam vents to climb higher and higher until you reach Spiral Balcony. The door up the stairs leads to Headwick. Don't speak with him until after you visit the nearby Water Gate and drop over the side of the tower. **Do not talk to Headwick until you are ready to continue to the final fight against Dreamcatcher!**

💧 WATERFALL FALL

Drop off the edge and guide your Skylander through each of the rings. You must go through all the rings to get phantom platforms to appear. Without the platforms, you can't reach the **Synchronized Swimming Cap**. You can take as many tries as you need to hit all the rings, so be patient!

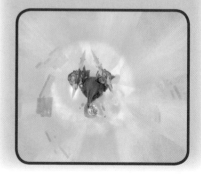

Library Lock Out

Drop from the roof to a ledge below. The door has a Lock Puzzle. Go right, down, up, left, up, left, down, right, up, right, down, right, left, down, right, up, right, up, left, down, left, down, right, left, up, right, up, left, and down to collect all the coins. Go right, left, up, right, up, left, and up to reach the exit.

Destroy all the stacks of books. Jump on the stone platforms. Use the steam vent to reach the highest platform and the **Legendary Cyclops Teddy Bear.**

Dreamcatcher

Attack sleeping Mabu to remove the shield protecting Dreamcatcher. In each stage, her shield becomes stronger as she adds more Mabu. Attack her every time her shield is down.

After she takes some damage, she alters the floor. Watch out for red tiles; they're about to fall away. While falling doesn't end the fight, your Skylander is dropped at the end of the battle area opposite Dreamcatcher.

She employs minions during the battle. She uses sheep as whirling projectiles, and the creatures that kept the scientists asleep wander after your Skylander.

Back at Skylanders Academy

Visit Persephone and give the surprisingly huge Legendary Cyclops Teddy Bear a home. Go to the Main Hall where you can find a new Skaletone Showdown challenger. You can also return to the hat shop and complete Hood Sickle's quest. Once you complete Hood Sickle's quest, speak to Hatterson to open up The Hat Store.

9

Mystic Mill

OBJECTIVES

STORY GOALS

▶ Regain control of the flagship

▶ Take out the Evilikin turrets

▶ Retake the Mill from the Evilikin

Quest Preparation

There are two quests to complete in Mystic Mill. Place Bomb Shell in a Magic trap and Shrednaught in a Tech trap.

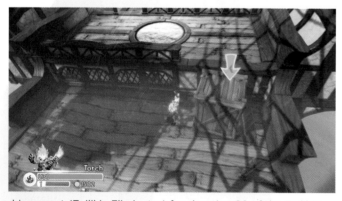

BOMB SHELL   SHREDNAUGHT

DARES

No Lives Lost

All Areas Found (19)

Enemy Goal (55)

Villains Defeated

Traptanium Gates

DIFFICULT DARES

Time to Beat: 12:25

Don't Switch

Complete all Villain Quests (2)

COLLECTIONS

1 Story Scrolls

4 Treasure Chests

3 Soul Gems

1 Winged Sapphires

1 Legendary Treasures

3 Hats

MAP KEY

(A)	Connector Point
	Hat
	Legendary Treasure
	Quest
	Skystones Smash Player
	Soul Gem
	Story Scroll
	Treasure Chest
	Villain Stash
	Winged Sapphire

Mabu Flagship

Guide the sliding crate into the stairwell. Repeat the process three more times to reach the flight deck and regain control of the flagship. Don't worry about trying to keep the crates on the deck. If one falls overboard, another appears shortly afterward.

Take control of Flynn's turret and clear the island's defenses. The controls remain the same as when you cleared out Chef Pepper Jack's zeppelin defenses. There are four Winged Gems to shoot again, and you can earn an achievement (Evilikin Eliminator) for shooting 20 of the Evilikin manning the cannons. Take out the larger enemies capable of firing on Flynn's ship. Shoot the Evilikin until no more appear to man the cannon.

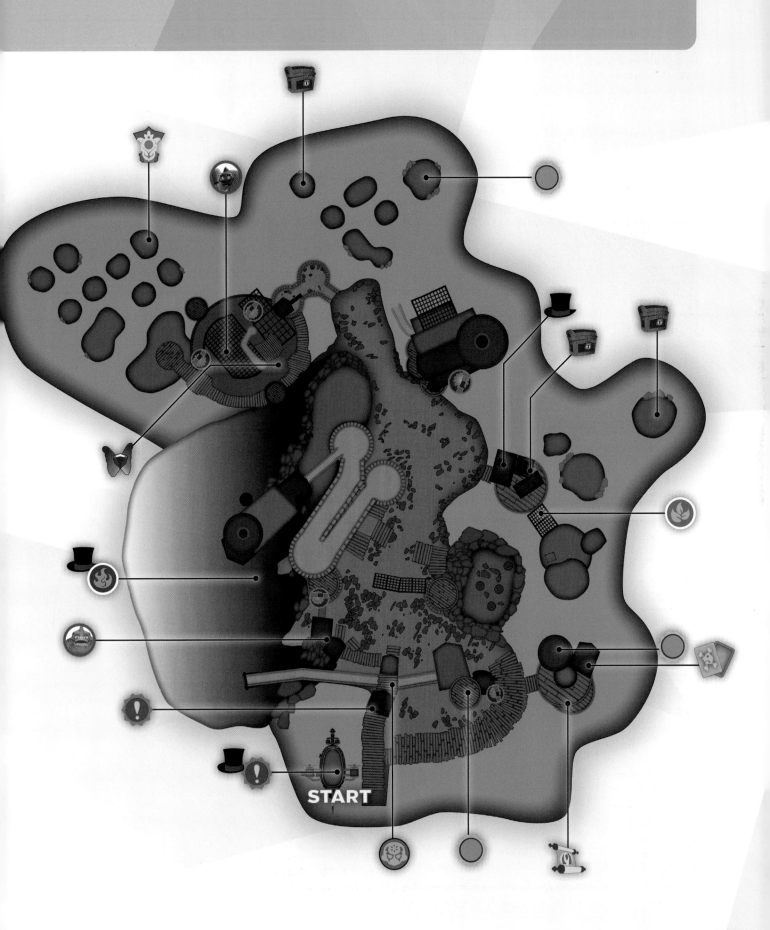

START

Loading Docks

Rizzo's crew joins your Skylander on the docks. Rizzo stays aboard his flagship, and he has a quest for Bomb Shell. The nearby building is the Lumber Mill Office. Drop off the left end of the dock for two big piles of coins. Use the Teleporter Pad to return to Rizzo's crew.

MISSION: DEMOLITION

Rizzo wants Bomb Shell to help blow up a Troll fortress. Bundles of dynamite are scattered around the fortress. They need to be planted at various weak points. You have 10 minutes to plant 8 bundles of dynamite.

Bomb Shell begins at the base of the fortress and must work upward to reach enough weak points. Troll guards are everywhere. Fortunately, the dynamite is not on a timer, so take the time to eliminate the Trolls when they block the path ahead (don't go out of the way to get them). For completing this quest, Rizzo hands over the **Garrison Hat**.

Lumber Mill Office

Loggins needs Shrednaught's help in his office.

SURE BEATS KEYS

Loggins asks for help getting into his office, and only Shrednaught can do what needs to be done. Keep Evolved Shrednaught available for the remainder of Mystic Mill. There are a number of doors and barriers that only they can handle.

Back in Loading Docks, follow the pier until the path is blocked by a locked gate. Interact with the Mabu icon to summon Rizzo's crew to build platforms to reach the gate's key.

Go up the short ramp near the locked gate. Claim the **Story Scroll** and go inside the two small buildings. The building on the right is the Packing House. The other building is Wheelhouse A. When you're done in both buildings, continue up the path through the previously locked gate to Mudder's Corner.

Packing House & Wheelhouse A

The Packing House has a Skystones Smash player named Packard, and a Troll Radio. Wheelhouse A has Tread Head's **Soul Gem (Rocket Boost)** and another Troll Radio.

Mudder's Corner

Evilikin Runners attack in groups and keep the uphill trip interesting. Look for a Troll Radio not far up the path on the left, between two doors. The door closer to the radio goes to the Western Storage Unit. The other doorway leads to Wheelhouse B. There's a third doorway, next to the Western Storage Unit, that can only be opened by an Evolved Shrednaught. It leads to Sawdust Processing. Walk under the metal walkway to reach Waterways.

Western Storage Unit

A few Chompies and Evilikin guard the floor of this small building. After you eliminate them, the real battle begins.

Sawdust Processing & Wheelhouse B

Destroy the barrels inside Sawdust Processing, and collect the pile of coins. Wheelhouse B has a **Villain Stash**.

Shield Shredder

The battle begins against three less-powerful Shield Shredders, which is a good opportunity to learn how they fight. When their shields are up and spinning, move away. The shields build up gusts of air that propel them forward. Attack after their burst of speed, but move away when their shields begin to spin again.

When the main Shield Shredder drops down, he's supported by a few Evilikin cannons. Take out the cannons when they drop to the lower level, then take out Shield Shredder.

Waterways, Eastern Storage Unit & Power House

The gate at the end of the Waterways is doubly locked. Summon the Mabu to build platforms to reach the Power House. Use the floor switches inside the Power House one time each to complete the circuit.

The second key floats atop the aqueduct, but there are a few places to explore before you need to get it. A Life Gate is near a locked door (the kind that needs Evolved Shrednaught to open) not far from the Mabu-built platforms. The locked door leads to Eastern Storage Unit, which has a **Treasure Chest** inside.

FLYING FLORA & PLANT PROCESSING...PLANT

Don't use the second Bounce Pad until after you grab the nut in the corner. Plant the nut and cross the flower bridge. Ride the balloon that drifts off by itself to the right. Open the **Treasure Chest** and pick up the nut. Ride the balloon up to the tiny platform and plant the nut. Walk to the chimney and jump down. Claim the **Mountie Hat** and exit the building.

FIRE FALLS

No enemies to worry about in Fire Falls, just platforms that wiggle a bit when Skylanders jump on them. Collect the coins on the way up to the **Volcano Hat**.

Walk up either wooden ramp that leads to the metal bridge overlooking the area. The Super Bounce Pad at one of the walkways sends your Skylander to a tree trunk. Torch's **Soul Gem (The Incinerator)** is there with a pile of coins.

Go up the aqueduct, but watch for cannon fire from above and logs rolling downward. Jump over the stone wall at the first rounded bend, where you can see a Fire Gate nearby. When you're done in the Fire Gate, retrace your steps but continue to the top of the aqueduct for the key.

Saw Mill Main Gate

Unlocking the gate doesn't mean the way ahead is clear! Shield Shredders and Chompies guard a Battle Gate. They're supported by a wizard who covers allies in air bubbles. When an enemy suddenly becomes invulnerable, look for a floating gem. Take out the enemy carrying the gem as fast as you can. Destroy the *Traptanium* crystal to create a bridge to Nature Bridges - North.

Nature Bridges - North

Destroy the *Traptanium* crystal here to create another bridge. Cross the bamboo bridge, then pick it up and set it on the other side. Cross the wooden bridge to reach the **Treasure Chest**. Go back to the bamboo bridge but don't cross it. Pick it up and move it to build a path back to the first platform in the area.

Pick up the wooden (not bamboo!) bridge and carry it over the bamboo bridge, then the *Traptanium* bridge. Place the wooden bridge to reach Flip Wreck's **Soul Gem (Sea Slammer)**.

Return to Saw Mill Main Gate and walk up the stone ramp. Keep the Evilikins occupied while the Mabu remove the door. Not far beyond the door, look for a **Winged Sapphire** behind a gate that requires Evolved Shrednaught's assistance.

The enemies on the wooden ramp guard a Battle Gate and fight from behind barricades. When the gate is down, walk past the metal ramp on the right (it leads to Pulp Shredder, the location of the battle against Krankenstein) and talk to Persephone for upgrades. Destroy the *Traptanium* crystal near her to build a bridge to Nature Bridges - West.

Nature Bridges - West

Alternate carrying the bamboo and metal bridges to reach the **Legendary Saw Blade** in the back corner platform. There are piles of coins on other platforms, so take some time to explore the area.

Pulp Shredder

Walk up the metal ramp to begin the final battle for Mystic Mill.

Krankenstein

Krankenstein comes to the fight with a large support group of Shield Shredders and Evilikin cannons. Krankenstein sends in Shield Shredders first, then jumps down with the cannons.

Back at Skylander Academy

Go to the Main Hall and place the Legendary Saw Blade over the fireplace. Check in with Auric, who has added Trinkets to his inventory.

AURIC'S INVENTORY

Trinkets	Price
Ulysses Uniclops	350
Medal of Mettle	350
Winged Medal of Bravery	350
Elemental Opal	350

Go up the stairs near the Skaletones to reach the Outer Walkway. Follow the Outer Walkway to The Grand Library. Look for

a trick bookshelf that leads to a coin-filled room, The Archives. Use a mini Skylander to speak with Quigley to explore hidden areas, including The Reading Room.

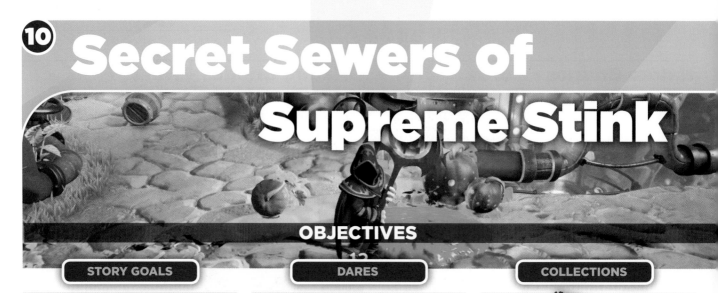

10

Secret Sewers of Supreme Stink

OBJECTIVES

STORY GOALS	DARES	COLLECTIONS

STORY GOALS

▶ Shut Down Krankcase's Goo Supply

▶ Prove You are a Skylander!

Quest Preparation

Before you take the plunge into the sewers, place Pain-Yatta in a Magic trap and Chomp Chest in an Earth trap.

PAIN-YATTA   CHOMP CHEST

DARES

No Lives Lost

All Areas Found (19)

Enemy Goal (135)

Villains Defeated

Traptanium Gates

DIFFICULT DARES

Time to Beat: 19:30

Don't Switch

Complete all Villain Quests (2)

COLLECTIONS

1 Story Scrolls

4 Treasure Chests

2 Soul Gems

1 Winged Sapphires

1 Legendary Treasures

3 Hats

MAP KEY

(A)	Connector Point
🎩	Hat
🛡	Legendary Treasure
❗	Quest
🃏	Skystones Smash Player
⬤	Soul Gem
📜	Story Scroll
🧰	Treasure Chest
◆	Villain Stash
🦋	Winged Sapphire

Goober's Trail & Outer Sewage Segue

Break down the wooden fence and be ready for two hazards on the other side. First, the green goo flowing on the ground damages Skylanders who touch it. The other hazard is the pool of goo that becomes a Goo Chompy.

Use the Bomb to destroy the gate. Take out the Chompy guards. Go around the left side of the Outer Sewage Segue to find a **Story Scroll**.

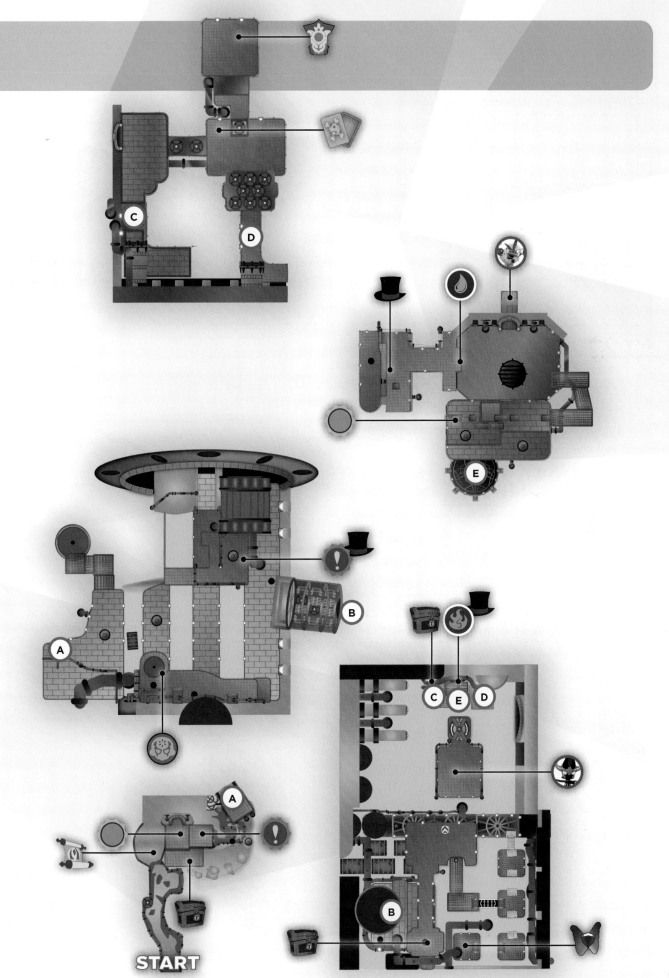

START

Walk around the front of the building. The tunnel entrance on the same level as the **Story Scroll** is Flam Bam's Retreat. Jump over the side of the ledge in front of the tunnel entrance to reach an identical entrance below, one that leads to Effluent Deck.

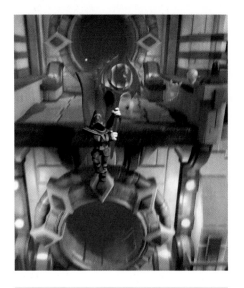

HOT DIGGITY DASH

Flam Bam wants Chomp Chest for a hot dog eating contest. The goal is to eat 75 hot dogs before the timer expires. The timer doesn't have much time on it, but eating a hot dog adds a few seconds. Eating a hamburger adds 10 seconds.

The hot dogs pop up one at a time, so no rushing ahead until the next hot dog appears. Enemies appear along the way, but don't stick around to fight them. Take out the enemies blocking the path you need to follow and don't bother with the others. Hamburgers are a nice time bonus, but they're not worth wasting time to get.

Effluent Deck & Flam Bam's Retreat

To get the **Treasure Chest** in Effluent Deck, you must use the Bomb from Goober's Trail. If you have trouble getting to the gate in time, use a Skylander with a dashing or flying ability.

Flam Bam is a dragon with a quest for Chomp Chest. Destroy the nearby *Traptanium* crystal to reveal a Bounce Pad. Bounce up and step outside for Echo's **Soul Gem (Call of the Siren)**.

The path beyond Flam Bam's Retreat is blocked by cascading goo falling from above. Step on the round platform on the lower ledge and walk in the direction of the arrows to shut off the flow of goo.

The last obstacle to entering the sewers is a Lock Puzzle. Go right to hit the water drop. Go left, down, left, and down to get past the first stage. Go left, up, left, down, right, down, left, down, up, right, up, left, down, right, down, right, and up to collect the coins. Go left, down, right, down, and left to pass the second stage. Go left, right, up, right, up, right, right, down, and down to get the coin. Go up and left to clear the Lock Puzzle. The Grit Chamber is on the other side of the door.

Grit Chamber & Runoff Falls

After an awkward introduction to the locals, go left to explore Runoff Falls. Collect the valuables here, and ride the jet of steam to get the coins floating above it.

You need to cross the channels of goo next. Use the barge floating in the goo to reach the platform in the middle of the goo. When the large barges appear, hop on one and ride it to Backflow Alley.

Backflow Alley

Backflow Alley has a Troll Radio and a skeleton looking for help.

I'M WITH THE BAND

Bag O' Bones wants Pain-Yatta to escort his talent (a singing gecko group) safely out of enemy territory. Stay close to the geckos and eliminate all the enemies that appear to stop them. The geckos occasionally drop their gramophone and scatter when they encounter an ambush. Guide the geckos to safety and Bag O' Bones hands over the **Rubber Glove Hat**.

Use the floating barges to get back to the Grit Chamber, or jump from the bridge that spans the goo channel (you need to hop over a pipe to get across the bridge). Eliminate the Evilikin cannons to start the flow of barges on the second channel of goo.

Use each switch near the laser puzzle one time to open the large tunnel that serves as the entrance to Flow Drain Dropoff. Don't go that way just yet. Smash the wooden fence and ascend the ramp to The Storm Drain.

The Storm Drain

Goo flows from the open pipes intermittently, so wait for a gap in the goo and hurry past. Use the steam vents to get more coins. Go down to the end of the area for a **Villain Stash**.

Flow Drain Dropoff

Avoid the goo spraying from the floor. Jump over the edge and guide your Skylander into the floating valuables. The ride ends in the Spoiled Sanctum.

⚙ Spoiled Sanctum

A Battle Gate blocks progress and you must deal with waves of Chompies and Evilikin forces that include cannons and a Scrap Shooter. Cross both rows of floating barges on the other side of the Battle Gate, then go to the left and ride the steam up to Persephone.

Head back to the right until Rage Mage introduces himself. Continue past the pipes (watch out for goo!) until you see a bamboo bridge. Re-use the bamboo a few times until you come to a metal bridge. Pick up the metal bridge and use it to reach the **Winged Sapphire**. Return the metal bridge to its original location. Cross the bridge and use the nearby Bounce Pad to reach Drainage Vista.

Drainage Vista & Catwalk Cubby

Ignore the laser puzzle for now. Go to the corner and walk down the catwalk to a **Treasure Chest**. Go back to the laser puzzle and use the switches farthest from the block one time each. Use the switch nearest the block twice to reveal a Super Bounce Pad. Use it to reach Drainage Central.

⚙ Drainage Central

The Rage Mage appears again, but then hides behind a Battle Gate while Evilikins and Chompies attack. Destroy the logs from under the Evilikin cannons to bring them into range.

✦ Rage Mage

Rage Mage joins the fight when the Scrap Shooter appears. Ignore Rage Mage and focus on eliminating the other enemies. Rage Mage lacks his own offensive abilities. He boosts his allies with angry magic.

The Battle Gate remains up until a final wave of Shield Shredders appears and is eliminated. Jump on the giant gear and walk in the same direction as the arrows on top of it. Jump down to the Fire Gate below.

🔥 INNER HEADWORKS

The **Trash Can Lid** Hat is behind a doubly locked gate, right at the entrance to the area. The only hazards in the area are jets of flame that add to the difficulty of jumps between some ledges. To get the first key, go to the right. Push the block into the hole and bounce up. Avoid the flames and hop over the gap. Use the Bounce Pad to reach the highest level. Cross one more gap, grab the key, and drop down to the locked gate.

The second key requires frequent use of the Bomb. Use it to blow up the piles of stones. Keep working toward the top ledge for the key. Keep going back to the Bomb after using it. Even if the path ahead is clear, there are piles of coins in side areas.

The two large pipes below the Fire Gate lead to two different spots in the same area (Digestion Deck). Walk around the leftmost pipe for a Lock Puzzle-blocked **Treasure Chest**. To solve the puzzle, go left, down, right, left, up, left, up, right, down, up, left, down, right, up, right, down, and right to douse the Lock Master. Go left, up, right, up, right, down, left, down, left, up, right, left, and down to smash the last jars. Go up, right, down, and right to reach the exit.

Digestion Deck & Going Down

The rounded shapes on the ground spout goo, so wait for a break in the stream before walking over them. Flam Bam is in the area, and he's a tough Skystones Smash player. The **Legendary Eel Plunger** floats near a pile of coins on the other side of two sets of goo spouts.

After your trip to Digestion Deck, jump down the large air shaft between the pipes. It's a wild, coin-filled freefall that ends at Splash Station.

Splash Station & Barge Basin

If you made it this far without touching any goo, you get the No Goo For You! Achievement. Go to the left and move the pipe blocks to change the flow of water. The water hits High Five's **Soul Gem (Organic Slam Apples)** and knocks it down to where your Skylander can reach it.

Go to the right and repeat the process with the pipe blocks there. Push them into place to restore the flow of water. The water level rises, allowing the barges in Barge Basin to float. Jump between barges and head for the Water Gate. Come back to the building on the right afterward.

AQUA DECK

Push the pipe block into the channel to knock out the Goo Chompy. Take out the other Chompies and claim the **Shower Cap**.

Prove You Are a Skylander Arena Battle

Go to the last building where the inhabitants of the sewers demand proof that you are a Skylander. The proof they want comes in the form of an Arena Battle.

Stage 1 has Evilikins and Chompies. It's a straightforward fight with no additional complications. Stage 2 is where things become interesting. A Rage Mage joins the fight. Take him down quickly for an extra reward. He'll escape if he's left alone too long. Watch out for the eye stalk that appears. It heralds the appearance of a trail of green slime. It's wide and difficult to jump over. Touching it doesn't do much damage, but it slows down your Skylander (and enemies if they get too close).

Stage 3 is more of the same, but multiple slime trails are possible. The fight becomes more challenging when Fisticuffs joins. He extends his larger arm and is vulnerable while it's stretched out. Don't move in to attack too quickly! He's able to pivot and change the direction of his arm thrust up to the split second before he extends it.

Back at Skylander Academy

Everything new is in the Main Hall. Brock has a new Arena for the Rumble Challenges. Go to the area past the Hat Shop entrance  to put the Legendary Eel Plunger in its proper place. Finally, there's a new Skaletone challenger. It's Mags!

Wilikin Workshop

OBJECTIVES

STORY GOALS	DARES	COLLECTIONS

STORY GOALS

▶ Defeat Dr. Krankcase

Quest Preparation

There are three quests to complete in Wilikin Workshop. Put Shield Shredder in a Life trap, Dreamcatcher in an Air trap, and keep a Fire trap handy for Scrap Shooter. His quest appears shortly after you trap him during Wilikin Workshop.

SHIELD SHREDDER

DREAMCATCHER

SCRAP SHOOTER

DARES

No Lives Lost

All Areas Found (19)

Enemy Goal (60)

Villains Defeated

Traptanium Gates

DIFFICULT DARES

Time to Beat: 16:30

Don't Switch

Complete all Villain Quests (3)

COLLECTIONS

 1 Story Scrolls

 4 Treasure Chests

 2 Soul Gems

 1 Winged Sapphires

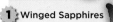 1 Legendary Treasures

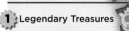 2 Hats

MAP KEY

 (A) Connector Point

 Hat

 Legendary Treasure

 Quest

 Skystones Smash Player

 Soul Gem

 Story Scroll

 Treasure Chest

 Villain Stash

 Winged Sapphire

Wilikin Worker's Town & Wilikin Band Café

Turn around and jump down to a lower ledge with a few coins and a Bounce Pad. Bounce back up and go through the door to the right of your starting spot. The Wilikins inside have a quest for Shield Shredder.

WOOD-BE BAND

Wilikin band wants Shield Shredder to help by making special noise.

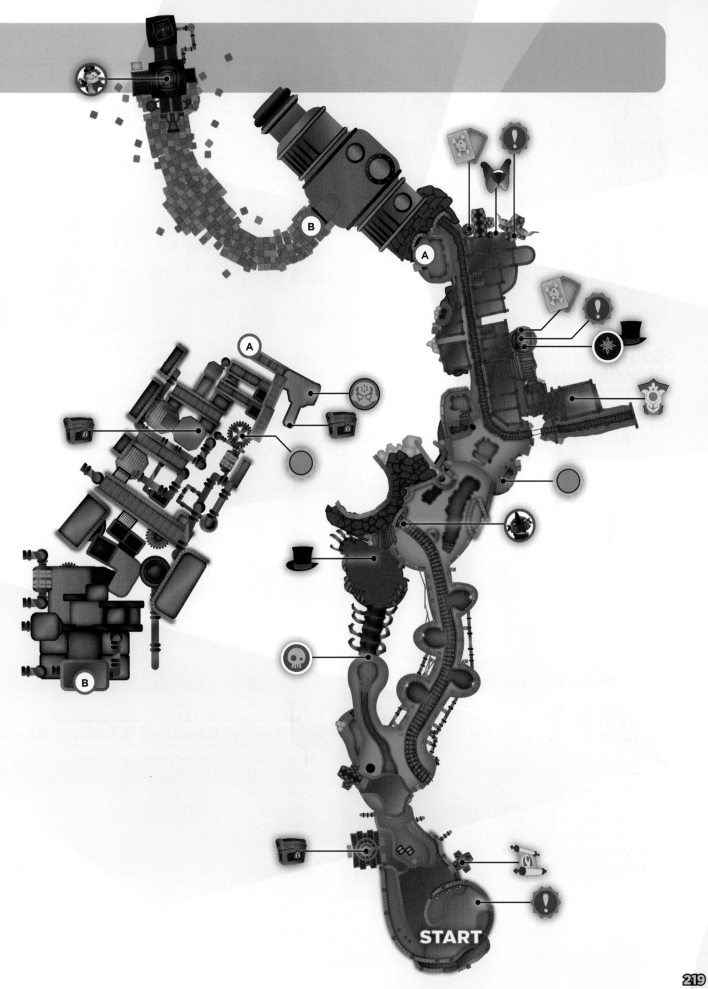

START

Approach Kaos, but don't follow him when he starts down the path. The door on the right leads to Spool Storage Shack. The door to the left of where Kaos stops and waits is Wilikin Break Room.

Spool Storage Shack & Wilikin Break Room

A **Story Scroll** is inside the Spool Storage Shack. Destroy everything else in the shack and step on the red button to drop the gate in front of a **Treasure Chest** in the nearby Wilikin Break Room.

Go back outside and arrange the pipe blocks to restore the flow of water and open the way to Railcar Repair Station.

Railcar Repair Station & Railcar Repair Shop

Conlan provides an update on the situation at the Workshop. The tracks are blocked, but wait to open them. The door near Conlan goes to the Railcar Repair shop (it has only a Troll Radio inside), and an Undead Gate is not too far away. When you're done exploring, pull the switch to start the Railcar Gauntlet.

TOY RETURNS

The bone-themed gates close behind your Skylander and gift packages fall from the sky. Some are gifts, but others are Evilikins. Additional packages appear while you're fighting. You must clear three gates to reach the **Clown Bowler Hat**. Use the Teleport Pad for a quick trip back to the entrance.

Railcar Gauntlet & Railcar Arena

Indestructible railcars spawn from a cave and roll down the tracks. To avoid the railcars, jump over them or step to the open areas on either side of the tracks.

The railcars stop coming when your Skylander crosses into the Railcar Arena and a Battle Gate appears. Evilikin cannons support a new type of enemy, an Evilikin that is invulnerable while it spins. The final enemy is a Scrap Shooter.

Scrap Shooter

Scrap Shooter has two barrel attacks. The first is a spread of barrels that rolls across the ground. Use the raised platforms to avoid the attack, but don't think you're completely safe there. Scrap Shooter has a second attack that fires barrels from its forehead. The key to the attacks is what its hands do before attacking. If it touches its mouth, it's the barrels on the ground attack (your window to attack is after the third wave of barrels). If its hands go to the ground, watch out for the forehead shot.

SAFE TOY DISPOSAL

The small gift packages inside this gate release gold. Open the hat box for the **Lil' Elf Hat**.

Big Train Loading Area

Leave Kaos waiting on the platform beyond the Battle Gate. Follow the wooden fence on the right until it ends. Drop off the side. Fling Kong's **Soul Gem (Make It Rain)** is on a ledge with a Bounce Pad.

When the trains start running, hop on one and ride it across the bridge. Ride the train to the End of the Line to earn the Ride the Rails achievement.

End of the Line

Pick up the **Legendary Masterpieces** floating above the platform where the train stops. Destroy the nearby *Traptanium* crystal to create a bridge to the nearby boat

and pile of gold. The ledge below has a Magic Gate and a Bounce Pad that goes back to the Big Train Loading Area.

Sneaky Pete's Saloon, Rochester's House & The Old Mill

The building above the Magic Gate is Sneaky Pete's Saloon. The two houses on the platform across from where Kaos waits are Rochester's House and the Old Mill. Sneaky Pete and Rochester both have quests for trapped Villains. The Old Mill has a Skystones Smash player named Yar Har and a **Winged Sapphire**, both hidden behind a wall of boxes. When you're done with the quests and Skystones Smash playing, meet up with Kaos. Once you enter the Factory, there's no way to return to the train yards.

PIRATES OF THE BROKEN TABLE

Yoho wants Scrap Shooter to fix his Skystones Smash table. After it's repaired, Yoho offers to play Skystones Smash.

SWEET DREAMS

Rochester wants Dreamcatcher's help with his sleeping problem.

The Factory

Ride the conveyor belt and pick up as many coins as you can. The ride ends at a *Traptanium* crystal and a blocked Bounce Pad. Take down a quartet of spinning Evilikins to remove the Battle Gate.

Open the **Villain Stash** and destroy the *Traptanium* crystal near it. Destroying the crystal clears the path to a **Treasure Chest**. Bounce to the higher conveyor belt and move against it to reach Persephone. A few enemies appear on the next conveyor belt, which carries your Skylander to the Smashing Area.

Smashing Area & Crane Loading and Dropping

Use the Bounce Pads to climb a few levels. A **Treasure Chest** is behind a Battle Gate; this gate is opened by a large red button on a nearby platform across the conveyor belt.

Ride the conveyor belts to another platform with a Bounce Pad. The higher platform has a *Traptanium* crystal with Head Rush's **Soul Gem (Horns Aplenty)** inside.

Avoid the welding arms and cross the conveyor belts to reach another Battle Gate. Eliminate the Evilikins to remove the gate. A ramp retracts and halts your progress. The switch that controls the ramp is not far, but the boxes on the conveyor belt needed to reach the switch turn into mines.

Lower the ramp and carefully cross over the conveyor belt. Use the crane controls to pick up Bombs and blow up the barriers.

Path to Dr. Krankcase

The area outside the Factory is filled with Evilikin forces. Large stone formations block your progress until you defeat the Evilikins in the immediate area.

Dr. Krankcase

Dr. Krankcase begins the battle by jumping into the air and landing hard on the ground. Avoid the red circles when they appear. After he lands, he slides around on spinning legs that deal hefty damage.

At 25% health lost, Dr. Krankcase returns to his high platform and flips a switch that activates goo pits. Barrels roll down conveyor belts and fall into the goo, where they grow legs similar to the doctor's. It's possible to destroy the barrels before they reach the goo. However, the goo-infused barrels may drop food when they're destroyed, so consider allowing one or two to change. Dr. Krankcase joins the fight between, and during, waves of barrels.

At 50% health, Dr. Krankcase fires off exploding goo bombs. Stay out of the green circles when they appear on the ground. The goo doesn't inflict damage, but it does slow down your Skylander. After a few rounds of goo, Dr. Krankcase sends in a powerful Evilikin. Avoid its melee attack and retaliate while it recovers from swinging its arms.

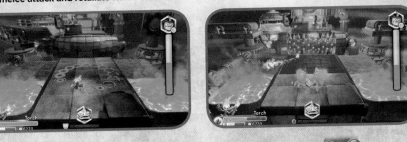

After you destroy the first Evilikin, the doctor breaks out a giant roller covered in spikes and turns part of the floor into a conveyor. He also sends out another Evilikin robot, and drops more goo bombs!

The roller works both ways. It damages anything, including Dr. Krankcase, caught in its spikes. Dr. Krankcase resumes dropping in from above and spinning his legs while sliding around the area until you deplete his health.

Back at Skylander Academy

Go to the Main Hall and place the Legendary Masterpieces above the fireplace. When you're ready to go to Time Town, talk to Flynn.

OBJECTIVES

STORY GOALS

▶ Rescue Kaos from the Clocktower

Quest Preparation

There are two quests to complete in Time Town. Have a Water trap ready for Cross Crow. You capture him in Time Town, but you need a return trip to complete his quest. Dr. Krankcase should be in a Tech trap. If you don't upgrade him, you miss out on some areas of Time Town.

DR. KRANKCASE

CROSS CROW

DARES

No Lives Lost

All Areas Found (19)

Enemy Goal (70)

Villains Defeated

Traptanium Gates

DIFFICULT DARES

Time to Beat: 11:50

Don't Switch

Complete all Villain Quests (2)

COLLECTIONS

1 Story Scrolls

4 Treasure Chests

2 Soul Gems

1 Winged Sapphires

1 Legendary Treasures

2 Hats

MAP KEY

(A)	Connector Point
	Hat
	Legendary Treasure
	Quest
	Skystones Smash Player
	Soul Gem
	Story Scroll
	Treasure Chest
	Villain Stash
	Winged Sapphire

Grand Approach

Destroy the Da Pinchy Statue. Destroy five total Da Pinchy statues to earn the achievement, Da Pinchy Defacer. Eliminate the nearby *Traptanium* crystal to gain access to a moving platform.

Ride the platform along the wires to reach a floating island. The island has Rocky Roll's **Soul Gem (Boulder Posse)** and three Da Pinchy Statues. Return to your starting point and walk over the edge to Father's Cog's Patio.

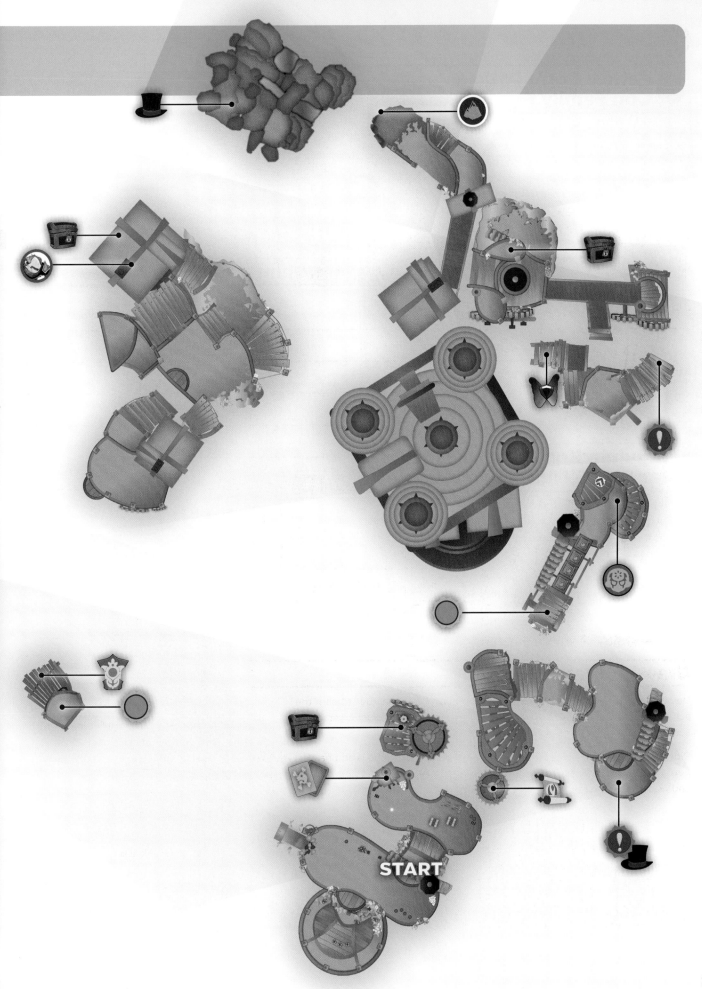

START

Father Cog's Patio & Cog Family Fortune

Eliminate the Buzzer Beaks, then step through the doorway. The Cog family fortune hangs from the gears in the room. Collect all the necklaces within reach. Step on the glowing button in the middle of the house to turn the gears and move the necklaces to where your Skylander can get them. You need to move the gears a few times to collect everything. Playing Co-op in this area makes it much easier to collect the necklaces.

Pendulum Bob's House, Moon Gear Rise & Musical Terrace

Head back to the Grand Approach and look for Da Pinchy. Before you move the gear blocks, investigate the building on the far left. The Mabu inside, Hans, wants to play Skystones Smash.

Return to Da Pinchy and push the gear blocks into place. Go to the red gear on the right for the **Story Scroll**. Use the gear with two Bounce Pads to reach the red gear on the left. The platform below that red gear is the Musical Terrace, which has a **Treasure Chest**.

Use the Bounce Pad near the **Treasure Chest** to return to Moon Gear Rise. Bounce up to the highest green gear and step up to the platform with blue planks. Wait for the mural that flips into place to go away, then hurry along the path to Chime Hammer Square.

Chime Hammer Square

Save Da Pinchy from the avian assault of Buzzer Beaks and a Cross Crow. Cross Crow fires nasty bolts from a crossbow. Avoid the missiles and take down Cross Crow while it reloads. Walk away from Da Pinchy after rescuing him. Drop off the wooden ledge for a quest.

DIORAMA DRAMA

Leyland wants Dr. Krankcase to see his diorama. Dr. Krankcase either isn't completely reformed or he's a harsh critic of dioramas. Whenever you encounter one, tag in the Evolved Dr. Krankcase.

Wayward Cog Storage

Step through the ruined diorama to reach Wayward Cog Storage. Destroy everything inside and open the hat box for **Skylanders Bobby**.

Use the Bounce Pad to return to Da Pinchy, who explains Steam Locks. Smash the steam tubes to break the lock. Should you miss-time a swing on a lock, it resets (just the current lock, not the entire puzzle).

The area beyond the Steam Lock is infested with feathered fiends. Defeat them to clear the Battle Gate from a button. Step on the button to pull up wooden steps. Watch for a skeleton diorama off the right side of the blocks.

Backstage & Main Spring Fly

Hop down and tag in Dr. Krankcase. The doorway he reveals leads Backstage. Ride the platform attached to the rotating central shaft to the **Villain Stash**. Use the Bounce Pad outside to reach the top of the building and a Super Bounce Pad. Go past the purple pad and cross the undulating line of blocks to Thunderbolt's **Soul Gem (Lightning Rain)**. Return to the Super Bounce Pad and go for a ride.

Speak with Florg, then look for Tessa nearby. She has a quest for Cross Crow.

SKYLANDS' BIGGEST FANS

Tessa wants Cross Crow's help in making Skylands safe for birds to fly again. You have 10 minutes to restore power to 10 fans. The area is crawling with Trolls and a few Bomb Shells. Note the locations of Super Bounce Pads. After you restore the power to all the fans you can find in an area, use the Super Bounce Pad to travel quickly to a new area.

Jump up to the conveyor belt near Florg, and immediately hop on the platform next to it. Stand on the button to summon a row of blocks that leads up to a **Winged Sapphire**. Use the Teleport Pad to return to the conveyor. Avoid the spring-loaded wall, then step on through to Sunny Side Narrows.

Sunny Side Narrows & Clockwork Innards

Move against the conveyor (flying Skylanders have an easier time with this) to reach a platform with a Troll Radio. There's another platform directly below the radio. Persephone is there, as is a Teleport Pad to return to the top. You could also use the rotating platform to move between levels.

Return to the conveyor and ride it until it ends. Deal with the enemies that appear, then drop down one level lower. Step on the button to rotate the nearby gear. Use the Bounce Pad to return to the higher level and walk on the green gear in the direction indicated by the arrows. Jump off the green gear and fall into the hole it left after being raised.

Clockwork Innards has a **Treasure Chest** behind a Battle Gate, and a group of crow-like enemies that you must clear out before you can get it. To reach the enemies on the higher levels more quickly, walk on the gear in the direction of the arrows. After you get the **Treasure Chest**, take the gear to its highest point and return to Sunny Side Narrows.

Spin the large, green gear to the top again and ride the conveyor on the other side of the spring-loaded flower design. The conveyor leads to a Steam Lock and an Earth Gate. Use the Super Bounce Pad beyond the Steam Lock to reach Clockwork Courtyard.

BROKEN TOE PLATEAU & WATERFALL CAVE

Cross the narrow bridge and eliminate the Buzzer Beaks. Walk upstream and under the bridge to reach Waterfall Cave. Grab the glowing pick and clear out the rubble that keeps the sliding block from moving into place.

Carry the pick outside and clear the rubble from the path up to the **Alarm Clock Hat**. The stream is strong enough to push around Skylanders, so be careful when they're standing in it and using the pick.

Clockwork Courtyard

Clockwork Courtyard has two Battle Gates. You must defeat waves of enemies to drop the first gate, and another to open the second. There are two points of interest in the area. The first is the diorama not far from where the Super Bounce Pad deposited your Skylander. Tag in Dr. Krankcase to open the way to Retired Clock Storage. The building beyond the first Battle Gate is Cogsworth's Bed and Brunch.

Cogsworth's Bed and Brunch & Retired Clock Storage

Explore both rooms, destroy everything you can, and loot all the valuables. Go back to Clockwork Courtyard after collecting everything.

Push the gear blocks into place on the right side of the courtyard, which starts up a rotating platform. The platform on the left has a Troll Radio. The right side platform has a Steam Lock. Solve the puzzle to start a battle against Cross Crow and some of his allies. Defeat the enemies that appear after trapping

Cross Crow to remove the Battle Gate and reveal a **Treasure Chest**. The topmost platform is a one-way trip to Tower Approach.

Tower Approach

Clear out the enemies to open the Battle Gate. Destroy the *Traptanium* crystal and ride the platform over the wires to a platform with the **Legendary Clocktower**. Return to Da Pinchy and solve the Steam Lock.

Owl Clock Gallery

The newly-opened building is the Owl Clock Gallery. Step on the flashing button to move the stairs. Ascend the stairs and stand on the flashing button there. Repeat the process again to rescue Kaos.

Back at Skylander Academy

Visit Persephone's Treehouse, where you can place the Legendary Clocktower. Check in with the Skaletones to learn about their newest member. Boom! When you're ready to go after Wolfgang, speak with Da Pinchy.

Cross Crow

This Cross Crow is slightly more powerful than the ones encountered up to this point, but fights the same. It fires bolts from a crossbow. Avoid the bolts and take it down while it's reloading.

13

The Future of Skylands

OBJECTIVES

STORY GOALS

▶ Enter the Big Bad Woofer

▶ Destroy the power conduits

▶ Defeat Wolfgang

Quest Preparation

Put Rage Mage in a Magic trap before you travel into the future. For Wolfgang, you need one trip through the Future of Skylands with an Undead trap ready, then a follow up trip to complete his quest.

RAGE MAGE   WOLFGANG

DARES

No Lives Lost

All Areas Found (13)

Enemy Goal (35)

Villains Defeated

Traptanium Gates

DIFFICULT DARES

Time to Beat: 12:40

Don't Switch

Complete all Villain Quests (2)

COLLECTIONS

1 Story Scrolls

4 Treasure Chests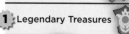

2 Soul Gems

1 Winged Sapphires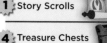

1 Legendary Treasures

3 Hats

MAP KEY

Ⓐ Connector Point

 Hat

 Legendary Treasure

 Quest

 Skystones Smash Player

 Soul Gem

 Story Scroll

 Treasure Chest

 Villain Stash

 Winged Sapphire

Arrival Platform

An energy barrier keeps your Skylander contained to the starting platforms. Look for a gap in the fence and drop down to be treated to a holograph of Wolfgang and a mystery element gate. Bounce back up to the higher platform and pull the switch to shut off the barrier.

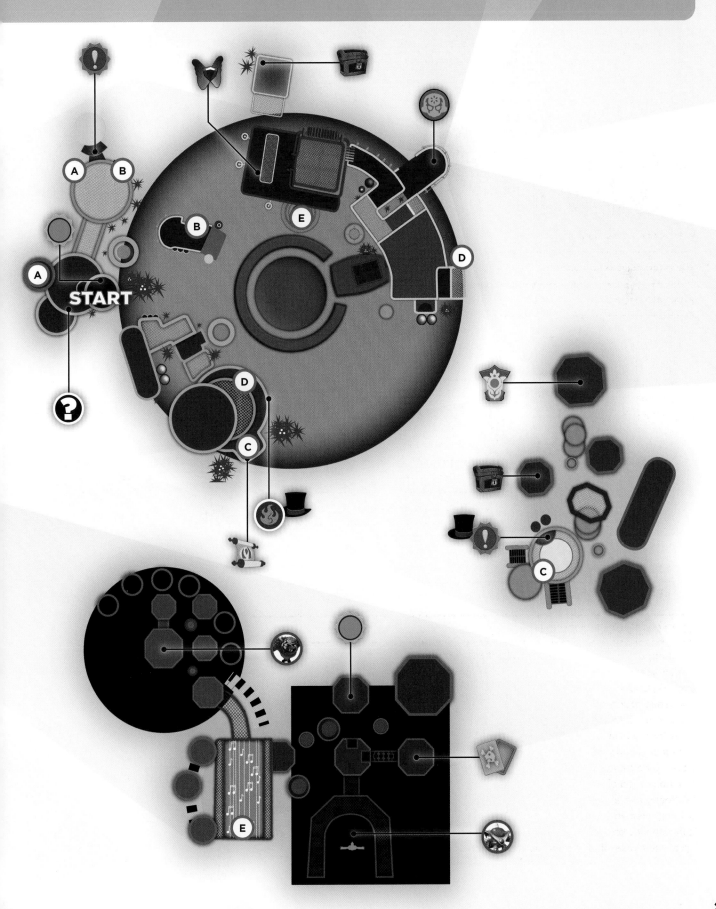

START

Ice Cream Planet

The first enemy in the future is a Blaster-Tron. Attack it from behind to take it down and avoid the blue lines when they appear from its gun. There are two taxis and a quest waiting for you afterward.

The taxi to the left is a one-way trip up to Gearshift's **Soul Gem (Swing Shift)**. Jump off the platform to return to the Arrival Platform. The ride from the right-hand taxi ends at Electro Bridge Controls.

ICE CREAM IN THE FUTURE?

Noobman needs help selling ice cream and he wants Rage Mage's help. Anger and ice cream are a winning combination in the future!

Electro Bridge Controls & Astro Bug Zapper

Use the switch next to the Mabu to extend the bridge. Cannons in the distance fire bombs to make the crossing dangerous. An energy barrier blocks the path near a Troll Radio. The switch to deactivate it is on the lower ledge. Drop down over the floating coins and deactivate the energy barrier.

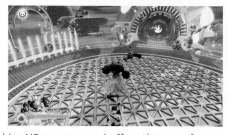 # Sub-Orbital Combat Plaza

Drop down into the Sub-Orbital Combat Plaza and defeat the array of futuristic enemies that includes cyclops and a pair of Blaster-Trons. A taxi driven by Snuckles X9 appears and offers the use of his transport.

Don't take him up on his offer until after you visit the Fire Gate and use the Super Bounce Pad. The Super Bounce Pad deposits your Skylander near a **Story Scroll** and an automated taxi that goes to Containment Corner.

MINI SUN

Avoid the flares emanating from the mini sun. They travel slowly around the sun. When they pass, walk behind them carefully. Follow the trail of coins to the **Extreme Viking Hat**. Wait for a gap in the flares and walk behind them again to return to the entrance.

AN INCONVENIENCE OF IMPS

Q.U.I.G.L.E.Y. wants Wolfgang's help with an overabundance of Lock Master Imps. You must lead 100 imps to the Vacuum Droid in 10 minutes.

Destroy the bags of blue grain to get the attention of the imps. Lure them toward the Vacuum Droid to make things go more quickly. The Droid moves slowly along a set path. Blue barriers fall when the area is clear of imps. For Energy Barriers, you must find the control switch to shut them off. After you complete the quest, Q.U.I.G.L.E.Y. hands over the **Tin Foil Hat**.

Containment Corner

Wolfgang's quest is here, as well as a *Traptanium* crystal. Destroy the crystal to create a bridge. Destroy the *Traptanium* crystals to build more bridges. Pick up the metal bridge and use it to reach both a **Treasure Chest** and the **Legendary Rocket**. To reach the Legendary Rocket, carry the bridge back to Q.U.I.G.L.E.Y.'s platform, and use the Super Bounce Pad. The taxi near Q.U.I.G.L.E.Y. is the return trip back to Sub-Orbital Plaza.

Anti-Grav Truck

Snuckles X9's transport is the Anti-Grav Truck. When the giant arms appear, push the boxes out of the way and use the cannon. You need to hit both arms to free the truck. The ride ends at Space Dog Field.

Space Dog Field

Persephone is behind an energy barrier to the left. The controls are across from her but you need to deal with a swarm of enemies first.

Speak with Zeta Blobbers and follow him up the ramp. He stops at an energy barrier near a Troll Radio. Jump over the railing down to a platform with the control switch and a **Villain Stash**. Cross the bridge beyond Zeta Blobbers to reach the Sub Atomic Particle Smasher.

Sub Atomic Particle Smasher & Planet Ham

Don't get too close to the spiked walls. The giant atoms that appear do some damage, but are not durable. Any attack breaks them up into smaller pieces and any follow up attack destroys a smaller piece. When the barrier is gone, use the Bounce Pad to rejoin Zeta Blobbers who points out your next destination, but don't go there yet.

The **Winged Sapphire** is almost directly over Zeta Blobber's head, but you need to push over a few nearby blocks to reach it. Push the blocks to the right into Planet Ham. Jump up to the higher area and open the **Treasure Chest** there.

Harmonic Hold

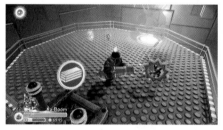

Defeat the swarm of enemies to open the Battle Gate. Destroy the nearby *Traptanium* crystal to create a bridge. Blaster-Tron is on the platform to the right past the bridge, along with a number of Brawlrus assistants.

Cross the metal bridge and carry it around. The platforms in the area have a Skystones Smash player named Gumbus the 10000th, A Troll Radio, and Trail Blazer's **Soul Gem (Heat Wave)**.

Return to Zeta Blobbers and follow him a short distance. Carry the metal bridge across two spans to reach the blueprints. Next up is a trip in a spaceship!

You have more control over this ship than in previous turret-type missions. You must first blast through the shielding (each hexagon can take one hit) while avoiding the subwoofer's defensive cannons and bombs. After clearing the shielding around a power conduit, turn the ship around and destroy it. To earn the Just to be Safe achievement, take down every shield unit during this flying sequence.

The exterior hull falls away, exposing additional power conduits. A robot orbits the subwoofer and restores the shield. That makes it even more important to clear the shield in one pass, then immediately turn around and blast the exposed power conduit. When all power conduits are destroyed, it's time to take on Wolfgang.

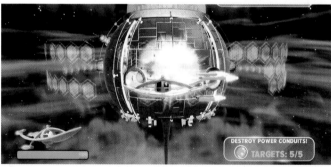

💀 Wolfgang

Wolfgang opens up with an array of music-enhanced melee attacks. He slides across the floor behind a wave of notes. He flashes red and does an overhead attack with his instrument, and uses the speakers to give himself an extra boost of speed. He's vulnerable immediately after each attack.

With one-third of his health gone, the battle shifts to a side view. Wolfgang continues his melee attacks, but you have fewer escape routes. Time your jumps to avoid his attack and retaliate quickly before he leaps back to the speaker to attack again.

Wolfgang begins a laser light show when he has one-third of his health remaining. When the beams are narrow, they're safe to touch. Listen for the buildup of energy and move away from the laser (whether it's to a side or jumping over it). When Wolfgang rejoins the fight, the laser show continues and you must avoid the lasers and Wolfgang's attacks. Have an Undead trap ready for when he falls!

Back at Skylanders Academy

Place the Legendary Rocket on the right side of the Game Room near the piano. A new Arena opens up in Brock's Rumble Club.

Auric has added a few items to his inventory.

AURIC'S NEW INVENTORY

Key	Price
Brock's Rumble Clubhouse	1200
Trinkets	**Price**
Pirate Pinwheel	600
Medal of Valiance	600
Hats	**Price**
Sherpa Hat	500
Tribal Hat	500
Croissant Hat	500
Weather Vane Hat	500
Toucan Hat	500

You found the Legendary Rocket in The Future of Skylands!

14

Operation: Troll
Rocket Steal

OBJECTIVES

STORY GOALS	DARES	COLLECTIONS

STORY GOALS

▶ Save the captive soldiers

▶ Break down the launch pad gate

▶ Confiscate the rocket

DARES

No Lives Lost

All Areas Found (17)

Enemy Goal (115)

Villains Defeated

Traptanium Gates

DIFFICULT DARES

Time to Beat: 11:15

Don't Switch

Complete all Villain Quests (2)

COLLECTIONS

1 Story Scrolls

4 Treasure Chests

2 Soul Gems

1 Winged Sapphires

1 Legendary Treasures

4 Hats

Quest Preparation

Put Krankenstein in an Air Trap. It might be a while before you can complete Bone Chompy's quest. They don't appear for another two Story Mode chapters!

KRANKENSTEIN   BONE CHOMPY

MAP KEY

(A)	Connector Point
🎩	Hat
🏅	Legendary Treasure
❗	Quest
🃏	Skystones Smash Player
⚪	Soul Gem
📜	Story Scroll
🧰	Treasure Chest
🔵	Villain Stash
🦋	Winged Sapphire

Mabu Main Base

Buzz has a quest for Bone Chompy near the starting point, and there's a Troll Radio just ahead. Go right at the fork to reach an Earth Gate. Go up the hill from the Earth Gate for the second villain quest.

When you're done with quests and *Traptanium* gates, move toward enemy lines and defeat the Troll forces to free Snuckles. The Mabu Base Entrance is just beyond his cage.

START

PAGING DR. BONE CHOMPY

Buzz wants Bone Chompy to become the medic for the Mabu Defense Force. After completing the quest, more of the Mabu Main Base is opened, and you get a Nurse Hat.

ONWARD WILIKIN SOLDIERS

Wooster wants Krankenstein's help building Wilikin soldiers. He hands over the Kepi Hat as a token of his appreciation.

Boomsticks! You truly have a gift, Bone Chompy!

Buzz

CRAWLER CANYON

The instructions are deceptively easy. Jump on increasingly higher moving platforms to reach the top and collect the **Sunday Hat**. The problem is the platforms are carried by insects in opposite directions at different heights. If your Skylander is hit by a platform, you are forced to begin again from the start. Each time you jump, watch for a platform coming from the opposite direction.

 ## Mabu Base Entrance

Free Nort from his cage. He points out the location of a Bomb, which is near a Health Reginifier. Gimpy explains how to get them to work. Grab the Bomb and destroy the Troll defenses and gate.

There are two doorways here. The left goes to Southwest Tower, and the right goes to the Southeast Tower. Continue on through the destroyed gates to reach the Battlements.

They call these things Health Regenifiers. Maybe it's because they heal you

Tortellinos

Southwest Tower & Southeast Tower

Grab the Bomb from outside and carry it inside the Southwest Tower to get to a **Winged Sapphire**. The Southeast Tower has a **Treasure Chest** behind a Puzzle Lock. Go right, down, left, down, right, down, left, down, right, up, right, up, left, down, right, up, right, and left to get all the coins. Go down, right, up, right, down, right, left, down, down, right, up, and right to break the last jar. Go up, left, down, right, down, up, left, down, right, down, right, up, left, down, right, down, right, down, and right to open the lock.

☠ Battlements

To clear the Lock Puzzle from the gate, go right, down, and left to get the coin. Go down, right, down, right, up, left, down, right, and up to clear the first stage. For the second stage, go down, right, down, left, down, right, down, left, up, left, down, right, and down. On the third stage, go up, right, up, and left to get all the coins. Go down, right, up, left, down, left, up, right, down, right, down, right, down, left, and up.

Free Rizzo from his cage. He points out the location of a Bomb. Summon the Mabu to build steps on the right and left. There's another Health Reginifier nearby to charge up.

Troll Firing Range, Tank Factory & Factory Storage

Use the steps on the right to reach the Troll Firing Range. Destroy the *Traptanium* crystal for a **Treasure Chest**. The steps on the left go the Tank Factory. Follow the stone ramp behind the Bomb to another **Treasure Chest**. Go through the nearby door for Cobra-Cadabra's **Soul Gem (Big Basket Bomb)**.

Back outside, jump on the blocks in the correct order. Activate the power coil at the top and head into the nearby Tech Gate.

⚙ FACTORY POWER PLANT

Get ready for some quick jumping between rotating platforms. Jump up to the top platform to avoid having it sweep your Skylander off the bottom one. However, the top platform isn't safe for long. Two boxes slide in and out and you must avoid those as well. Perfect your quick jumping between the platforms to get the **Cubano Hat**.

239

Back in the Battlements, use the Bomb to blow up the gate. When prompted, step back and use the switch to activate the Mabu Catapult. A Lock Puzzle appears on the gate ahead.

Go left, down, up, and up to get to the water. Go down, right, left, down, left, right, left, up, and up to clear the first stage.

For the second stage, go up, left, down, left, down, right, up, left, up, and right to reach the water. Go down, right, down, up, left, down, left, and up to get the coins. Go right, down, right, up, right, up, left, up, left, and up.

For the final stage, go left, down, left, up, right, right, down, and left to get to the water. Go up, left, down, right, and right to smash the pots. Go left and down to finish.

![icon] Troll Base Entrance

The two doorways on the other side of the gates are the Northwest and Northeast Towers. Look for a Health Regenifier on the right. Destroy the timberworks behind the Health Regenifier to clear the way to the **Legendary Mabu Parachute**.

Northwest Tower & Northeast Tower

Each tower has a pile of valuables, but only the Northeast Tower has a Lock Puzzle guarding it. Go left, up, left, down, right, down, right, right, up, up, and left to open the lock.

Troll Main Base

The Trolls are massed at the gate and have heavy reinforcements. Let the Mabu (and Evilikin, if you have them) handle the bulk of the

fighting. Go back to the Regenifier as often as you need. Look for a path on right. Smash the timberworks to reach the Troll Weapons Lab.

![icon] Troll Weapons Lab

Beyond the battle against Grinnade, Troll Weapons Lab also has a **Villain Stash**.

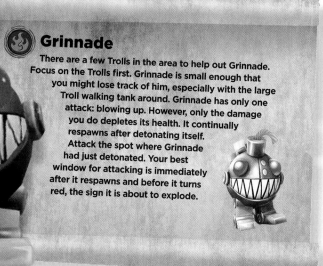

![icon] Grinnade

There are a few Trolls in the area to help out Grinnade. Focus on the Trolls first. Grinnade is small enough that you might lose track of him, especially with the large Troll walking tank around. Grinnade has only one attack: blowing up. However, only the damage you do depletes its health. It continually respawns after detonating itself. Attack the spot where Grinnade had just detonated. Your best window for attacking is immediately after it respawns and before it turns red, the sign it is about to explode.

Follow the winding path past the Troll Weapons Lab. There's a Bomb to use against the Troll forces. Continue up higher and the path ends at a Teleport Pad near a **Story Scroll**. Use the Teleport Pad to jump to Enigma's **Soul Gem (An Eye For Several Eyes)**. The Teleport Pad is a one-way trip. You need to jump down to rejoin the battle.

Mission Con-Troll

Professor Nilbog initiates an Arena Battle. The battle opens against a swarm of Grinnades and Trolls carrying maces. Stage two adds a hazard from the skull-marked doors. When one opens, it's about to fire a jet of flame. Don't stand in front of that one! Lob Goblins and a tank join the fight. Stage three builds on the second. Multiple doors open at the same time and the Professor joins the battle as Threatpack. If you manage to complete this arena battle without getting hit by rocket exhaust, you get the Achievement, Exhaust All Possibilities.

💧 Threatpack

Threatpack's only offensive ability is cluster missiles. Avoid the red circles where they appear on the ground. Fortunately, Threatpack always hovers close to the ground so you don't need to rely on ranged attacks to hit him.

⚙ Mech Factory

Look for the tower from which the Troll walking tanks appear. Go inside that doorway and take out the Trolls inside. That swings the tide of battle in your favor!

Back at Skylander Academy

Place the Legendary Mabu Parachute on the path near the steps leading down to Persephone. Visit the Main Hall where Brock has a new addition to the Rumble Club and the Skaletones have an awesomely awesome new member.

15

Skyhighlands

OBJECTIVES

STORY GOALS

▶ Take out the Sky Pirates

▶ Beat Hawkmongous to get the Prism

Quest Preparation

The quests in Skyhighlands feature the two villains captured in Operation: Troll Rocket Steal. Keep Threatpack in a Water trap and Grinnade in a Fire trap and you're set.

GRINNADE   THREATPACK

DARES

No Lives Lost

All Areas Found (12)

Enemy Goal (50)

Villains Defeated

Traptanium Gates

DIFFICULT DARES

Time to Beat: 20:30

Don't Switch

Complete all Villain Quests (2)

COLLECTIONS

1 Story Scrolls

4 Treasure Chests

1 Soul Gems

1 Winged Sapphires

1 Legendary Treasures

2 Hats

MAP KEY

(A)	Connector Point
	Hat
	Legendary Treasure
	Quest
	Skystones Smash Player
	Soul Gem
	Story Scroll
	Treasure Chest
	Villain Stash
	Winged Sapphire

Defend the Dreadyacht

The level begins with you in control of a flying ship armed with a cannon. Press Up on the D-Pad to invert the flight controls if you prefer. Shoot down the pirate ships attacking the Dreadyacht. Look for green heart icons to appear and fly through them if your ship takes too much damage.

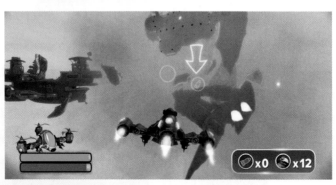

Fly close to Flynn's ship for boost. Use boost for a quick burst of speed. Looks for Mags next. Her ship carries rockets. Rockets track enemies and are more powerful than the cannon. Shoot down a total of 30 Air Pirates to clear the way for your landing. If you manage to shoot down 30 Air Pirates without using rockets, you earn the Achievement, Look Ma, No Rockets! Picking up rockets is fine, just don't use them.

START

Landing Platforms & Stolen Property Room

Go down the ramp on the left to meet up with Tessa, who has a quest for Threatpack, near a broken turret and a **Story Scroll**.

Follow the ramp up, past the starting point, until you encounter a locked gate. The key, and a Troll Radio, are in the Stolen Property Room. Its entrance is near the locked gate. You need to take out a few pirates before you can grab the key and unlock the gate.

YOU BREAK IT, YOU FIX IT

Tessa asks for help fixing a cannon. Completing the quest begins a turret sequence and unlocks homing rockets for future turret events, provided Threatpack is in the *Traptanium Portal*.

A Battle Gate blocks the path farther along the ramp. A new enemy, Bad Juju, appears here. Bad Juju is a wizard who summons whirlwinds that spin Skylanders in place. It doesn't do any damage, but does make it difficult to aim properly. Hawkmongous appears next and you must defeat him in Skystone Smash to continue.

Lower Defenses, Lower Elevator & Digger's Dungeon

Tessa flies past and asks for help with the pirates chasing her. Jump in the turret and blast the pirates out of the sky. There are two gems that appear as well. Shoot them for a bonus.

The gates behind the turret open. The ramp ends at a large gear. Jump on top of the gear and walk in the direction of the arrows. Stop partway up the hut for Digger's Dungeon, which has a quest and a **Villain Stash**. Take the gear to the top to reach Middle Defenses.

MINER TROUBLES II

Diggs can't break apart a certain type of ore and asks for Grinnade's help. After completing this quest, an Evolved Grinnade can destroy the purple ore formations found throughout Skyhighlands.

Middle Defenses

A closed gate near a turret halts your progress. Before jumping into the turret, you must defeat a group of sky pirates! The turret sequence is similar to the previous ones, but this time there are three gems to hit while shooting down the pirate ships.

Hawkmongous appears on the other side of the gate, demanding a Skystones Smash rematch. After defeating him, nab the nearby **Legendary Geode Key**.

Upper Elevator

Hop on the gear and spin it upward. Jump over to the smaller gear. Spin it up high enough to reach the platform with Blastermind's **Soul Gem (Lock Puzzle Psychic)** and the doorway to the Greenhouse.

Greenhouse

The Greenhouse has a **Treasure Chest**, Persephone, and a Life Gate. The Life Gate doesn't lead to a new area, your Skylander remains in the Greenhouse.

 GREENHOUSE

Push the blocks on the other side of the gate down to the lower level. Push one of the blocks over to the depression in the ground. Use the block to reach the higher ledge and the **William Tell Hat**.

Spin the larger gear halfway up, jump away from the smaller gear and look for a Water Gate. Spin the smaller gear to its highest point to reach Upper Defenses.

 THE WATERWORKS

Go into the building and open the **Treasure Chest**. Walk up the ramp to the right and stand on the button to raise the water level. Continue your ascent and watch for additional buttons that raise the water level. When you reach the top, a plank extends out to the **Radar Hat**. Another plank extends from the opposite wall. Use the button at the end of it to drain The Waterworks and head back outside.

Upper Defenses & Lost and Found

Here you find another gate, more enemies to defeat, and another go with a turret. This time, Mags asks for help with the "blueberries" chasing her. The doorway on the opposite side of the platform of the turret is the entrance to Lost and Found.

Lost and Found has a **Winged Sapphire** and a *Traptanium* crystal. Destroy the crystal and break the floor to reveal a **Treasure Chest**.

I call pirates, "blueberries" for some reason, can't remember why, but anyway,
Mags

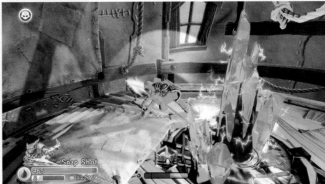

Snap Shot
465

Cutting Platform

Hawkmongous sends in waves of minions at first. Watch out for the large energy weapon in the back of the battle area. The crystals rise and glow when it is about to fire. After you clear out his pirates, Hawkmongous joins the battle as Tae Kwon Crow. Tae Kwon Crow moves quickly and strikes with a sword that emits an energy wave through the ground. Once you've defeated Tae Kwon Crow, return to Skylanders Academy.

Back at Skylanders Academy

Auric has added the Molekin Mountain Hat to his inventory, for 1000 gold. Speak with Flynn when you're ready to travel to the Golden Desert.

even have the slightest idea what those things are but I am still the best pilot in
Flynn

16

The Golden Desert

OBJECTIVES

STORY GOALS

▶ Clear out the Chompy Worms

▶ Save Cali from the Golden Queen

Quest Preparation

You are unable to complete the quests for this level at this time.

DARES

No Lives Lost

All Areas Found (10)

Enemy Goal (55)

Villains Defeated

Traptanium Gates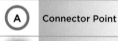

DIFFICULT DARES

Time to Beat: 15:50

Don't Switch

Complete all Villain Quests (2)

COLLECTIONS

1 Story Scrolls

4 Treasure Chests

1 Soul Gems

1 Winged Sapphires

1 Legendary Treasures

2 Hats

MAP KEY

(A)	Connector Point
	Hat
	Legendary Treasure
	Quest
	Skystones Smash Player
	Soul Gem
	Story Scroll
	Treasure Chest
	Villain Stash
	Winged Sapphire

X's Shifting Sands

The quest Diggs offers is for Blaster-Tron, an enemy who can't be captured yet. The **Story Scroll** is to the right, up on a large, flat stone. Step on the Super Bounce Pad to travel over the chasm.

Rocky Roll
390
6968

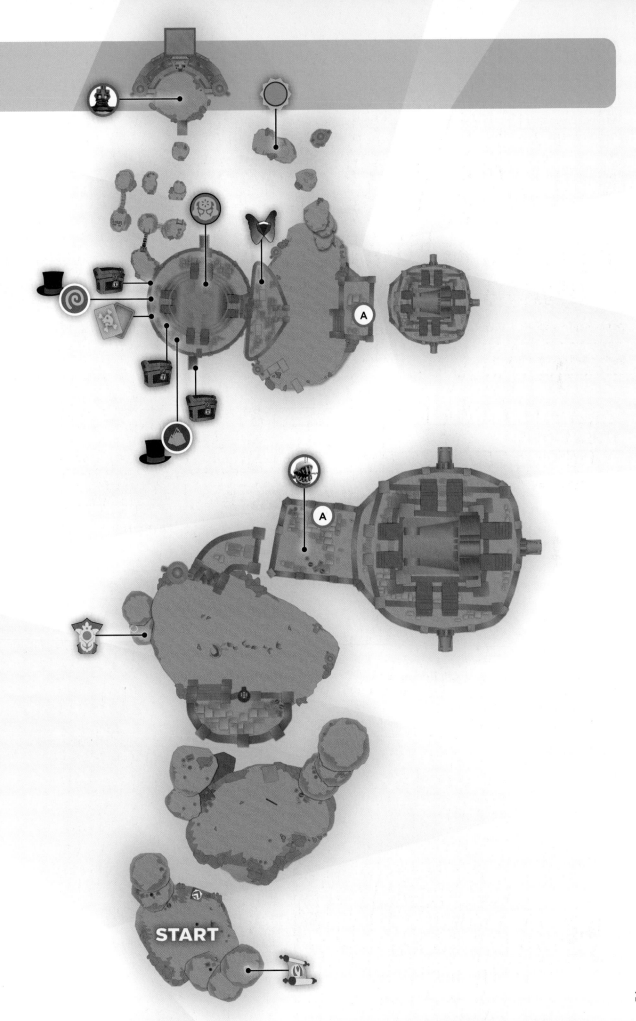

START

Defeat the skeletal enemies to clear the Battle Gate from the Super Bounce Pad. Strike the shield-wielding skeletons from behind, or goad them into an attack you can avoid. When their swords are extended, they're vulnerable. If you're the patient type, you can destroy the shields slowly. You can also destroy the entrance they use to enter the area. Bounce ahead to the Dust Bowl.

Dust Bowl

Speak with Cali who explains how to deal with the giant Chompy Worms. While you're manning the cactus-flinging catapult, aim for cacti and any statues in your field of fire. The statues turn into coins. If you destroy 10 cacti during this chapter (you have more opportunities at cacti later) you earn the Garden Gladiator Achievement/Trophy.

When the Chompy Worm flies off, follow Cali into the cleared bowl. Collect the loose coins and look for a platform off the left side. Grab the **Legendary Dragon Head**, and then use the explosives near Cali.

Use the Super Bounce Pad to reach an open courtyard. Enemies spill out of a doorway into a balcony just out of jumping range. Grave Clobbers are huge and powerful, but slow. When a green ring appears on the ground, you might be able to snag a Bomb out of the air by jumping at just the right time. Otherwise, stay clear! Eventually a Bone Chompy makes an appearance, though he isn't the last enemy to appear. A Super Bounce Pad is unlocked when the final enemy falls.

Bone Chompy

Bone Chompy likes to chew brains. Watch out for its dash attack. If it hits one of your Skylanders, it starts chewing on their heads! Avoid the charge and this should be a relatively easy capture.

The Temple of Topaz

Cali needs cover from the Chompy Worm again. This time, Masker Mind-controlled Bomb Shells join the Chompy Worm. The Chompy Worm is more aggressive, charging the catapult on more than one occasion. After it takes enough damage, it flies off again.

Destroy the *Traptanium* crystal on the left. Then do the same on the right to form a bridge. Walk over the bridge and destroy a third *Traptanium* crystal to reach Tuff Luck's **Soul Gem (Garden of Pain)**. Use the Super Bounce Pad for a quick trip back to Cali. After the Golden Queen appears and leaves, push the three blocks into the holes. Step on each flashing button to open the gate ahead and extend a bridge. Get the **Winged Sapphire** from the corner of the raised area.

The Howling Caverns & Hole in the Wall

Persephone waits just inside the doorway. Stepping down into the lower area begins a long fight to clear a Battle Gate on a Bounce Pad. A second Bounce Pad appears below Persephone, allowing you to reach the doorway where your foes appeared. It leads to Hole in the Wall, and a **Treasure Chest** behind rows of spikes.

Bounce up to the Lock Puzzle. Go left, down, right, down, left, and up to get to the water. Go down, left, right, down, up, left, down, left, down, left, up, left, down, right, up, right, down, up, left, up, and down to hit the coins and vases. Go up, left, and down to clear puzzle and open the door to The Golden Springs.

The Golden Springs

Visit the Earth Gate first. When you're done inside the gate, push the block one spot. Use the switch nearest the block once. Flip the switch nearest the molekin once and wait next to it. When the pulse passes through the beam, use the switch again to send the pulse over to the other side.

THE EARTHEN ALCOVE

Push the blocks in place to reach the **Desert Crown**.

Walk up the newly opened stairs. The left path ends at a Lock Puzzle guarding a **Treasure Chest** inside a *Traptanium* crystal. Go right, and up to collect the coins. Go down, left, up, right, down, left, up, left, up, right, up, left, down and right to clear the lock.

The path that goes off to the right is trapped. Watch out for the spikes that pop up from the ground! The door goes back to The Howling Caverns, near the **Villain Stash** shown earlier. Go down the stairs away from the Villain Stash first. The door at the bottom goes back out to The Golden Springs, near a Skystones Smash player and an Air Gate. The hall near the Villain Stash is a one way trip back to a different area of The Temple of Topaz.

THE WINDY WATCH

Jump between the floating balloon tops and platforms. After you get the **Batter Up Hat**, use the Teleport Pad to return to the area's entrance.

The Windy Heights

There's a **Treasure Chest** to the left of the entrance to the area. In the Windy Heights, pick up and move the bamboo bridge so you can retrieve the wooden bridge. Move the wooden bridge to the center platform, then move the bamboo bridge to the opposite side. Move the metal bridge across the bamboo bridge and place it there. Finally, get the wooden bridge and use it to reach the platform with the Super Bounce Pad.

The Jeweled Coliseum

The first stage begins with a steady stream of shielded skeletons, followed by Bone Chompies and a Bad Juju. Watch out for eyebeams from the statue overlooking the arena floor. When the bomb-tossing enemies appear, try to catch a bomb and throw it at the statues under Cali. Take out all the statues to send the wall behind her crashing into the enemies below.

Things pick up when the Chompy Worm appears in the center of the arena floor and creates a quicksand pit. The edges of the floor are safe from the pit, but not from the enemies that keep appearing!

Grave Clobber

Grave Clobber stomps around the arena until it draws close enough to swing its two massive fists. It drives both fists into the ground and causes a minor earthquake. Avoid the attack and move behind the stone creature before hitting back. Grave Clobber moves slowly, so ranged attacks on the move can be effective.

Back at Skylanders Academy

Place the Legendary Golden Dragon Head at the doors of the Main Hall. Check in with Brock, who has a new arena for the Rumble Club. Talk to Flynn to go to the Lair of the Golden Queen.

17

Lair of the Golden Queen

OBJECTIVES

STORY GOALS

▶ Find and defeat the Golden Queen

Quest Preparation

Keep Grave Clobber in the Earth trap you used in the last chapter, and have an Air trap ready for Bad Juju. However, you'll need a return trip to complete that quest.

GRAVE CLOBBER   BAD JUJU

DARES

No Lives Lost

All Areas Found (10)

Enemy Goal (55)

Villains Defeated

Traptanium Gates

DIFFICULT DARES

Time to Beat: 13:40

Don't Switch

Complete all Villain Quests (2)

COLLECTIONS

1 Story Scrolls

4 Treasure Chests

1 Soul Gems

1 Winged Sapphires

1 Legendary Treasures

3 Hats

MAP KEY

(A)	Connector Point
	Hat
	Legendary Treasure
	Quest
	Skystones Smash Player
	Soul Gem
	Story Scroll
	Treasure Chest
	Villain Stash
	Winged Sapphire

Tomb of the Forgotten Queen

Speak with Cali, who is standing not too far from a Troll Radio. Push the blocks past Cali to create a clear path for the energy beam emanating from the wall to the crystal in the middle of the room. Turn the switch near the door twice to open the way to the Halls of Treachery.

Torch
435
7286

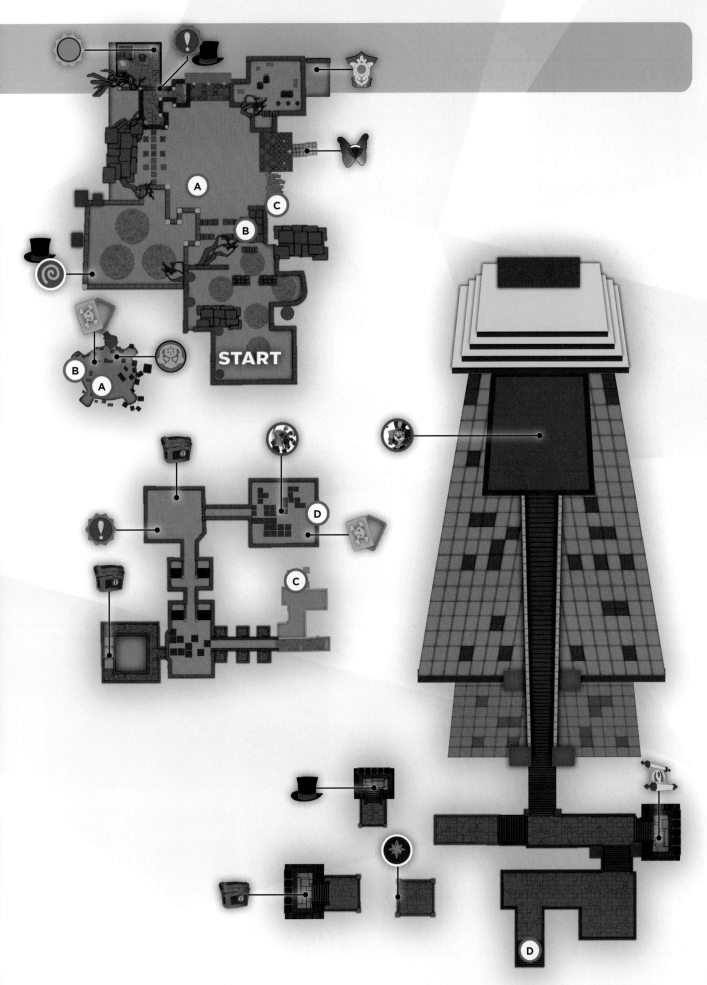

START

The Halls of Treachery

The nearby bridge leads to an area with a Battle Gate and an Air Gate. Cali appears with a warning about the bridge ahead that you should heed. Before you press on, break out one of your Giants and step on the small blue button in the corner.

 CRADLE OF THE FOUR WINDS

Weave between the vortices produced by the large fans on either side of the room. They do minor damage, but will carry your Skylander back toward the starting point should they come in contact with them. Your reward for getting through the whirlwinds is the **Classic Pot Hat.**

The tiles Cali warned you about can support a Skylander's weight long enough to grab the coins floating on them and hop back off. Falling into the sand below sends your Skylander to The Darkest Reach.

The Darkest Reach

Fight against skeletal dragons and eyeballs. Look for a **Villain Stash** in one corner. Defeat Mut, the Mabu, near the gate in Skystones Smash to reach the Teleport Pad that leads back to the Halls of Treachery.

Glumshanks has a quest for Bad Juju at the end of the bridge with the shaky tiles in the Halls of Treachery. Just beyond him are Short Cut's **Soul Gem (Scissor Stilts)**, and a *Traptanium* crystal. You must destroy the *Traptanium* crystal to get to the block you need to reach the **Soul Gem**.

REMOTE LOCATION

Glumshanks needs help moving sand to get a spare remote for Golden Queen's Ultimate Weapon. After getting Bad Juju's help, he hands over the Beetle Hat.

The second bridge with shaky tiles has an additional surprise: spear trap tiles. Watch out for the tiles with holes in them. Step on every tile on the bridge to reach a hidden path ahead.

The Secret Vault

Walk to the back of the room with the crystal beam puzzle. If you missed any tiles on the bridge, the wall remains in place. You can see the **Legendary Hippo Statue** but you can't reach it until you step on every tile on that bridge.

Move the blocks to provide a clear path between the crystals in the room just outside the Secret Vault. Use the switch in the corner twice to open the door.

The bridge beyond the opened door has two new tiles. Avoid the glowing tiles (they deal damage) and use tiles with green crosses that heal your Skylander. The key in the corner unlocks the door off one side of the bridge.

Walk toward the key on the second row of tiles to the left of where you start (it's entirely fall-away tiles), pick up the key and come back on the row that touches the stone path that leads to the locked gate.

This key is used in two places, but it can be used only one time per trip this level. Unlock the gate and collect the **Winged Sapphire**. If you already have the **Winged Sapphire**, carry the key across the bridge to the doorway beyond it. The door leads to the Parade of Broken Soldiers, and there's no returning to this area after passing through the door.

☠ The Parade of Broken Soldiers

Push the three blocks on the lowest level forward to build a path to the higher ledge. Push the blocks from both sides of the golden pool into it.

Cali pops up again and offers a warning about the Spy Guys. Avoid their beams of light (if you're caught, you must begin at the front edge of the Spy Guy's patrol area) by stepping into corners or hopping on top of platforms.

The pit directly ahead of where you passed the first Spy Guy has a **Treasure Chest** in the back. Push the three blocks in the lower area into a line in the center of the floor. There is now a gap between the first and second block, but your Skylander can make the jump.

The next area has a pair of Spy Guys. Attack the statues on the left side of the path to topple them on the Spy Guys. Cali appears not far from a *Traptanium* crystal, with Grave Clobber's quest.

WHERE IS FLYNN?

Cali wants Grave Clobber to rescue Flynn from captivity. The goal is to locate three blue buttons in ten minutes or less. Don't try to fight every enemy that spawns. Focus on finding either a Teleport Pad or one of the blue buttons that opens Flynn's cage. Stay on the move and don't worry about enemies coming up from behind. They can't use the Teleport Pads.

Destroy the crystal to reveal a key, one of two required to unlock a gate in front of a **Treasure Chest**. If you carried the key from the previous area, this is where to use it. Sneak past the two Spy Guys and get ready for a long fight against a few waves of skeletal enemies, and a chance to capture Bad Juju. After the fight ends (there's more fight after Bad Juju goes down), take on Nut in Skystones Smash to open the gate.

Bad Juju

Bad Juju remains in the middle of the chamber and relies on whirlwind attacks and allies to do the dirty work. The whirlwind is only annoying at first, spinning its target around and around, throwing off your aim and keeping your Skylander locked in place. Watch out for the lightning strikes from above. They fall exactly on a whirlwind, so get out as soon as possible.

The Seat of Flowing Gold, Heart of Gold & The Temple of the Divine Treasure

Go left at the first intersection. The solid path ends at a large bridge of various tiles (damaging, breakaways, and so on). Run straight across the bridge (avoid the damaging tiles!) to the Magic Gate.

THE EVERSHIFTING ABYSS

The bridge tiles behind the Magic Gate change every second. Most are familiar, but there are two new tiles. The blue tiles give experience, and the tiles with the round shape give coins.

Go straight across the bridge for a **Treasure Chest**. Go left from the Treasure Chest to reach the **Crazy Light Bulb Hat**.

From the Magic Gate entrance, angle to the left across the bridge. Go down the hallway (not up the stairs on the left!) and hop on the stone railing on the right. Avoid the Spy Guy (stay on the railing as much

as possible) and go to the end of the long hallway. There's a **Story Scroll**, and a Lock Puzzle that you don't need to worry about.

Return to the stairway and go up to the top. It's an uneventful climb until Cali pops up at the top with one last warning.

Golden Queen

The Golden Queen begins the battle by creating expanding and contracting gold circles on the ground. Only the edges inflict damage. Jump over the edges and get in your shots on the Queen. Get used to dealing with these circles; they appear often over the course of this battle. Using a flying Skylander makes avoiding the circles easier.

After she takes some damage, she ejects rings on the ground. Collect the rings quickly, or she absorbs them back, restoring some of her health.

The Golden Queen summons golden wings that fly around the area while she hides behind a shield. She also sends out blades that spin around on the ground. Avoid the blades and attack the wings. The Queen is vulnerable to attacks up until the point she shields herself, but you also need to eliminate the wings to advance the fight on to the next stage.

For the next stage of the battle, the outermost rows of tiles vanish, shrinking the battle area. The battle continues with more golden circles, the wing firing out blades that bounce around the area, and tiles being eliminated from the floor.

When the floor is down to three rows, the Golden Queen vanishes. The floor shrinks down to 3 x 3 grid of tiles. When a new one appears, run or jump to it to avoid a golden sphere crashing down from above.

The floor resets and then becomes a 3 x 3 grid in the middle. Four wings appear, one on each corner of the grid. Long lines of blades bounce off the walls and tear through the area where your Skylander is fighting. Jump over blades and attack wings. Focus on one wing at a time and eliminate it before moving on to the next.

The gold globe appears again and slams down into the file. The tiles vanish in a rippling wave. Wait until the last possible moment and jump over the wave of vanishing tiles. The row behind should reappear as your Skylander hits the ground.

The Golden Queen hits a growth spurt and takes up an entire side of the battle arena. She emits huge streams of blades that you must avoid. She's invulnerable while the blades are out, but requires a brief period of rest. As soon as she's down, jump in and attack.

The following two rounds of spinning blades are accompanied by gold circles. Keep on jumping to avoid both. When the floor shrinks, the golden circles are gone, replaced with wings. Eliminate the wings quickly, while avoiding the spinning blades.

The final stage involves one simple strategy: run! Follow Cali down the steps and do not stop. Quickly remove any debris in the way and get moving again. One touch from Golden Queen takes out any Skylander and you must start over again from the top of the stairs, with a new Skylander. At the bottom of the stairs, attack the support columns of the arch to end the battle.

Back at Skylander Academy

Take the Legendary Hippo Head to the staircase just outside the Game Room. Talk to Flynn to thwart Kaos one more time!

18

The Ultimate Weapon

OBJECTIVES

STORY GOALS

▶ Reach the Top of the Great Machine

▶ Defeat Kaos!

Quest Preparation

Keep the Golden Queen in an Earth trap. You'll need one trip through The Ultimate Weapon to trap Smoke Scream, and another to complete his quest.

GOLDEN QUEEN   SMOKE SCREAM

DARES

No Lives Lost

All Areas Found (11)

Enemy Goal (40)

Villains Defeated

Traptanium Gates

DIFFICULT DARES

Time to Beat: 29:55

Don't Switch

Complete all Villain Quests (2)

COLLECTIONS

1 Story Scrolls

4 Treasure Chests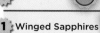

1 Soul Gems

1 Winged Sapphires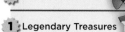

1 Legendary Treasures

2 Hats

MAP KEY

(A)   Connector Point

    Hat

    Legendary Treasure

    Quest

    Skystones Smash Player

    Soul Gem

    Story Scroll

    Treasure Chest

    Villain Stash

    Winged Sapphire

Loading Zone & Receiving Dock

The Loading Zone has the Golden Queen's quest and destructible objects. Go up the steps to reach a Super Bounce Pad.

Chopper
417
7
2215

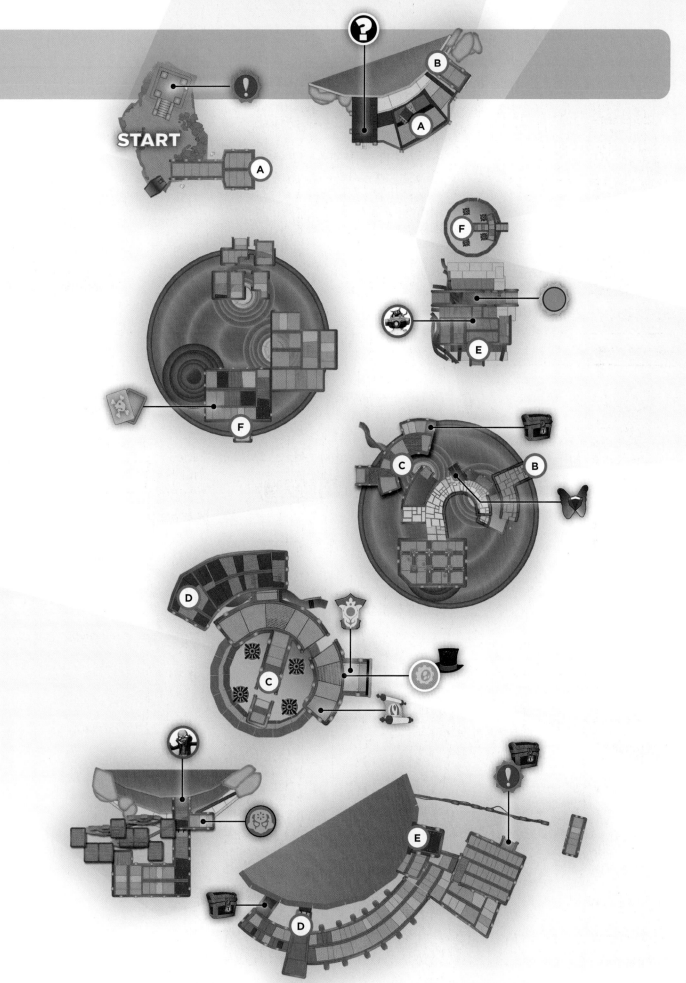

START

BANK ON THIS

Dr. Noobry's invention, the Piggybank-o-matic 3001 isn't working as intended. He wants the Golden Queen's help in getting his machine working. Look for Piggybank-o-matic 3001 objects throughout the Ultimate Weapon. The Evolved Golden Queen can get a load of valuables from each one.

The Super Bounce Pad deposits your Skylander near a mystery element gate. A Battle Gate on the ground hides a Bounce Pad. Bounce up to the walkway above and go through the door to enter the Relay System.

Relay System

Use every switch in the room one time, except the one to the left of the two horshoe magnets hanging from the ceiling, to bring up the bridge and open the nearby door. The door goes to the Matter Refactoring Room.

Matter Refactoring Room

Follow the catwalk until it ends. Drop down and take on the Smoke Scream and Grinnades that guard a Battle Gate. The Bounce Pad under the Battle Gate sends your Skylander up to a higher catwalk, but save that trip until after you drop down one level near the Bounce Pad for a **Winged Sapphire**.

Bounce up to the higher catwalk. There's a Troll Radio to the left and a laser puzzle to

the right. Use the switch one time to start the giant wheel turning. Hop on one of the platforms and ride it out to collect all the coins. Hop off at the top. Go left past the Lock Puzzle for a **Treasure Chest**.

To clear the first stage of the Lock Puzzle, go right, down, left, up, down, left, down, right, up, left, right, up, left, down, right, down, left, and up to collect all the coins. Go left, right, left, up, down, right, down, up, down, right, up, left, and down.

To clear the second stage, go up, right, down, right, left, down, right, up, left, down, left, right, and up to go through the water. Go right, right, and up to collect the final coin. Go down, left, down, right, and down.

On the third stage, go right, up, down, left, up, left, down, left, up, right, down, down, up, down, left, up, left, down, right, down, left, up, left, and down.

Step on the large, red button that is revealed. It sends your Skylander plummeting downward. If you manage to collect 9 coins here, you earn the achievement, Do a Barrel Roll.

Repair Platform H

Jump over the right side gap, visit the Tech Gate, and grab the **Story Scroll**. Go back to the left and interact with the purple and gold tube to gain access to a Bounce Pad.

THE BALLOON RETURN

Hop on the balloon and ride it to a spinning gear. Ride the gear around to its lowest point. Step on the balloon there and float over to the **Legendary Weird Robot**. Return to the giant gear and ride a platform around to the other balloon. Jump between balloons and another large gear to reach the **Brainiac Hat**.

The Bounce Pad drops your Skylander into another fight. When all the enemies are defeated, a door opens and a warning about the power is displayed. Go through the newly opened door to go out to the External Power Sorter.

External Power Sorter

Persephone is directly outside the door. Turn around and follow the walkway back to a **Treasure Chest**. Avoid the red light bursts passing between the statue mouths. Use each switch once at the laser puzzle to form the bridges needed to reach Buzz and the door to Power Exhaust Ports.

FIGHT DOOM WITH BOOM

Buzz wants Smoke Scream's help busting through a gate so he can plant explosives to destroy the Ultimate Weapon after Kaos is defeated. Completing the quest clears the way to a **Treasure Chest**.

Power Exhaust Ports

Smoke Scream attacks immediately, but he's not alone! After you defeat Smoke Scream, additional enemies, including Hood Sickle and Broccoli Guy, continue to fight.

 Smoke Scream

Smoke Scream uses two attacks. The first is a short-range flamethrower. He kneels slightly just before using it. Smoke Scream's second attack is a bouncing barrel. He pauses and lowers the grate just below his turret before releasing a barrel.

When all the enemies are defeated, a bridge extends from across the room. Jump up the platforms to reach Ka-Boom's **Soul Gem (Missile Rain)**. You need to start on the right and work back to the left to reach the **Soul Gem**. Jump under the vacuum in the circular area behind the **Soul Gem** to be whisked away to the Grinder.

The Fly Wheels

The Grinder

Glumshanks would like to play Skystones Smash, and is appreciative even in defeat. Use the two switches for the laser puzzle one time each to raise two platforms to span a gap in your path.

The next area becomes incredibly hazardous after spinning arms pop up from the floor. Weave between the arms toward the large, red button behind them. Step on the button, avoid the arms again, and head for the door in the back of the area.

Clear out the enemies that spawn. Use the switch one time to activate the fly wheel. Ride it around to the balloons on the left side. There are two more fly wheels to ride around to reach the top. Go to the right for a **Villain Stash**. Step on the platform straight ahead to fight Kaos.

Kaos

Kaos opens the fight with *Traptanium*-powered circles that are similar to what the Golden Queen used. Avoid the edges and attack when you can, including while Kaos charges up his attack and after the attack, while he engages in taunting. Use flying Skylanders to more easily avoid the circles.

Kaos switches to using two types of "bullets" as an attack. One type depends on your Skylander. It is the same element as your Skylander and restores health. The other is a different element that deals more damage than the other bullets restore. Make sure you have a Villain on the portal. When Kaos uses the bullets, tag between Skylander and Villain to avoid taking damage from the bullets.

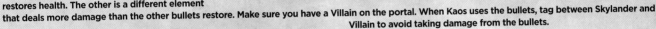

Resorting to an old trick, Kaos sends out Doom Sharks. Move just around the edges of the Doom Sharks to restore health. Continue to hit Kaos when you can.

Kaos powers up (and heals a bit) by adding *Traptanium* crystals in the form of swords and dashes in a straight line, chopping downward. Fortunately, he telegraphs the attack, making it easier to avoid.

Kaos powers up and heals again, adding wings this time. He ditches the dashing sword attack, and opts for covering the battle area with laser beams. Stay away from the beams as best you can. Not every beam indicates an attack, but his attack could run along any of the beams.

Kaos continues to mix up his various attacks, except for when he flies out of range and covers the arena with laser lines. He uses different patterns each time.

He has an enormous health pool to get through, but keep at it and you should have Kaos in his specially-designed trap soon enough!

Back at Skylanders Academy

Completing the Story Mode unlocks the Nightmare Mode, Difficult Dares, and awards you different Arkeyan Helms, based on what level of difficulty you completed. There's much more left to do (as the assembled people at Skylanders Academy let you know!), so keep on adventuring Portal Master! Your first trip should be to the Kitchen, where the Legendary Weird Robot will make his home.

Mags
Now hold your hungry horses there, fellas, there's still a lot to do

Nightmare Express

OBJECTIVES

STORY GOALS

▶ Find the artifact in the temple

▶ Take down the Troll Mega Tank

▶ Retake the Trolly Grail

Quest Preparation

The quest during this level is for a Tech Villain, Trolling Thunder. You cannot complete the second Villain Quest at this time.

TROLLING THUNDER

DARES

No lives Lost

All Areas Found (24)

Enemy Goal (70)

Villains Defeated

Traptanium Gates

DIFFICULT DARES

Time to Beat 11:50

Don't Switch

Complete All Quests (2)

COLLECTIONS

1	Story Scrolls	
4	Treasure Chests	
0	Soul Gems	
1	Winged Sapphires	
1	Legendary Treasures	
4	Hats	

MAP KEY

(A)	Connector Point
	Hat
	Legendary Treasure
	Quest
	Skystones Smash Player
	Soul Gem
	Story Scroll
	Treasure Chest
	Villain Stash
	Winged Sapphire

Temple Ruins Approach

Before speaking to Cali to officially start the chapter, run up the hill to the right to find a new area and seek out Da Pinchy.

Temple Site Overlook

Speak to Gobler to get a hint about a chest in a remote location. Walk up to the Bomb at the end of the cliff to record this new area but the only way to get to this chest is to complete the Trolling Thunder Quest. Speak to Da Pinchy at the bottom of the hill to find out what needs to be done.

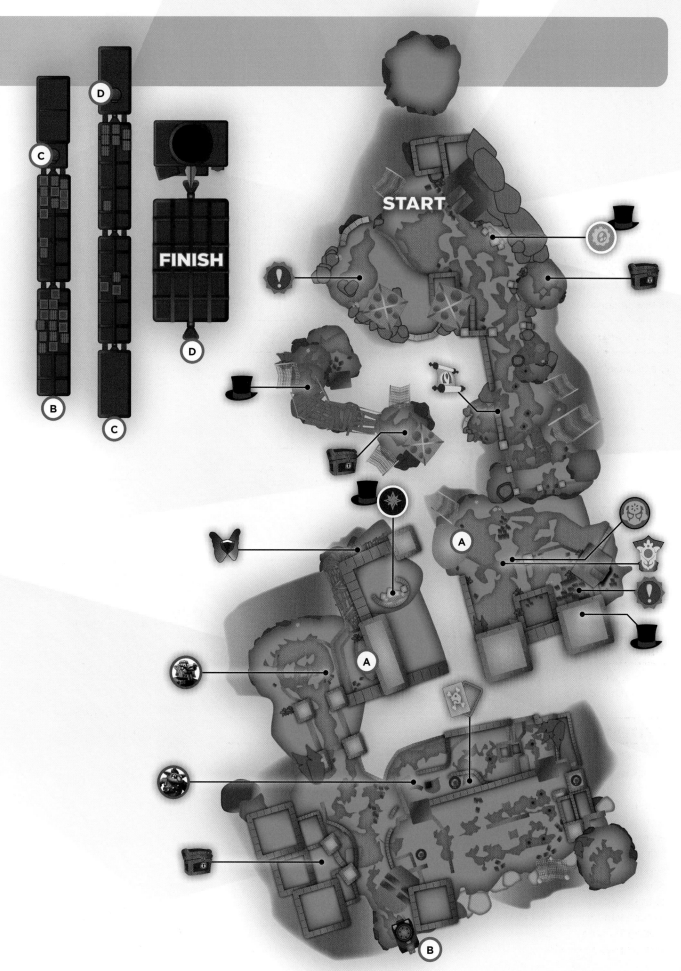

START

FINISH

267

STATUE OF LIMITATIONS

The artist carved a beautiful statue of Captain Flynn but there is a big boulder blocking it. To complete this quest, trap Trolling Thunder later in this chapter and return to this location with it in the Tech Trap. Speak to Da Pinchy and Trolling Thunder automatically blows up the boulder and a little more.

Talk to Cali and listen to her tale of the Trolly Grail. Flynn went after the artifact alone and got into trouble. To find him you need to use the automatic bomb builder (the blue glowing circle) to make a large rolling bomb that can blow up walls and other structures. Jump on the blue circle and push the large bomb into the blockade ahead. Before going to the Rubble Pathway use a Trap Master of the Tech Element to open the gate on the right.

Suspended Island Ruin

Removing the boulder also knocks down the large statue of Flynn, but the good news is that it makes a bridge to another area. Cross the makeshift bridge and grab the **Cycling Hat**.

Continue to the wooden bridge and push the large rolling bomb into the gate with a bomb symbol to blow it up. Open the now accessible **Treasure Chest** and return to the starting spot of the chapter.

⚙ VERTICAL CHALLENGE BOMB CLOSET

The goal in this vertical level is to get the bomb to the top to remove the barricade. However, the only path is using the escalators that are rolling the wrong way. These are too slow to make it to the top carrying the bomb. Jump up the escalators and push two blocks down to make an alternate route using the staircase to the left.

Leap up the steps and blocks on the left to get to the top quickly and toss the bomb at the wall to get the **Outback Hat**.

Return to the start of the level and activate the automatic bomb builder and push another large rolling bomb down the same path. Instead of trying to roll it up the wooden bridge, push it over the edge to the right.

Forgotten Ledge & Hidden Cavern

Push the bomb into the wall that has the red bomb icon to blow it up. The explosion reveals a secret entrance to the Hidden Cavern. Collect the **Story Scroll** "Meditations on Boom"—Appendix III. Pick up the bomb and go back outside to the Forgotten Ledge. Use the Bounce Pad to return to the top level. Move as quickly as you can and toss the bomb into the barricade to get access to the Tank Terrace Ruins.

🍃 Rubble Pathway

Rush into the area to deal with the Lob Goblins and use the Bounce Pad to the left to leap up to a ledge and find a **Treasure Chest**.

Hint: Blow up wall with Bomb.

Tank Terrace Ruins

There are three tanks in this area and each is guarding a key. You need all three keys to unlock the door to the Temple of Boom. Grab the first bomb in front of you and toss it at the tank to the left before it can lock in on your location. Pick up the bomb again and toss it at the tank at the bottom of the stairs. Wipe out the enemies that are hiding near the key and go up the hill. Once again, pick up a bomb and destroy the last tank at the top of the hill, then talk to Peebs.

GRAND THEFT PLAN

Behind some extremely locked gates are the Trolls' secret plans for their latest tank. However Peebs can't crack the combination to the lock. There is only one Troll that knows all the codes, the Lob Goblin. After trapping this enemy later in this chapter, return here. Speak to Peebs as the Lob Goblin to automatically unlock the gate and receive the Coconut Hat as a reward.

Before using the three keys to go after Flynn, smash the *Traptanium* crystal on the lower level in between the location of the two tanks. The crystal blocks the entrance to another secret area, but make sure you grab a bomb before entering.

Underground Ruins

Switch to a Villain from one of your *Traptanium* traps and open the **Villain Stash** to the left. Go back outside and grab a bomb if you don't have one, then toss it at the Stone Cage to free the artifact. Leap up the ledges on the right and jump to the **Legendary Flynn Statue**.

Go back outside to the Tank Terrace Ruins and finally continue your mission searching for Flynn. Use all three keys in the mouth of the statue to unlock the way into the temple.

Temple of Boom

Flynn got trapped trying to snag the Trolly Grail and needs some help getting loose. To free Flynn you need to step on the two blue circular switches, but that is not as easy as it sounds. First, the wall to the right must be destroyed to reach that section. This takes a bit of block pushing to maneuver the cannon down to a breakable part of the wall.

Before running to the newly opened section on the right, move the three blocks that were near the cannon into a straight line. This makes a bridge connecting the left and right sections. Cross the bridge and step on the first button.

Go to the back of the room and jump up a series of ledges, watching out for the floor spikes. Continue on that path around the back of the room to get to the right side. Step on the second glowing button to free Flynn. Leave through the newly made opening. Unfortunately for Flynn he doesn't get to enjoy the Trolly Grail for long as Noodles, the overgrown green cylcops, steals it.

Temple Battle Arena

As soon as you exit the temple there is an opportunity to catch Trolling Thunder.

Trolling Thunder

The tank's turret fires several shots in a row that can be avoided if you move around the tank in the same direction. There are other enemies to deal with while battling the tank and they should be dealt with only when they get in your way. Close in on Trolling Thunder and circle around to its back to attack. Keep moving around the tank and wait until it stops firing to counter attack.

Wipe out any remaining enemies and go up the narrow wooden planks where you first entered the area (on the left side of the screen) to reach the Cliffside Sanctuary.

Cliffside Sanctuary

Drop off the edge of the cliff and use your puzzle solving skills to complete the Lock Puzzle. Move to the right to slide across the red bumpers, then slide up and down to smash through the breakable blocks to collect the coins in the bottom left corner. Go straight up through the gate and around to the left to line up with the next gate on the right. Pass through this gate and collect the coins to the left, then return to the top right corner going up and left to line up with the next gate. Go down through this gate and move to the left to finally slide up and complete the first puzzle.

Go to the right and smash through the breakable block below. Move to the left corner, breaking a few more blocks, and ride through the red bumpers. Go up through the gate to gain the water ability and then through the gate to the left. Repeat the previous path to smash through the breakable block at the end of the red bumpers. Use the water ability to put out the flames in the bottom left to get to the exit.

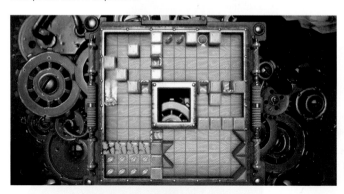

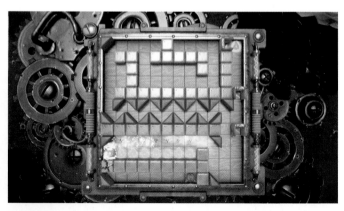

Once you've opened the giant lock, get the **Winged Sapphire** and bounce back to the Cliffside Sanctuary above. Use the Bounce Pad near the end of the walkway to access a *Traptanium* Gate.

⭐ MYSTICAL RECESS

This is a pretty straightforward room. Simply jump on the lowest platform to the right and leap across the next several platforms when they are lower than the one you are currently on. The top platform has the **Medic Hat.**

Backtrack to the Temple Battle Arena and forward through the open gate between two large stone columns.

Iron Tank Confrontation

Return to where you defeated the Trolling Thunder and Cali mentions that Flynn and Noodles went down this path. However, a Troll Mega Tank shows up and complicates things. This tank is too tough for a regular bomb! You need to find a way to get one of the large rolling bombs into this ravine. Don't stand in the crossfire of the tank for long while battling the enemies, instead make a quick retreat to the right by smashing the wooden poles.

Bomb Closet

Talk to Elbow to reinforce that the smaller bomb will not affect the big tank. However, this bomb can destroy the wall on the left side of the ravine, allowing access to a new area. Before grabbing the explosive, drop down a ledge and smash the *Traptanium* crystal to reveal a **Treasure Chest.**

Bounce back up to Elbow, grab the bomb, and run back to the Iron Tank Confrontation area to toss the explosive at the wall. Run up the steps and speak to Musgrove.

⭐ Lower Rolling Bomb Range

Step on the button to release a large bomb. It can't be pushed down into the ravine and must be maneuvered there the long way. Push the rolling bomb down into the next area and bowl over the enemies while trying to get it into the back corner on the elevator.

Talk to Persephone if you want to upgrade your Skylander and press the button to raise the elevator when the bomb is in place. Stepping on the button also lowers the gate blocking the way ahead.

Roll the bomb into the grove to the left of the steps. Use the nearby button to activate the Vertical Bomb Launcher and send the bomb to the upper level. Stand on one more blue button to open the last set of bars to finally have the rolling bomb smash into the Mega Tank.

Upper Rolling Bomb Range

Position the rolling bomb on the two rising platforms and roll it through the enemies. If you are up for a game of Skystones Smash, Da Pinchy is on the left and is eager to play.

The bomb-tossing goblin can be tough to deal with far away but it's easier to win with melee attacks. For an instant victory, simply roll the large bomb into the Lob Goblin.

274

KABOO-oose

Automatically hop aboard the Nightmare Express and follow Flynn to chase after Noodles. Grab the bomb on a crate and leap up a series of crates to toss the explosive at the hatch. Jump across to the next car and drop down to the interior of the train.

Box Car & Special Delivery

Smash all the breakable goodies inside the train and push the crate near the ledge at the back room to use it as a stepping stone. Back on top of the train, leap down and grab the bomb to use against the tank. Return to get another bomb and leap up a very tall stack of crates to blow up another hatch. Leap down once again to reenter the train.

Dining Car

A group of enemies, including a Lob Goblin, Chill Bill, and several others, tries to prevent your progress to the front of the train. Smash them if you like or simply run to the back of the room and leap up the crates to escape.

Noodles

The first round of foes consists of a pair of Troll Welders, Shield Trolls, and a Lob Goblin. Hunt down the bomb thrower first and clean up the rest. Reinforcements soon arrive, including waves of Chill Bills and Grinnades. Follow the drop ships and switch sides to wipe out the enemies as soon as they appear.

The last several foes include Trolling Thunders. Circle around these tanks to avoid their fire and attack their backs. The final confrontation is out of your hands. Flynn takes care of Noodles personally and gets some revenge for Cyclops's earlier attack.

Mirror of Mystery

OBJECTIVES

STORY GOALS

▶ Construct a Troll Mech

▶ Destroy Persephone's Tree

▶ Defeat Evilon

Quest Preparation

The quests during this level are for Mad Lobs, requiring a Tech Trap, and a Chompy, requiring a Life Trap.

MAD LOBS   CHOMPY

DARES

No lives Lost

All Areas Found (18)

Enemy Goal (45)

Villains Defeated

Traptanium Gates

DIFFICULT DARES

Time to Beat: 8:55

Don't Switch

Complete All Quests (2)

COLLECTIONS

1 | Story Scrolls

4 | Treasure Chests

0 | Soul Gems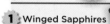

1 | Winged Sapphires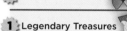

1 | Legendary Treasures

3 | Hats

MAP KEY

A | Connector Point

 Hat

 Legendary Treasure

 Quest

 Skystones Smash Player

 Soul Gem

 Story Scroll

 Treasure Chest

 Villain Stash

 Winged Sapphire

Tubtub Hub

Welcome to a mirror universe where everything is opposite. That means Trolls and Kaos are the good guys while Evilon and the Mabu are the enemies. At the start of the level, talk to Kaos to get a new Quest.

FISHINESS PROTECTION PROGRAM

An impending attack on the village leaves Kaos with no choice but to scare away his fish friend. The problem is that Kaos is too nice to raise his voice and needs Mab Lobs to scare his fishy friend away. Capture Mab Lobs later in this level and return here to frighten the fish.

FINISH

START

Troll Village

Run down the spiraling hill. After crossing the wooden bridge, talk to Moonbeam the Troll. Unfortunately, the Trolls peace rally will have to be postponed, thanks to an upcoming attack on the village. Help the Trolls defend their home by assembling a Mech that has three pieces scattered around the village. While searching the village for the Mech Parts, there are several items to collect and a Quest from Butterfly.

WORKERS' CHOMPENSATION

A lazy Troll is supposed to be helping out on the farm, but he's sleeping the day away. Butterfly needs a Chompy to come by and give the sleepy Troll a good bite to wake him up. Capture the Chompy in back of Uncle Ziggy's garage and return to give the slumbering Troll a good biting.

Butterfly
I knew it! I knew that a good biting would wake him up.

Rainbow Harmony Farms

To the left is a farm where you can pick up an Boingo Nut and plant it in the holes with the purple icons to grow crops. Jump up a few ledges to go to the top section with more planting holes and the first **Mech Part** can be found.

Rainbow Rockside

Go to the left end of Rainbow Harmony Farms and jump down where the guard rope has been cut to get to a grassy ledge. The **Legendary Treasure: Legendary Windmill** is a short distance ahead. Use the nearby Bounce Pad to return to the farm above.

Pawn Shop

In the Troll Village's center, find the doorway on the left that is below a Bounce Pad. Enter to find the Pawn Shop and win a game of Skystones Smash against Strawberry to lower the bars in the back of the room. Once the bars are lowered, go up the stairs by a pair of barrels to get the **Carnival Hat**.

Sage's Stewhouse

Walk to the village's top level and go to the Rainbow Harmony Farm's right to find another house. Sage is in the back, and he has a **Mech Part**; however, he uses it for cooking, laundry, baths, and other things. The Troll wants some treasure for the part, but he only asks for 20 gold.

Before getting the last Mech Part, there is an important collectible to grab. To the right of Sage's Stewhouse, leap across the wooden walkways to go above Uncle Ziggy's garage and find the **Winged Sapphire**.

Uncle Ziggy's Garage

The last piece is in Uncle Ziggy's garage, and it takes a bit of block-pushing to get to. The blocks need to be pushed to allow access to the **Mech Part** in the corner, as well as to create a path to the garage's rear entrance. Push the left block to the right, and the other left block forward once. Then push both blocks in the middle column to the right as far as possible to leave a clear path to the back of the garage. It's possible to push the blocks to prohibit access to the rear exit; if that happens, simply leave and return to the garage.

Chomp Dudes Rest

Chompy

This little green guy is super aggressive and leaps forward with biting attacks. Let the Chompy jump at you, then dodge and run to get some distance. Try to keep the Chompy at the best distance to land your attacks while staying out of the range of its biting move.

When all three Mech Parts are collected, Moonbeam automatically assembles a group of Mechs. Hop into the all-blue robot and wipe out the parachuting Mabu. The other Trolls help blast the barricade, opening a new section across the wooden bridge.

Totally Trail

Evil Flynn drops bombs on the Mechs, destroying them, but several Trolls, armed with clubs, join the fight. A Life Gate is a short distance on the right.

LAZY LOOKOUT

This is a simple section with only a few Chompies to tackle. Jump up the series of ledges to get the **Cornucopia Hat** at the top.

Flower Power Fields

Before taking on Mab Lobs, check to the right side and destroy the *Traptanium* crystal to reveal a **Treasure Chest**.

Paisley Perch

Head left to free a couple of Trolls in cages. Then go to the right and destroy a barricade by the Troll Radio to find the **Story Scroll: "Meditations on Boom"** – Appendix IV.

Return to the Flower Power Fields and follow the path while fighting Mabu soldiers and a tank. Let the Trolls distract the enemies and safely attack them from the side.

⊘ Mab Lobs

When you finally catch up with Mab Lobs, several Mabu and tanks join the fight. Try to take down Mab Lobs before a lot of reinforcements can join the battle. Also, make sure your Troll buddies provide some backup before jumping into the heat of battle. First, knock Mab Lobs off the stump to really open him up to damage. After he throws a bomb, dodge it and close in for a combo attack.

Use your Troll friends to help deal with the waves of enemies at the tree's base in order to lower the gate.

Charge the tree and jump to the top level to hit the enemies as soon as they emerge. Evil Persephone unleashes Mabu super soldiers, bomb enemies, and Chompies. The soldiers can take a lot of damage, but it's best to take out the bomb throwers first. There are several waves of enemies to deal with, so fight conservatively or switch out your Skylander if needed.

Secret Stashaway

Evil Persephone uses her fairy magic to summon several waves of enemies. Before climbing to the tree's top tier, go to the right side and drop off the round platform. Grab the **Treasure Chest** and use the Bounce Pad to return to the foot of the tree.

When all the enemies are defeated, Stardust appears in the area leading to the Secret Stashaway. Pick up the bomb he brought and toss it at the tree to destroy it.

DoomHelm Pass

Moonbeam was somehow able to make it ahead of you, and he has some advice on how to get through the battlefield. The trick is to hit the  big green buttons in the safe areas to deactivate the energy gates. All of these domed areas with the large green buttons are a good place to take a break, as they block the falling bombs.

CONTEMPLATION CASCADES

Walk off the first edge, following the water to the platforms below. Avoid the damaging spray of water on the next several platforms by following the slow spinning patterns. Continue to drop to get the **Gondolier Hat**.

Don't be too eager to use the Bounce Pad, as there is a very tricky item to find. Walk to the back of the screen and jump to a hidden platform that has a **Treasure Chest**.

Lonely Locale

Bounce up to the DoomHelm Pass and resume your progress on the battlefield. To complete the goal of finding all areas, make sure to go all  the way to the right and drop off the ledge at this spot.

As you dodge the shower of bombs and continue to deactivate the energy gates, look to the left edge by the final green button. Just below this area is a grassy ledge that has a **Villain Stash.**

Peaceful Palace

For the final assault on Evilon and his castle, it's time to take to the air. Automatically hop aboard the airship and look for the yellow/red  target rings to appear below. Blast the giant Mabu guns before they can lock-on and fire back. Feel free to shoot the Mabu and tanks, but the large guns fire back.

Flying foes also join the battle! Target the aerial enemies quickly and blow them out of the sky before they can bring you down.

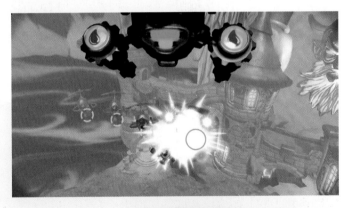

The final confrontation is an air battle with Evil Flynn, but you have a trick up your sleeve. An Elemental Attack charges up and  can be used on Flynn to do massive damage. Continue firing on Flynn's ships and unleash the Elemental Attack to knock him out of the sky.

Skylanders Academy

Skylanders Academy is the hub where your Skylander first appears when you select Story from the main menu (after completing Chapter 1: Soda Springs), and where your Skylander returns after completing a story Chapter, an Arena (if you spoke with Brock), or Kaos Challenge Mode (if you interacted with the Kaos statue). The buildings are under construction and unavailable at first, but Mags opens new areas as you complete chapters of the adventure.

The Courtyard

Your Skylander begins each trip to Skylanders Academy on a stone path overlooking the Courtyard. The character at the other end of the path is often the one you talk to in order to begin the next part of the adventure. The Villain Vault is a few steps farther. Use the Villain Vault to learn more about Villains, and to switch them into your traps.

The floating platforms near the Villain Vault lead to a mysterious portal. When you place the Magic Items Mirror of Mystery or Nightmare Express on your *Traptanium Portal*, use this portal to reach those worlds. Descend the steps on the side opposite of The Courtyard of the mysterious portal to reach Persephone.

Where does it lead to? Some very special places. That's why it's such a special

Persephone's Treehouse

Persephone remains in The Courtyard, trading Skylander upgrades for gold, but she's not far from her Treehouse. Go inside her treehouse to collect a few coins and the **Elemental Diamond** Trinket.

Courtyard Tower

Complete Chapter 2: Know-It-All Island and hop over the gap between the mysterious portal area and the red carpet. Use the switch to enter Courtyard Tower. It's a large, open room filled with coins that you can visit one time during each trip to Skylanders Academy. The coins reappear each time, and there's a Trinket you can collect once, **Iris' Iris**.

Main Hall

When the Main Hall first opens after Know-It-All Island, there are more closed off areas than spots to visit. Auric's shop is available immediately, and he adds to his inventory throughout the adventure. Interact with the hot air balloon image near the fireplace to create a shortcut between the Main Hall and The Courtyard.

The first new area in the Main Hall appears after Chapter 3: Chompy Mountain. Mags has a slot machine-like device that spits out valuables. Brock opens the Rumble Club after Chapter 4: Phoenix Psanctuary, and Crossbones introduces Skaletone Showdown at the same time.

The Great Chimney

Inside the Main Hall, look for a switch near the fireplace. It opens the way to The Great Chimney. It's similar to the Courtyard Tower, where you can visit it once per trip to Skylanders Academy and it also has a Trinket, the **Big Bow of Boom**.

Upper Hallway

Opened after completing Chapter 6: Rainfish Riviera, the Upper Hallway doesn't have any attractions of its own, but houses the Hat Store and Game Room.

The Kitchen

The Kitchen appears off the Main Hall after the completion of Chef Zeppelin. Hit the floating dodecahedrons in the cauldron

with an attack from a Skylander of the proper element to destroy them. Destroy all the dodecahedrons to earn rewards. Each trip back from a Story chapter adds new elements to the cauldron. The Kitchen is also the location of Kaos' quest.

The Crystal Caverns

Opened by placing the Legendary Geode Key in the Kitchen, the Crystal Caverns are a special area only available to Mini-Skylanders.

Hat Store

Hatterson opens a store off the Upper Hallway. He has a quest for Hood Sickle, and once it's complete he offers a selection of Legacy Hats for sale. His inventory includes hats for sale in previous Skylanders adventures.

HAT STORE INVENTORY

Hats	Price	Effect
Fancy Hat	25	+2 Armor, +1 Speed
Cowboy Hat	25	+2 Critical Hit, +2 Armor
Plunger Head	25	+2 Critical Hit, +2 Elemental Power
Purple Fedora	25	+1 Speed, +2 Armor
Turban	25	+5 Armor
Biter Hat	25	+5 Critical Hit
Propeller Cap	100	+3 Speed
Coonskin Hat	100	+7 Critical Hit
Royal Crown	100	+10 Critical Hit
Mariachi Hat	100	+10 Armor
Archer Hat	100	+10 Critical Hit
Toy Solider Hat	100	+5 Critical Hit, +2 Speed
Pirate Hat	250	+20 Armor
Rocket Hat	250	+6 Speed
Traffic Cone Hat	250	+15 Critical Hit
Princess Hat	250	+3 Speed, +7 Elemental Power
Wabbit Ears	500	+5 Speed, +12 Armor
Unicorn Hat	500	+12 Critical Hit, +12 Armor
Firefighter Helmet	500	+8 Critical Hit
Future Hat	500	+10 Speed

WHO WANTS KAOS KAKE?

After you capture Kaos, take him to Blobbers in the kitchen. Blobbers wants Kaos' help in creating a competition-winning dish.

HATATROSPHE!

Hatterson wants to improve business at his Hat Store, and Hood Sickle is the perfect candidate to help him. Hood Sickle needs to destroy eight counterfeit hat machines in 10 minutes or less. Each machine has Troll guards that try their best to keep Hood Sickle from completing the task. Clear out the guards as quickly as you can, then use Hood Sickle's big swing to destroy the machines.

Skaletone Showdown

Skaletone Showdown is a rhythm game where you take on some of the most famous (and infamous) characters from all of Skylands. It's not just for Skylanders, either. Captured Villains can play, too!

Look for the Skaletone's frontman, Crossbones, in the Main Hall. The statues behind him represent the people trying to join the band. Complete additional Story chapters to unlock the full roster of showdown challengers.

Interact with a statue to begin a showdown against that character. You must select a difficulty. Higher difficulties offer more gold, but you need to be good to earn it.

There are three stages to a showdown. The first and last stages prompt you to press the proper button when it crosses into the gold box on the screen. Accuracy increases your score multiplier, so no missing means bigger scores. The middle stage is a freestyle jam. Mash buttons and shake the controls sticks as quickly as possible to fill the meter. Fill the meter to earn a medal.

Game Room

The Game Room opens after events in Chapter 6: Rainfish Riviera. Dreadbeard offers to play Skystones Smash inside. Jump on the nearby Element-based platforms with a matching Skylander to move up higher. Reach the top and claim your prize. After you collect the Legendary Rocket in Chapter 13: Future of Skylands, the Game Room has the portal to reach the Observatory.

Academy Defense Tower

Once you complete Chapter 7: Monster Marsh, a new area opens up off the Main Hall. Go past Mags and her slot machine to reach the Academy

Defense Tower. There are coins to collect in the area, a Trinket to find, and a Troll Radio for entertainment.

Outer Walkway

Go up the stairs near Crossbones to reach the Outer Walkway. The Outer Walkway connects the Main Hall to The Grand Library.

The Grand Library

The Grand Library opens after your visit to Mystic Mill. It has two hidden areas, which both contain Trinkets, to explore. One is The Archives. Look on the wall not far from the quick travel portal. The other secret location involves Quigley and a mini Skylander. The book in the upper right corner of the library brings up the Skylander collection menu.

Legendary Treasures

Use the Legendary Treasures you collected during Story chapters to decorate Skylanders Academy. Most Legendary Treasures are simple visual upgrades, but some do more than improve the Academy's visual appeal.

Treasure	Chapter Found	Where to Place it	Effect
Legendary Tribal Statue	CH 2: Know-It-All Island	Courtyard	Floating statue appears
Legendary Chompy Statue	CH 3: Chompy Mountain	Main Hall	Large statues appear
Legendary Golden Egg	CH 4: Phoenix Psanctuary	Main Hall	Attack it to open it up
Legendary Pepper	CH 5: Chef Zeppelin	Kitchen	Kitchen decoration
Legendary Bubble Fish	CH 6: Rainfish Riviera	Courtyard	Decoration near quick travel spots
Legendary Golden Frog	CH 7: Monster Marsh	Outer Walkway	Changes the look of the area
Legendary Cyclops Teddy Bear	CH 8: Telescope Towers	Courtyard	Floats between buildings
Legendary Saw Blade	CH 9: Mystic Mill	Main Hall	Wall decoration
Legendary Eel Plunger	CH 10: Secret Sewers of Supreme Stink	Outer Walkway	The Eel pops up from pools
Legendary Masterpieces	CH 11: Wilikin Workshop	Main Hall	Paintings appear over the fireplace
Legendary Clocktower	CH 12: Time Town	Persephone's Treehouse	Grandfather clock appears
Legendary Rocket	CH 13: The Future of Skylands	Game Room	Opens the Observatory
Legendary Mabu Parachute	CH 14: Operation: Troll Rocket Steal	Courtyard	It's raining Mabu
Legendary Geode Key	CH 15: Skyhighlands	Kitchen	Opens the Crystal Caverns
Legendary Golden Dragon Head	CH 16: The Golden Desert	Main Hall	Door decorations
Legendary Hippo Head	CH 17: Lair of the Golden Queen	Upper Hallway	New pillar base
Legendary Weird Robot	CH 18: The Utlimate Weapon	The Kitchen	A new kitchen helper
Legendary Windmill	Mirror of Mystery	Courtyard	Windmill appears
Legendary Flynn Statue	Nightmare Express	Upper Hallway	Statue of Flynn appears

The Archives

The Archives is a coin-filled room you can revisit one time for each trip to Skylanders Academy. There is also a Trinket to collect here.

The Reading Room

Speak with Quigley while a mini Skylander is on the *Traptanium Portal*. He sends your Skylander to The Reading Room. Here you can find **Stealth Elf's Gift**.

The Observatory

To get to the Observatory, you need to find the **Legendary Rocket** in The Future of Skylands. On your next trip to Skylanders Academy, go to the Game Room and place the **Legendary Treasure** to create a portal to the Observatory. The Observatory has a telescope you can use to observe the rocket orbiting a moon. If it looks familiar, you might remember it from the opening credits! You can find **Spyro's Shield** in the Observatory as well.

Skystones Smash

Skystones Smash is a new game played in Skylands. Almost every chapter during the adventure includes one or more Skystone players ready to challenge you to a card battle. Batterson teaches you the game during Chapter 5: Chef Zeppelin, but you meet the first Skystone player while battling The Gulper in Chapter 1: Soda Springs. When you defeat other Skystones Smash players, you earn an amount of gold based on how challenging the other player was.

Building Your Skystone Collection

There's only one way to get more Skystones, and that's to defeat the Villains listed at the beginning of each chapter of the adventure. Their portraits appear while the level is loading, and again on the Dares screen. After you defeat one of these Villains for the first time, whether you trap them or not, their Skystone is added to your collection.

New Skystone:
Eye Scream

Tips for Winning Skystone Smash

Don't use powerful Skystones when they're not necessary

A Skystone's "extra" attack value does not carry through to damage the player. If your opponent's Skystone with three attack hits a Skystone with 1 health, the two extra attack points go to waste. This is important to keep in mind when your Skystones are not as good as your opponent's. Your 1 Attack/1 Health Sheep Creep is just as effective at stopping the 3 Attack/1 Health Brawl and Chain as your own Brawl and Chain would be.

Save your Fireball Skystones until they can do maximum damage

Chef Pepper Jack and Wolfgang are the only characters who get to attack every Skystone your opponent has in play. Save Fireball for a time when it will hit multiple cards. You might even clear out the opponent's entire side and free all of your cards to hit the other player.

High attack/low health Skystones are good for one attack; make it count and don't think you've wasted the Skystone

Eye Five, Masker Mind, and Threatpack might only get one attack. Put that attack to good use by hitting the opponent directly, or taking down a powerful Skystone like Smoke Scream.

Special Ability Skystones

Some Skystones have a special ability that is activated when they are played. These abilities are the first action taken after the Skystones have been placed. So, for example, if you place Chef Pepper Jack, he immediately hits the opponent's Skystones for one damage. Each effect takes place only when the Skystone is placed. In subsequent rounds, it is treated as a regular Skystone.

Fireball

Damages every opponent Skystone currently in play. The number of fireballs on the Skystone indicate how much damage is done to each Skystone.

Chef Pepper Jack   **Wolfgang**

Heart Boost

Restores your health. With Heart Boost you can push your health above its original starting value (10). The number of hearts on the Skystone indicate how much health is restored.

Chompy Mage   **Golden Queen**

Lightning

Damages the other player directly. The number of lightning bolts on the stone indicates how much damage is done.

Dreamcatcher

Sheepify

Changes one of the other player's Skystones into a sheep with one health. The target is always the Skystone directly across from where you place the Sheepify Skystone, unless the slot is blank. Then it targets the opponent's most powerful Skystone.

Dr. Krankcase   **Kaos**

Skystones Checklist

Sheep Creep 1

Tussle Sprout 2

Broccoli Guy 3

Chill Bill 3

Chomp Chest 4

Chompy 4

Rage Mage 4

Buzzer Beak 1

Slobber Trap 1

Bruiser Cruiser 2

Cuckoo Clocker 2

Eye Scream 3

The Gulper 3

Bone Chompy 4

Fisticuffs 4

Lob Goblin 4

Pain-Yatta 4

Brawl and Chain

Shrednaught

Bomb Shell

Brawlrus

Grinnade

Mab Lobs

Scrap Shooter

Cross Crow

Grave Clobber

Krankenstein

Shield Shredder

Blaster-Tron

Eye Five

Masker Mind

Threatpack

Bad Juju

Hood Sickle

Trolling Thunder

Tae Kwon Crow

Smoke Scream

Kaos Doom Challenges

Overview

Welcome to Kaos' ultimate challenge! He has created a task so ridiculously difficult it will take an entire army of Skylanders to beat it. Well, at least that is what he is hoping. Kaos cursed the training simulator and each challenge gets progressively harder. These can be found to the left in the Main Menu or in the Academy at the status of Kaos. The statue shows the current waves completed in gold numbers.

There are 100 waves of enemies to survive and they are separated in to nine groups of Challenges. Each Challenge must be completed in order to unlock the next one. The reward for completing these is Kaos' treasure as well as Stars. There are a total of 50 Kaos Mode Stars to boost your Portal Master rank.

Survival Basics

Each minion unleashed by Kaos attempts to knock out the Skylander or to break open the locks on the Mystery Box of Doom. The status of the box is shown on the right side indicated by the green gauge. However, the goal is actually to survive and if the box is opened you wont fail the Challenge. Also, if a Skylander is knocked out it is possible to restart the challenge or simply continue with another Skylander.

When entering the Challenges it is important to have a wide selection of Skylanders to activate Towers as well as provide backup if one gets knocked out. A key factor in surviving the Challenges is to use the Towers to help defeat enemies. Also, conserve food for when it is really necessary. On higher difficulty settings enemies do more damage and food is a lot more scarce.

Challenge Phases

Each Wave consists of a Build Phase and "Combat Phase." Move a Skylander near a Tower Spot to build defenses against Kaos' army. When you are ready to start the Combat Phase use the wave switch that is held by the hovering robot. Note that each time you play a wave the enemy pattern is different. If all Towers survived that Combat Phase there is nothing to build and the Towers are upgraded. After completing all Waves in a challenge, Kaos' treasure is yours! Also, after the last wave of an area Persephone appears to upgrade any Skylanders. To proceed to the next challenge or quit the game, step onto the exit portal.

Towers

A specific Skylander or Villain of the same element as the Tower spot must be used to create a Tower, except for the few special spots that show elements of all types. Towers can be chosen from all elemental types and each Tower damages enemies with their own element attack. Several Tower spots are covered and may require a Trap Master to break the Traptainium Crystals or a Giant to lift a huge boulder.

Each time a tower survives a wave it is upgraded. Note that Towers are completely regenerated after each Wave. The upgrades are an important part of survival, as Towers get significantly more powerful as they are upgraded. Visually, The Tower changes when it is upgraded and a gold star is added to the base of the Tower. A Tower can be upgraded three times, then it gets a treasure bonus starting with +1 and ending with +5 each time after the fifth upgrade. If a Tower is destroyed it loses all of its upgrades.

Mystery Box of Doom

The Mystery Box of Doom does not have to survive the Wave to complete the Challenge. However, if it is opened a huge evil creature is unleashed. Once it is defeated, a new box appears for the next wave. The contents of the Mystery Box of Doom are random and it can contain any of following enemies:

So It Begins

Waves 1-3 (Tutorial)
Suggested Skylander Level: 1-5
Reward: ★★★
Enemies: Plant Warrior, Grinnade, Cuckoo Clocker

The first three waves are a tutorial, which illustrates how to play. Defeat the first group of Grinnades and Plant Warriors as they charge towards the Mystery Box of Doom. Create your first tower and start the second wave. Learn to work with the newly built Tower to defeat the same group of enemies.

During the next build phase, create a second tower and start wave three. Heavy enemies (Cuckoo Clockers) appear in this wave and it is important to intercept these tough enemies or they can quickly destroy a Tower. Stand near the tower it is attacking to protect it while using powerful attacks to work with the Tower to defeat the heavy foes.

Enfuego Rain Temple

Waves 4-10
Suggested Skylander level: 2-6
Reward: ★★★
Enemies: Cuckoo Clocker, Troll Warrior, Bomb Shell, Grinnade

From now on you must use a Skylander or Villain of the same elemental type to activate various Tower spots. There are three enemy doors and dealing with incoming foes revolves around monitoring where they emerge from the gates. Starting in Wave 5, pay attention to the warning about an incoming Chompie rain. Watch the ground for the red targets to avoid falling flaming Chompies.

Let the Towers deal with smaller foes and directly deal with the Cuckoo Clockers and Bomb Shells. The big birds are strong against Towers and should be attacked directly before they take one down. Bomb Shells launch projectiles that explode and continue to damage the area they hit. Lure these enemies away from the Towers if possible and make sure to fight near the Towers as much as possible to regenerate them.

Horrible Something Temple

Waves 11-20
Suggested Skylander level: 3-8
Reward: ★★★★
Enemies: Cuckoo Clocker, Troll Warrior, Eggsecutioner, Bomb Shell, Grinnade

Activate all the Tower spots and prepare for several traps. Wave 11 starts with fire that surrounds the Towers. Keep close to them but don't stand over the vents unless the Tower is in really bad shape. However, Fire Skylanders can actually be healed from these flames! Wave 12 introduces floor spikes that can pop up from time-to-time. To deal with these hazards stay on the cobbled stone section in the center of the area and use long-range attacks. Only travel outside this spot to deal with heavy enemies like the Cuckoo Clocker and Bomb Shells.

After a few waves the enemies start appearing from the sides as well as the front. Stay further back to keep an eye on the flow of enemies and alternate sides to deal with the largest threat. Upgraded Towers can deal with smaller foes but the Lob Goblins and heavy enemies should be tackled by the Skylanders. The traps shouldn't present too much trouble, but when the Chompy rain starts it can become chaotic.

Shift to each side depending which needs the most attention, and stick close to the Towers, However, be careful of the ring around the Towers that can be set ablaze.

Worst Nightmare Marsh

There are only two towers to support your efforts in this challenge and making sure they survive and upgrade is a pretty big priority. In Wave 22 tombstone traps appear and you must destroy them to get rid of the pesky bat clouds. The bats aren't a real threat but they are a big distraction, so smash the tombstones as soon as they appear. The initial enemies can be handled easily but the Ooglers are very fast and they can cause a lot of damage to the Towers if they aren't dealt with quickly. Their long range electric attack covers a lot of area but luckily they are not that tough to wipe out.

The real threats in this series are the heavy enemies such as the Pain-Yatta and Eye Five. The Eye Five travel in groups of two or three but they are relatively slow and should allow enough time to battle them personally. Don't let them get too close to the Towers or it falls quickly. On the other hand, The Pain-Yatta makes a dash for your Towers or Mystery Box of Doom. They usually arrive in pairs and they require using your Skylander directly. Try to get the attention of the heavy enemies and remain close to the Towers. Stay toward the back of the marsh to keep an eye on the Mystery Box of Doom and intercepts the Pain-Yatta to distract them from their target.

Twice Doomed Marsh

In the first build phase there is a boulder covering a Tower Spot. Only Giants can move the rock to create a Tower. The bat generating tombstones are back, along with a new trap called wicked water. The aptly named traps appear randomly in water and do a small amount of damage when touched. The first few waves are short but heavy enemies appear from the start and must be fought to save the Towers. Shield Shredders start to emerge and although they are small in stature they are very quick and can cut up Towers. They are not as resilient as the heavy enemies but you should wipe them out quickly to protect the Towers.

Stand towards the rear of the center island to survey the three enemy gates and stay out the water. Allow the Towers to do their job and deal with smaller enemies while you focus on the heavy damaging foes. The new heavy enemy in this challenge is the Brawl and Chain. It is similar to the Eye Five in that it moves pretty slowly but it does a ton of damage to Towers. A fully upgraded Tower should be able to withstand a Brawl and Chain, but in pairs they'll destroy a Tower in no time. Use the combined attack power of a Tower and a Skylander to bring down these tusked enemies.

Itchy Lilies Marsh

There are five Towers this time but don't think this will be an easy challenge. In fact, the two Towers near the enemy spawning points are difficult to protect. The same water and bat traps are back but, more importantly, the pace has significantly increased! Once again, stay in the center isle to engage the biggest threats emerging from the enemy gates. Speedy foes like Pain-Yatta, Oogler, and Shield Shredder can be tough to chase down before they overtake a Tower. Use attacks or traps that cover multiple areas to cope with enemies on all sides. For melee Skylanders, attack heavy enemies and after several hits switch to the next one to let the Towers finish them off.

The last several waves send out lots of heavy enemies at the same time. A small army of Eye Five or Brawl and Chain are tough to eliminate. They can wreck a Tower pretty quickly and tear through the Mystery Box of Doom in a few hits. Take on these large groups directly with the most damage attacks that hit a small cluster of enemies. Of course other enemies will try to attack as well, but don't become distracted by them.

Avoid chasing enemies around the entire area or spending too much time trying to save every Tower. Retreat to the back if necessary and try to keep the bad guys from getting to the Mystery Box of Doom.

Kaos Fury Docks

Waves 51-65

Suggested Skylander level: 15-18

Reward: ★★★★★★

Enemies: Cross Crow, Cuckoo Clocker, Shield Skeleton, Krankenstein, Grinnade, Grave Clobber, Scrap Shooter

Kaos Fury is a new gameplay element added to this challenge. The machine continues to build pressure until the meter is completely filled. If this happens, the area is covered in a dark mist and a new set of powerful enemies emerges from the gates. Activate the switch in the center of the machine to release pressure and drop the gauge all the way down. When Kaos Fury is trigged it continues into the next wave so make sure to hit the switch whenever there is a break in battle.

The battlefield is really small compared to the previous outdoor challenges. This means there is less running around but it also packs enemies in really close. The ideal place to stand your ground is between the two Towers, switching to whatever side needs assistance. There are a lot of heavy foes in this challenge and it adds two new ones, Krankenstein and Scrap Shooter. Soften up the big bad guys and switch to the next target while the Towers attempt to finish them off. Get the big enemies' attention and fight them head on even if it costs some HP. However, in the later waves there will probably be too many to hold off and it is better to let the Tower fall as a decoy.

Twisted Twister Docks

Waves 66-80

Suggested Skylander level: 17-20

Reward: ★★★★★★★

Enemies: Cross Crow, Cuckoo Clocker, Shield Skeleton, Krankenstein, Grinnade, Grave Clobber, Raven Warrior, Pain-Yatta

There are four Tower spots and one requires a Giant Skylander to move a boulder. The gauge on the Kaos Fury machine builds up a lot faster than the last challenge so use any break in the action to release the pressure. The best opportunity to do so is during a rush of small enemies that can be handled by the Towers. The new trap in this challenge is a twisted spinner that can whirl a Skylander around, immobilizing them for a short time. Every moment counts in the higher Waves and getting caught in the twister at the wrong time can be a big problem.

Stand guard in the center of the four Towers and fire off long-range attacks until enemies close in. Staying in the center allows you to change sides quickly to deal with enemies as well as regenerate any of the Towers. Big bad guys, especially Krankenstein, can take out a Tower pretty quickly and they often appear in groups of two or more. Weaken the heavy foes on one side and let the Towers finish them off while switching to the other side. Spending too long near any one Tower or on a single side probably means the others Towers are in jeopardy.

Finally Final Docks

Waves 81-100

Suggested Skylander level: 20

Reward: ★★★★★★★★★★ +

Enemies: Cross Crow, Cuckoo Clocker, Shield Skeleton, Krankenstein, Grinnade, Grave Clobber, Raven Warrior, Pain-Yatta, Brawlrus, Brawl and Chain, Scrap Shooter, Rocket Launchers

This area is a lot larger than the previous one, which means there is a lot more running around. Also due to its size and the armor/HP of the enemies it is tough to reach the switch to release the pressure on the Kaos Fury machine. Activate the switch anytime there is an absence of heavy foes, but that won't be very often. To further complicate matters, there are two twisters to contend with. Even with these traps, the best place to camp out is far back enough in the level to track enemies from all four gates.

Even with five Towers this challenge requires great time and resource management. Use your time effectively doing as much damage to a group as quickly as possible and switching to the next horde. Trying to fight and finish each foe leaves other areas vulnerable. Use the Skylander's powers to the best of their ability, firing off long range attacks or setting traps before enemies close in on the Towers. Piercing moves that go through enemies are great for groups that stay together in straight lines. Also use area effect attacks to weaken larger groups but switch to high damage single attacks for the heavy enemies.

Arena

Brock is back again and is excited about the Rumble Club that is filled with new Arena challenges. There are six brand new Arenas with four challenges each. All of the challenges have three stages and, as you would imagine, each stage and each Arena is progressively harder. As you complete a challenge, you unlock the next one in that set. However, to unlock Brock's Rumble Clubhouse you must first go to Auric's Store, after returning from Chapter 13: The Future of Skylands, and fund its construction for 1200 gold. To directly access the Arenas from the Main Menu, select the option on the right of the screen. They can also be found in game at the Academy by going through the double doors to the Main Hall and looking for Brock on the left.

Rewards

Beside the fun and pure challenge of the Arenas, there is a lot of incentive to go through the entire series. There are 30 Stars to earn and that can really raise your Portal Master level and earn you lots of rewards. The first three challenges earn one Star and the final one of each set is worth two Stars. There is also a decent amount of gold to earn, as shown in the following chart, as well as six powerful exclusive Hats. Last but not least, Arena Challenges are one of the best ways to level up a Skylander due to the quick and constant battles.

Arena Name	Match	Stage 1 Loot	Stage 2 Loot	Stage 3 Loot (first win)
Phoenix Nest	1	50	100	500
Phoenix Nest	2	50	100	600
Phoenix Nest	3	50	100	700
Phoenix Nest	4	50	100	1000 + Eggshell Hat
Dream Quake	1	100	150	800
Dream Quake	2	100	150	900
Dream Quake	3	100	150	1000
Dream Quake	4	100	150	1500 + Night Cap
Drain of Sorrows	1	100	150	1100
Drain of Sorrows	2	100	150	1200
Drain of Sorrows	3	100	150	1300
Drain of Sorrows	4	100	150	2000 + Candle Hat
Exhaust Junction	1	150	250	1500
Exhaust Junction	2	150	250	1700
Exhaust Junction	3	150	250	1900
Exhaust Junction	4	150	250	3000 + Planet Hat
Quicksand Coliseum	1	150	250	2500
Quicksand Coliseum	2	150	250	2700
Quicksand Coliseum	3	150	250	2900
Quicksand Coliseum	4	150	250	5000 + Pyramid Hat
Brock's Rumble Clubhouse	1	200	300	4000
Brock's Rumble Clubhouse	2	200	300	4500
Brock's Rumble Clubhouse	3	200	300	5000
Brock's Rumble Clubhouse	4	200	300	25000 + Wizard Hat (7000 second time)

Survival Tips

Each challenge has it's own set of rules along with unique trials. Here are some general guidelines that can help you get through the daunting task of trying to complete them all.

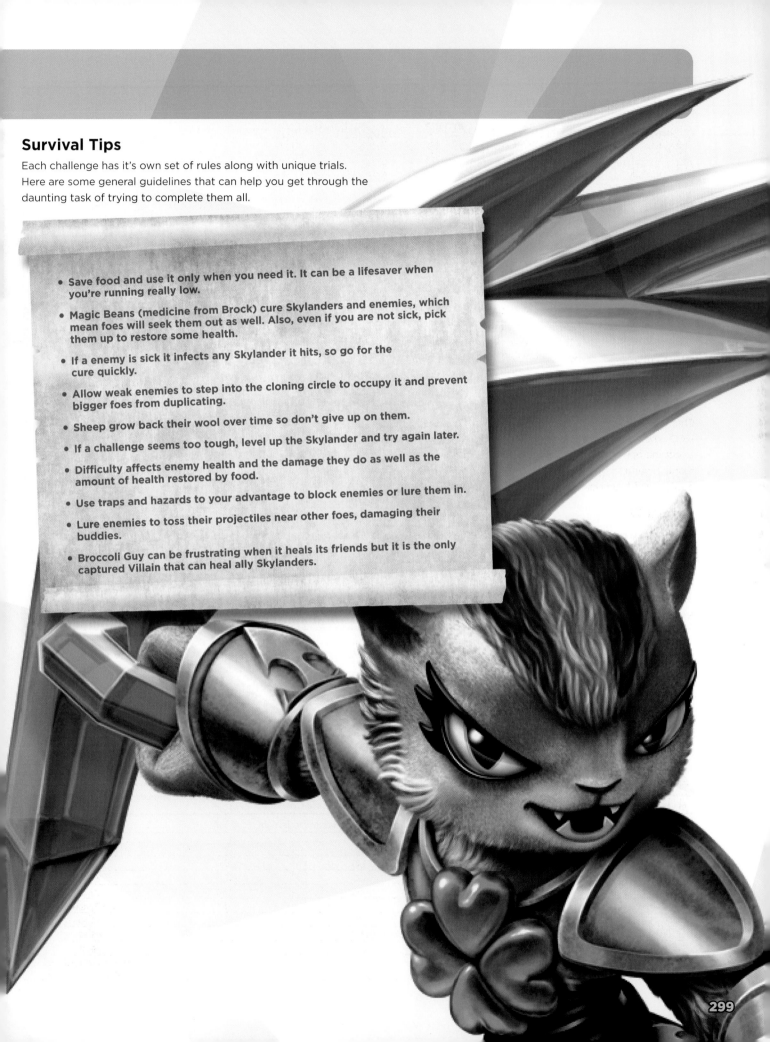

- Save food and use it only when you need it. It can be a lifesaver when you're running really low.

- Magic Beans (medicine from Brock) cure Skylanders and enemies, which mean foes will seek them out as well. Also, even if you are not sick, pick them up to restore some health.

- If a enemy is sick it infects any Skylander it hits, so go for the cure quickly.

- Allow weak enemies to step into the cloning circle to occupy it and prevent bigger foes from duplicating.

- Sheep grow back their wool over time so don't give up on them.

- If a challenge seems too tough, level up the Skylander and try again later.

- Difficulty affects enemy health and the damage they do as well as the amount of health restored by food.

- Use traps and hazards to your advantage to block enemies or lure them in.

- Lure enemies to toss their projectiles near other foes, damaging their buddies.

- Broccoli Guy can be frustrating when it heals its friends but it is the only captured Villain that can heal ally Skylanders.

Phoenix Nest

A huge nest is the perfect place for an arena challenge. However, there are three areas where pink baby birds can pop out and peck at anyone who gets close. The birds do very little damage but they can be really distracting. When they peek out they raise the platform above them, which provides a great vantage point to hit enemies below. Also the raised platforms can be used to hide behind to recover in the heat of battle.

Artillery Attack

Stage	Enemies	Reward
Stage 1	Tussle Sprout, Buzzer Beak, Plant Warrior, Chill Bill, Broccoli Guy, Slobber Trap, Lob Goblin, Bruiser Cruiser	50 Gold
Stage 2	Lob Goblin, Bruiser Cruiser, Chill Bill, Plant Warrior	100 Gold
Stage 3	Tussle Sprout, Chill Bill, Broccoli Guy, Lob Goblin, Bruiser Cruiser	500 Gold

The nest is under siege by pirates and bombs are falling from the sky. The bombs drop in a long straight pattern and the best way to avoid them is to stay on the move. Wipe out the freezing foes and bomb-tossing enemies first to reduce the amount of flying objects. Stay towards the center to see the incoming artillery (as red circles on the floor) and quickly move towards the nearest group of enemies attacking as you move. The exception is the charging Bruiser Cruiser that needs to be avoided and attacked from the side or rear.

Nest Ball

Stage	Enemies	Reward
Stage 1	Chompy, Troll Warrior, Eggsecutioner, Broccoli Guy, Lob Goblin, Chill Bill, Cuckoo Clocker	50 Gold
Stage 2	Chompy, Troll Warrior, Eggsecutioner, Broccoli Guy, Lob Goblin, Chill Bill, Shrednaught	100 Gold
Stage 3	Chompy, Troll Warrior, Eggsecutioner, Broccoli Guy, Lob Goblin, Chill Bill, Cuckoo Clocker, Shrednaught	600 Gold

Whoever is in possession of the magic football moves faster and does more damage. Try to keep possession of the ball as much as possible to gain a huge advantage. Any single hit causes a fumble and retrieving the ball is essential due to the boosts it provides to you or an enemy. Stand on one of the circular platforms and wait for the birds to pop up to get a lofty place to damage enemies below. Used range attacks as much as possible to avoid getting hit in order to hold on to the ball.

Birdy Bombs

Stage	Enemies	Reward
Stage 1	Chompy, Troll Warrior, Eggsecutioner, En Fuego Chompy, Buzzer Beak, Lob Goblin, Cuckoo Clocker, Chill Bill	50 Gold
Stage 2	Troll Warrior, Eggsecutioner, En Fuego Chompy, Buzzer Beak, Lob Goblin, Cuckoo Clocker	100 Gold
Stage 3	Troll Warrior, Eggsecutioner, Broccoli Guy, Lob Goblin, Chill Bill, Cuckoo Clocker, Shrednaught	700 Gold

All the enemies are carrying mines and when they are knocked out they drop the mine behind. Use a Skylander's long range attacks to wipe out enemies from afar and the mines fall where they are and assist in knocking out the survivors. When using melee attacks, apply a hit and run strategy. Knock out several at a time and back up out of the range of the bombs, allowing the explosives to hit other enemies that chase after you.

Perilous Perch Skirmish

Stage	Enemies	Reward
Stage 1	Chompy, Tussle Sprouts, Troll Warrior Melee, Eggsecutioner, Lob Goblin, Cuckoo Clocker, Chill Bill	50 Gold
Stage 2	Chompy, Tussle Sprouts, Troll Warrior Melee, Eggsecutioner, Lob Goblin, Cuckoo Clocker, Chill Bill, Broccoli Guy, Bruiser Cruiser	100 Gold
Stage 3	Chompy, Tussle Sprouts, Troll Warrior Melee, Eggsecutioner, Lob Goblin, Cuckoo Clocker, Chill Bill, Broccoli Guy, Bruiser Cruiser, Shrednaught	1000 Gold

The final challenge has elements of the previous levels. It starts out with falling bombs that keep you on the move. The next stage adds the magic football and keeping possession of the ball is the best way to get through the round quickly. Finally, the last stage adds mines from fallen enemies and the magic football is still in play. Hold onto the ball and try to use long-range attacks to create clusters of bombs that enemies have to travel through before they can reach you.

Dream Quake

This dreamscape is a floating cobblestone platform that separates into sections during the challenges. When the main section splits, it creates gaps that can be jumped by Skylanders, but it can also be used to separate enemies. Foes appear from the floating houses surrounding the main platform and in bubbles that float through the dreamscape. The space between sections is a great way to control the flow of enemies or to retreat to recoup. Also, keep in mind that falling does not cause any damage.

Monster Multiplier

Stage	Enemies	Reward
Stage 1	Chompy, Brawlrus, Cross Crow, Lob Goblin, Bruiser Cruiser	100 Gold
Stage 2	Chompy, Cross Crow, Lob Goblin, Brawl and Chain, Broccoli Guy	150 Gold
Stage 3	Chompy, Brawlrus, Cross Crow, Lob Goblin, Bruiser Cruiser, Brawl and Chain	800 Gold

The series of green rings marks a cloning spot that can duplicate enemies. This isn't too much of a problem for smaller foes but it can be a big issue if a really tough enemy starts to mass-produce. Stand near or on this spot to keep enemies away. This is especially true when the Brawl and Chain arrive since they are tough and take a while to defeat. Keep on eye on the clock and wipe out the enemies quickly or the time bomb will explode!

Flag, You're It

Stage	Enemies	Reward
Stage 1	En Fuego Chompy, Chill Bill, Lob Goblin, Cuckoo Clocker, Pirate Henchman	100 Gold
Stage 2	En Fuego Chompy, Lob Goblin, Broccoli Guy, Brawl and Chain, Pirate Henchman	150 Gold
Stage 3	En Fuego Chompy, Chill Bill, Lob Goblin, Cuckoo Clocker, Brawl and Chain, Broccoli Guy, Pirate Henchman	900 Gold

Stand near the flagpoles and raise your flag to send out a green damaging shockwave. However enemies can do the same thing and even take over your flagpoles. It's very difficult to take over and maintain more than one pole so pick one and camp out protecting it from enemies. Fire at foes while staying close to the flagpole and only leave if the area is overrun or to deal with long range bad guys like Lob Goblins or Chill Bills. Note that the shockwave from the opposite flagpole does not reach across to the other side of the platform.

Counting Sheep

Stage	Enemies	Reward
Stage 1	En Fuego Chompy, Plant Warrior, Oogler, Eye Five, Bomb Shell	100 Gold
Stage 2	En Fuego Chompy, Bomb Shell, Chill Bill, Plant Warrior, Oogler, Cuckoo Clocker	150 Gold
Stage 3	Plant Warrior, Chill Bill, Oogler, Eye Five, Bomb Shell, Cuckoo Clocker	1000 Gold

Nobody knows how the sheep made it into the Arena but you have to protect the flock. Be a good shepherd and stay close to the flock to prevent them from getting swarmed by smaller foes. Target the heavy damage enemies that use projectiles but always return to the flock. Be sure to stay close to the flock when you notice a powerful foe like the Eye Five. When a sheep takes damage its white skin is exposed, indicating it has little health left. Try to protect all three sheep but note that, to succeed, only one needs to make it through the challenge.

Bad Dream Brawl

Stage	Enemies	Reward
Stage 1	Brawlrus, Eye Scream Cuddles, Broccoli Guy, Bomb Shell, Bruiser Cruiser, Eye Scream	100 Gold
Stage 2	Brawlrus, Lob Goblin, Cuddles, Broccoli Guy, Bruiser Cruiser, Slobber Trap	150 Gold
Stage 3	Bomb Shell, Lob Goblin, Broccoli Guy, Cuddles, Eye Scream, Bruiser Cruiser, Brawl and Chain	1500 Gold

This challenge kicks off with the Super Damage Football. Quickly grab the ball and use its power boost to hunt down the enemies. The next stage adds three flagpoles and it gets hectic to try to maintain one. If you can't hold one, keep moving and jump the red shockwaves when they get close. The final stage adds the cloning circle and time bomb. Try to keep the big enemies out of the cloning circle and clear out the Broccoli Guys that keep helping their allies.

Drain of Sorrows

Brock booted the fishy owner and took over the endless good pond. Combat takes place on a raft that is floating on a toxic pool. Many of the enemies are sick and if they touch your Skylander it becomes ill as well. Brook throws out medicine from time-to-time and it is essential to cure your sickness or your health steadily drops. Watch out for the giant slug that coats a large section in green slime. Standing in those poison trails reduces your health but can also damage enemies and be used to lure them to their doom. The slime trails do not make anyone sick.

Germ Wars

Stage	Enemies	Reward
Stage 1	En Fuego Chompy, Cross Crow, Oogler, Broccoli Guy	100 Gold
Stage 2	En Fuego Chompy, Cross Crow, Lob Goblin, Oogler, Broccoli Guy, Krankenstein	150 Gold
Stage 3	En Fuego Chompy, Cross Crow, Lob Goblin, Oogler, Broccoli Guy, Krankenstein	1100 Gold

Getting sick from an enemy is not the end of the world but walking into the large slime trails can compound the problem. Once the raft is slimed, stay away from the green goo and let the enemies come to you. The big threat in this challenge is Krankenstein. It has a very long sweeping attack that can hit and make you sick if it touches you. The big damage from this foe and its long reach make it very hard to deal with if you get stuck in a corner. Attack it from long range and keep your distance even if it means treading through some slime.

Sheep Flush

Stage	Enemies	Reward
Stage 1	Troll Warrior, Evilikin Cannon, Shield Shredder, Bomb Shell, Masker Mind	100 Gold
Stage 2	Troll Warrior Melee, Evilikin Cannon, Chompy, Brawlrus, Bomb Shell, Shield Shredder, Masker Mind	150 Gold
Stage 3	Troll Warrior Melee, Evilikin Cannon, Shrednaught, Masker Mind, Brawlrus, Bomb Shell	1200 Gold

Three silly sheep made there way down to this goo pond and they must be protected. Fortutnely they are smart enough not to wander into the sickening streaks. The challenge becomes increasingly difficult when the slime trails start closing off large sections of the raft. Stay by the sheep and draw their attention. Also chase down the long-range foes to stop their bombardment. Hold your ground against the Shrednaught, even if it cost HP, to avoid letting it deal a ton of damage to the helpless sheep.

Sewer-Ball

Stage	Enemies	Reward
Stage 1	Grinnade, Cuddles, Fisticuffs, Chill Bill, Slobber Trap	100 Gold
Stage 2	Grinnade, Fisticuffs, Bomb Shell, Slobber Trap, Broccoli Guy, Brawl and Chain	150 Gold
Stage 3	Cuddles, Bomb Shell, Fisticuffs, Broccoli Guy, Slobber Trap, Chill Bill, Brawl and Chain	1300 Gold

This is a combined challenge that has a cloning ring and the magic football. Keep possession of the ball to grant extra speed to chase after foes trying to create a clone and to dodge bombs from the Bomb Shells. Also, the extra damage from the football adds a lot of power for long range attacks. Lure enemies into the slime while using long range attacks. However close in on the Fisticuffs to prevent them from using their extended reach.

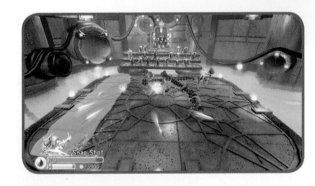

Slime Time Tournament

Stage	Enemies	Reward
Stage 1	Pirate Henchman, Lob Goblin, Eye Scream, Evilikin Cannon, Broccoli Guy	100 Gold
Stage 2	Lob Goblin, Cuckoo Clocker, Pain-Yatta, Evilikin Cannon	150 Gold
Stage 3	Lob Goblin, Evilikin Cannon, Cuckoo Clocker, Eye Scream, Broccoli Guy, Pain-Yatta	2000 Gold

Enemies carry mines and drop them when defeated. This becomes a problem when your mobility is restricted by slime trails and there are big foes like the Pain-Yattas. Try to lure foes into the slime and use hit and run tactics. The last stage adds flagpoles and Super Damage Football. Hold on to the ball as long as possible and try to take over one flag pole to gain the damage boost while preventing the enemies from controlling the entire raft.

Exhaust Junction

The Trolls have been kicked out but their rocket remains and Brock thinks he knows how to operate it. Unfortunately, as he fiddles with the controls the exhaust from the rocket shoots fire through any of the four chutes below. Needless to say, the large walls of fire must be avoided and your best bet is to keep an eye on the floor to lookout for the arrow pattern. The yellow arrows mark the lanes that will soon be filled with a column of fire. Stand between them to lure enemies to their doom. There is also a ledge on the far left where enemies can hide.

You're MINE

Stage	Enemies	Reward
Stage 1	Buzz Beak, Plant Warrior, Oogler, Blaster-Tron	150 Gold
Stage 2	Plant Warrior, Raven Lobber, Buzz Beak, Hood Sickle, Broccoli Guy, Oogler	250 Gold
Stage 3	Plant Warrior, Raven Lobber, Blaster-Tron, Broccoli Guy, Oogler, Hood Sickle, Buzz Beak	1500 Gold

A cloning spell and mine carrying enemies make this challenge tricky. Try to keep the big bad guys like the Blaster-Trons out of the cloning ring and let the smaller foes occupy it. Stay in the safe lanes and use long-range attack to let enemies wander through the fire and trip on mines dropped by their fallen comrades. The Blaster-Trons are the biggest problem due to their shields and projectiles. Circle around back to attack them but stay clear of the fire lanes.

Artillery 2: With a Vengeance

Stage	Enemies	Reward
Stage 1	Pirate Henchman, Evilikin Cannon, Shield Shredder, Bomb Shell, Pain-Yatta	150 Gold
Stage 2	Pirate Henchman, Cross Crow, Scrap Shooter, Bomb Shell, Shield Shredder, Evilikin Cannon, Mega Chompy	250 Gold
Stage 3	Pirate Henchman, Bomb Shell, Shield Shredder, Evilikin Cannon, Cross Crow, Scrap Shooter	1700 Gold

Pirate artillery rains down, making it really hazardous to maneuver. The arena can quickly become cluttered with barrels, bombs, and arrows. Use long range attacks while in a safe lane but it wont be possible or practical to just sit still. When there is a break in the flames, wipe out the big bad guys with your most powerful attacks to clear the arena and reduce the amount of projectiles to dodge. Also, look out for lurking foes on the far left ledge.

Don't Get Hit

Stage	Enemies	Reward
Stage 1	En Fuego Chompy, Pirate Henchman, Oogler, Pain-Yatta	150 Gold
Stage 2	En Fuego Chompy, Bomb Shell, Pirate Henchman, Oogler, Pain-Yatta, Raven Lobber	250 Gold
Stage 3	Pirate Henchman, Oogler, Grinnade, Shreadnaught, Bomb Shell, Pain-Yatta	1900 Gold

This is a true test of skill as Brock reduces your health to 1. It's really tough not to get hit but grabbing a Shield power-up provides one hit protection. Ignore the food and try to use long-range attacks to avoid too much direct contact. The big bad guys are a problem but can be dealt with using hit and run tactics. The Bomb Shells and rocket launchers are your worst enemies and should be wiped out quickly to prevent your tripping on their explosives.

Flaming Flag Finale

Stage	Enemies	Reward
Stage 1	Chompy, Bad Juju, Cross Crow, Fisticuffs, Goo Chompy	150 Gold
Stage 2	Chompy, Bad Juju, Cross Crow, Fisticuffs, Goo Chompy	250 Gold
Stage 3	Chompy, Goo Chompy, Cross Crow, Fisticuffs, Bomb Shell, Scrap Shooter	3000 Gold

Start out by taking over the center spot and raise the flag. The second stage adds pirate artillery and it becomes increasingly hard to protect the flagpole. Finally, you are reduced to 1 HP in the last stage. It is really tough not to get hit and the Shield power-up is critical. If it gets too hard to hold the flag pole, move down the center lane and remember that dropping of the edge does not cause damage even at 1 HP. Look out for the Goo Chompies that leave a deadly pool behind!

Quicksand Coliseum

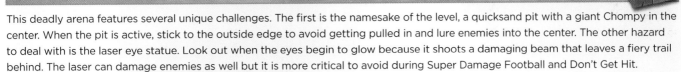

This deadly arena features several unique challenges. The first is the namesake of the level, a quicksand pit with a giant Chompy in the center. When the pit is active, stick to the outside edge to avoid getting pulled in and lure enemies into the center. The other hazard to deal with is the laser eye statue. Look out when the eyes begin to glow because it shoots a damaging beam that leaves a fiery trail behind. The laser can damage enemies as well but it is more critical to avoid during Super Damage Football and Don't Get Hit.

MightyBall Bombardment

Stage	Enemies	Reward
Stage 1	Bone Chompy, Plant Warrior, Tussle Sprout, Lob Goblin, Hood Sickle	150 Gold
Stage 2	Bone Chompy, Lob Goblin, Tussle Sprout, Broccoli Guy, Eye Five	250 Gold
Stage 3	Bone Chompy, Tussle Sprout Hood Sickle, Shield Skeleton, Eye Five, Broccoli Guy, Blaster-Tron	2500 Gold

Combine pirate cannonballs with Super Damage Football and you've got an intense challenge. Grab the ball and stay on the move to dodge falling bombs and enemy attacks. Staying on the move helps you avoid the teleporting Hood Sickles as well. Run around the outer edge to stay away from the giant Chompy in the center and use hit and run tactics. The extra speed and damage from the football should allow you to dominate enemies but be careful of Eye Five and tons of bombs from the Lob Goblins.

Multiplication Fever

Stage	Enemies	Reward
Stage 1	Brawlrus, Pirate Chompy, Pirate Henchman, Slobber Trap	150 Gold
Stage 2	Pirate Chompy, Evilikin Cannon, Slobber Trap, Broccoli Guy, Eye Five	250 Gold
Stage 3	Brawlrus, Evilikin Cannon, Broccoli Guy, Pirate Henchman, Tussle Sprout, Eye Five, Slobber Trap	2700 Gold

The big Chompy in the center appears a lot in this challenge so stay close to the outside of the arena. Enemies are sick and eager to pass along their disease. Avoid them as much as possible by using long range attacks and if you get sick quickly chase down some medicine from Brock. As you run around fighting and fleeing the sick foes, keep an eye on the cloning circle. Don't worry about smaller foes occupying the ring but it can be a big problem if Eye Fives cluster around it. Immediately chase them down and wipe they out before you are overrun by a horde of them.

Flames and Flags Forever

Stage	Enemies	Reward
Stage 1	En Feugo Chompy, Shield Skeleton, Lob Goblin, Scrap Shooter	150 Gold
Stage 2	En Feugo Chompy, Shield Skeleton, Bad Juju, Scrap Shooter. Lob Goblin, Blaster-Tron	250 Gold
Stage 3	Transformed Barrel, Shield Skeleton, Scrap Shooter, En Feugo Chompy, Lob Goblin, Bad Juju, Blaster Tron	2900 Gold

Each stage increases the number of flagpoles. It's possible to secure one flag but don't expect to be able to secure two or three. There are far too many tough enemies to stay in one spot and the barrels and bombs flying around ensure you have to keep on the move. Watch the ground to jump the red shockwaves and focus on taking out the enemies camping by the poles. Try to stand your ground and attempt to take over one flag or go to the back of the area to get a better view of all the foes and upcoming shockwaves.

Scorched Sand Showdown

Stage	Enemies	Reward
Stage 1	Bone Chompy, Shield Skeleton, Oogler, Lob Goblin, Grave Clobber	150 Gold
Stage 2	Bone Chompy, Shield Skeleton, Pain-Yatta, Oogler, Lob Goblin	250 Gold
Stage 3	Bone Chompy, Oogler, Lob Goblin, Shield Skeleton, Eye Five, Grave Clobber, Pain-Yatta, Rage Mage	5000 Gold

This challenge starts with a time bomb and enemy mines. Take on the enemies quickly, even if it means losing some health, to avoid setting off the bomb and failing the challenge. Stage two has a cloning spell with the quicksand Chompy. Stick to the outer rim and keep the Pain-Yatta out of the cloning circle! Stage three is a one-touch challenge so don't get hit! Grab the Shield power to gain an extra hit. This is very tough and the only way to get through it is to hit and run while avoiding enemies' attacks and the laser eye statue.

Brock's Rumble Clubhouse

Welcome to Brock's state of the art arena. This round ring has pinball bumpers, lasers, cannonballs, and lots and lots of fire! The outer perimeter lights on fire to keep Skylanders from trying to run from the action. However, the real threats are the flamethrower and laser turrets that pop up from the square floor panels. These can be pointed in any direction so pay close attention and use them to lure enemies to their doom. The enemies and traps are the toughest in the series; enter this arena with a fully upgraded Skylander that has leveled up a lot!

The Flame Game

Stage	Enemies	Reward
Stage 1	En Fuego Chompy, Raven, Evilikin Cannon, Bomb Shell, Trolling Thunder	200 Gold
Stage 2	En Fuego Chompy, Raven, Evilikin Cannon, Threatpack, Scrap Shooter, Trolling Thunder, Smoke Scream	300 Gold
Stage 3	En Fuego Chompy, Raven, Transformed Barrel, Bomb Shell, Evilikin Cannon, Threatpack, Trolling Thunder, Scrap Shooter, Raven Lobber, Smoke Scream	4000 Gold

Watch the flamethrowers when they appear and move to a favorable position before the enemies arrive. If they flames point outward take over the center of the arena and if they aim in at each other go to a safe edge avoiding the outmost ring. The flames cut off a lot of the battleground, which makes it difficult to maneuver. Use long range attacks and lure enemies into the flames. If there is nowhere to run, charge in and try to take out projectile foes fast.

Combusti-Ball

Stage	Enemies	Reward
Stage 1	Chill Bill, Threatpack, Cuddles, Eye Scream, Grave Clobber, Shield Shredder, Eye Hive, Broccoli Guy, Chompy	200 Gold
Stage 2	Raven Lobber, Chompy, Shield Shredder, Chill Bill, Cuddles, Grave Clobber, Broccoli Guy, Threatpack, Cyclops Dragon	300 Gold
Stage 3	Cuckoo Clocker, Cross Crow, Chompy, Shield Shredder, Grave Clobber, Broccoli Guy, Eye Scream, Eye Hive, Threatpack, Cyclops Dragon	4500 Gold

Pinball bumpers seem like a harmless hazard but with all the projectiles flying around they add a ricochet effect that makes the arena filled with mayhem. The outer ring is safe in this challenge so use it to hide behind the bumpers and circle around to take out the long-range foes first. The big bumpers can be used as limited protection and they can very useful to dodge attacks especially from the dangerous and resilient Cyclops Dragon.

Laser Invader

Stage	Enemies	Reward
Stage 1	Buzzer Beak, Grinnade, Cuddles, Lob Goblin, Brawl and Chain, Pirate Chompy, Tae Kwon Crow	200 Gold
Stage 2	Grinnade, Lob Goblin, Shreadnaught, Oogler, Eye Five, Bomb Shell, Grave Clobber, Pirate Chompy	300 Gold
Stage 3	Cuddles Cuckoo Clocker, Buzzer Beak, Pain-Yatta, Oogler, Grinnade, Cyclops Dragon	5000 Gold

Rotating laser turrets can be an ally or a real burning pain! The key to dealing with the lasers is to follow the patter and move with them, jumping only when necessary. This should allow you to avoid getting hit while the beams cut up the enemies. It is tricky to shoot and run/jump and often it is best to wait for an opening to attack the bad guys. Many of the foes in this challenge are tough, so don't expect to take them out too quickly. Let the lasers soften them up and then finish them off.

A Fight to Remember

Stage	Enemies	Reward
Stage 1	Chompy, Shield Skeleton, Eggesecutioner, Mega Chompy, Evilikin Spinner, Bruiser Cruiser, Cuckoo Clocker, Scrap Shooter, Transformed Barrel, Chomp Chest, Sheep Creep	200 Gold
Stage 2	Evilikin Spinner, Chompy, Raven Lobber, Eggesecutioner, Bad Juju, Trolling Thunder, Shield Skeleton, Bruiser Cruiser, Transformed Barrel, Cuckoo Clocker, Cyclops Dragon, Chomp Chest, Sheep Creep	300 Gold
Stage 3	Chompy, Bad Juju, Mega Chompy, Raven Lobber, Transformed Barrel, Trolling Thunder, Scrap Shooter, Cuckoo Clocker, Bruiser Cruiser, Sheep Creep, Cyclops Dragon, Chomp Chest	25000 Gold

This challenge has it all; fire ring, pinball bumpers, flamethrowers, lasers, etc. It also showcases just about every foe you've battled before. Each stage is long and filled with a wide array of enemies. No single trick or tactic will work, you have to check out the traps and adjust your game plan when they change. Stay calm and use the same techniques from the previous challenges to use the traps to your advantage. Remember these are long battles so save food for when it is really needed.

Hats & Trinkets

Skylanders can wear one Hat and one Trinket at the same time. Hats convey positive statistical effects while they're worn. Trinkets are purely cosmetic. To change your Skylanders Hat and Trinket, select the Outfit option from the Skylanders overview screen. Villains can also get in on the fun by wearing Hats and Trinkets as well.

Hats

There are 99 hats to collect. Most Hats are found in one of the Story Mode Chapters, hidden behind *Traptanium* Gates, or given as a reward after completing a Villain Quest. Others become available for purchase from Auric, in the Main Hall of Skylander Academy, or from Hatterson in The Hat Store after completing Hood Sickle's quest.

Hats

Hats from Story Mode

 ALARM CLOCK HAT
CH 12: Time Town

MAXIMUM HEALTH	0
SPEED	4
ARMOR	10
CRITICAL HIT	0
CRITICAL HIT MP	0
ELEMENTAL POWER	0

 BATTER UP HAT
CH 16: The Golden Desert

MAXIMUM HEALTH	0
SPEED	0
ARMOR	12
CRITICAL HIT	15
CRITICAL HIT MP	0
ELEMENTAL POWER	0

 BEETLE HAT
CH 17: Lair of the Golden Queen

MAXIMUM HEALTH	0
SPEED	0
ARMOR	30
CRITICAL HIT	0
CRITICAL HIT MP	0
ELEMENTAL POWER	0

 **BRAIN HAT**
Mystery Gate

MAXIMUM HEALTH	?
SPEED	?
ARMOR	?
CRITICAL HIT	?
CRITICAL HIT MP	?
ELEMENTAL POWER	?

BRAINIAC HAT
CH 18: The Utlimate Weapon

MAXIMUM HEALTH	0
SPEED	6
ARMOR	0
CRITICAL HIT	15
CRITICAL HIT MP	0
ELEMENTAL POWER	0

 BRONZE ARKEYAN HELM
Beat Game on Easy Difficulty

MAXIMUM HEALTH	0
SPEED	4
ARMOR	15
CRITICAL HIT	25
CRITICAL HIT MP	0
ELEMENTAL POWER	0

 BUCKET HAT
CH 1: Soda Springs

MAXIMUM HEALTH	0
SPEED	0
ARMOR	5
CRITICAL HIT	0
CRITICAL HIT MP	0
ELEMENTAL POWER	0

 CARNIVAL HAT
AP: Mirror Of Mystery

MAXIMUM HEALTH	0
SPEED	4
ARMOR	0
CRITICAL HIT	10
CRITICAL HIT MP	0
ELEMENTAL POWER	0

CEILING FAN HAT
CH 4: The Phoenix Psanctuary

Stat	Value
MAXIMUM HEALTH	0
SPEED	0
ARMOR	5
CRITICAL HIT	5
CRITICAL HIT MP	0
ELEMENTAL POWER	0

CLOWN BOWLER HAT
CH 11: Wilikin Workshop

Stat	Value
MAXIMUM HEALTH	0
SPEED	0
ARMOR	0
CRITICAL HIT	20
CRITICAL HIT MP	0
ELEMENTAL POWER	0

CLOWN HAT
Mystery Gate

Stat	Value
MAXIMUM HEALTH	?
SPEED	?
ARMOR	?
CRITICAL HIT	?
CRITICAL HIT MP	?
ELEMENTAL POWER	?

COCONUT HAT
AP: Nightmare Express

Stat	Value
MAXIMUM HEALTH	0
SPEED	3
ARMOR	20
CRITICAL HIT	0
CRITICAL HIT MP	0
ELEMENTAL POWER	0

COLANDER HAT
CH 5: Chef Zeppelin

Stat	Value
MAXIMUM HEALTH	0
SPEED	0
ARMOR	10
CRITICAL HIT	0
CRITICAL HIT MP	0
ELEMENTAL POWER	0

CORNUCOPIA HAT
AP: Mirror Of Mystery

Stat	Value
MAXIMUM HEALTH	0
SPEED	2
ARMOR	0
CRITICAL HIT	0
CRITICAL HIT MP	0
ELEMENTAL POWER	15

CRAZY LIGHT BULB HAT
CH 17: Lair of the Golden Queen

Stat	Value
MAXIMUM HEALTH	0
SPEED	12
ARMOR	0
CRITICAL HIT	0
CRITICAL HIT MP	0
ELEMENTAL POWER	0

CUBANO HAT
CH 14: Operation: Troll Rocket Steal

Stat	Value
MAXIMUM HEALTH	0
SPEED	7
ARMOR	0
CRITICAL HIT	0
CRITICAL HIT MP	0
ELEMENTAL POWER	7

CYCLING HAT
AP: Nightmare Express

Stat	Value
MAXIMUM HEALTH	0
SPEED	8
ARMOR	0
CRITICAL HIT	0
CRITICAL HIT MP	0
ELEMENTAL POWER	7

DAISY CROWN
CH 4: The Phoenix Psanctuary

Stat	Value
MAXIMUM HEALTH	0
SPEED	2
ARMOR	0
CRITICAL HIT	5
CRITICAL HIT MP	0
ELEMENTAL POWER	0

DESERT CROWN HAT
CH 16: The Golden Desert

Stat	Value
MAXIMUM HEALTH	0
SPEED	0
ARMOR	0
CRITICAL HIT	0
CRITICAL HIT MP	0
ELEMENTAL POWER	27

DRAGON SKULL HAT
CH 7: Monster Marsh

Stat	Value
MAXIMUM HEALTH	0
SPEED	0
ARMOR	10
CRITICAL HIT	5
CRITICAL HIT MP	0
ELEMENTAL POWER	0

EXTREME VIKING HAT
CH 13: The Future of Skylands

Stat	Value
MAXIMUM HEALTH	0
SPEED	0
ARMOR	0
CRITICAL HIT	15
CRITICAL HIT MP	0
ELEMENTAL POWER	10

GARRISON HAT
CH 9: Mystic Mill

Stat	Value
MAXIMUM HEALTH	0
SPEED	0
ARMOR	20
CRITICAL HIT	0
CRITICAL HIT MP	0
ELEMENTAL POWER	0

GOLD ARKEYAN HELM
Beat Game on Hard Difficulty

Stat	Value
MAXIMUM HEALTH	0
SPEED	8
ARMOR	20
CRITICAL HIT	37
CRITICAL HIT MP	0
ELEMENTAL POWER	0

GONDOLIER HAT
AP: Mirror Of Mystery

Stat	Value
MAXIMUM HEALTH	0
SPEED	0
ARMOR	5
CRITICAL HIT	0
CRITICAL HIT MP	0
ELEMENTAL POWER	10

HEDGEHOG HAT
CH 2: Know-It-All Island

Stat	Value
MAXIMUM HEALTH	0
SPEED	2
ARMOR	0
CRITICAL HIT	0
CRITICAL HIT MP	0
ELEMENTAL POWER	2

HORNS BE WITH YOU
CH 3: Chompy Mountain

Stat	Value
MAXIMUM HEALTH	0
SPEED	0
ARMOR	0
CRITICAL HIT	0
CRITICAL HIT MP	0
ELEMENTAL POWER	7

HUNTING HAT
CH 3: Chompy Mountain

Stat	Value
MAXIMUM HEALTH	0
SPEED	0
ARMOR	2
CRITICAL HIT	2
CRITICAL HIT MP	0
ELEMENTAL POWER	0

IMPERIAL HAT
CH 6: Rainfish Riviera

Stat	Value
MAXIMUM HEALTH	0
SPEED	2
ARMOR	7
CRITICAL HIT	0
CRITICAL HIT MP	0
ELEMENTAL POWER	0

JUICER HAT
Mystery Gate

Stat	Value
MAXIMUM HEALTH	?
SPEED	?
ARMOR	?
CRITICAL HIT	?
CRITICAL HIT MP	?
ELEMENTAL POWER	?

KEPI HAT
CH 14: Operation: Troll Rocket Steal

Stat	Value
MAXIMUM HEALTH	0
SPEED	2
ARMOR	0
CRITICAL HIT	25
CRITICAL HIT MP	0
ELEMENTAL POWER	0

KOKOSHNIK
Mystery Gate

Stat	Value
MAXIMUM HEALTH	?
SPEED	?
ARMOR	?
CRITICAL HIT	?
CRITICAL HIT MP	?
ELEMENTAL POWER	?

LIL' ELF HAT
CH 11: Wilikin Workshop

Stat	Value
MAXIMUM HEALTH	0
SPEED	8
ARMOR	0
CRITICAL HIT	0
CRITICAL HIT MP	0
ELEMENTAL POWER	0

MABU MEDIC HAT
AP: Nightmare Express

MAXIMUM HEALTH	0
SPEED	0
ARMOR	**22**
CRITICAL HIT	0
CRITICAL HIT MP	0
ELEMENTAL POWER	0

MELON HAT
CH 1: Soda Springs

MAXIMUM HEALTH	0
SPEED	0
ARMOR	0
CRITICAL HIT	0
CRITICAL HIT MP	0
ELEMENTAL POWER	**5**

METAL FIN HAT
CH 6: Rainfish Riviera

MAXIMUM HEALTH	0
SPEED	0
ARMOR	0
CRITICAL HIT	**12**
CRITICAL HIT MP	0
ELEMENTAL POWER	0

MOUNTIE HAT
CH 9: Mystic Mill

MAXIMUM HEALTH	0
SPEED	0
ARMOR	**15**
CRITICAL HIT	0
CRITICAL HIT MP	0
ELEMENTAL POWER	0

NURSE HAT
CH 14: Operation: Troll Rocket Steal

MAXIMUM HEALTH	0
SPEED	0
ARMOR	**30**
CRITICAL HIT	0
CRITICAL HIT MP	0
ELEMENTAL POWER	0

OLD-TIME MOVIE HAT
CH 8: Telescope Towers

MAXIMUM HEALTH	0
SPEED	0
ARMOR	0
CRITICAL HIT	0
CRITICAL HIT MP	0
ELEMENTAL POWER	**15**

OUTBACK HAT
AP: Nightmare Express

MAXIMUM HEALTH	0
SPEED	**6**
ARMOR	0
CRITICAL HIT	0
CRITICAL HIT MP	0
ELEMENTAL POWER	0

PAPERBOY HAT
CH 3: Chompy Mountain

MAXIMUM HEALTH	0
SPEED	**4**
ARMOR	0
CRITICAL HIT	0
CRITICAL HIT MP	0
ELEMENTAL POWER	0

PARROT NEST
CH 4: The Phoenix Psanctuary

MAXIMUM HEALTH	0
SPEED	**7**
ARMOR	0
CRITICAL HIT	0
CRITICAL HIT MP	0
ELEMENTAL POWER	0

POT HAT
CH 17: Lair of the Golden Queen

MAXIMUM HEALTH	0
SPEED	0
ARMOR	**30**
CRITICAL HIT	0
CRITICAL HIT MP	0
ELEMENTAL POWER	0

RADAR DISH HAT
CH 15: Skyhighlands

MAXIMUM HEALTH	0
SPEED	0
ARMOR	**15**
CRITICAL HIT	**5**
CRITICAL HIT MP	0
ELEMENTAL POWER	0

RUBBER GLOVE HAT
CH 10: Secret Sewers of Supreme Stink

MAXIMUM HEALTH	0
SPEED	0
ARMOR	**12**
CRITICAL HIT	**12**
CRITICAL HIT MP	0
ELEMENTAL POWER	0

RUGBY HAT
CH 8: Telescope Towers

MAXIMUM HEALTH	0
SPEED	**3**
ARMOR	0
CRITICAL HIT	**7**
CRITICAL HIT MP	0
ELEMENTAL POWER	0

SCOOTER HAT
CH 5: Chef Zeppelin

MAXIMUM HEALTH	0
SPEED	0
ARMOR	0
CRITICAL HIT	0
CRITICAL HIT MP	0
ELEMENTAL POWER	**10**

SHADOW GHOST HAT
Mystery Gate

MAXIMUM HEALTH	?
SPEED	?
ARMOR	?
CRITICAL HIT	?
CRITICAL HIT MP	?
ELEMENTAL POWER	?

SHOWER CAP
CH 10: Secret Sewers of Supreme Stink

MAXIMUM HEALTH	0
SPEED	**6**
ARMOR	0
CRITICAL HIT	0
CRITICAL HIT MP	0
ELEMENTAL POWER	0

SILVER ARKEYAN HELM
Beat Game on Medium Difficulty

MAXIMUM HEALTH	0
SPEED	**6**
ARMOR	**17**
CRITICAL HIT	**30**
CRITICAL HIT MP	0
ELEMENTAL POWER	0

SKIPPER HAT
Mystery Gate

MAXIMUM HEALTH	?
SPEED	?
ARMOR	?
CRITICAL HIT	?
CRITICAL HIT MP	?
ELEMENTAL POWER	?

SKYLANDERS BOBBY
CH 12: Time Town

MAXIMUM HEALTH	0
SPEED	0
ARMOR	**20**
CRITICAL HIT	0
CRITICAL HIT MP	0
ELEMENTAL POWER	**7**

SLEUTH HAT
CH 2: Know-It-All Island

MAXIMUM HEALTH	0
SPEED	0
ARMOR	0
CRITICAL HIT	**7**
CRITICAL HIT MP	0
ELEMENTAL POWER	0

STEAMPUNK HAT
CH 6: Rainfish Riviera

MAXIMUM HEALTH	0
SPEED	0
ARMOR	**17**
CRITICAL HIT	0
CRITICAL HIT MP	0
ELEMENTAL POWER	0

SUNDAY HAT
CH 14: Operation: Troll Rocket Steal

MAXIMUM HEALTH	0
SPEED	0
ARMOR	0
CRITICAL HIT	**10**
CRITICAL HIT MP	0
ELEMENTAL POWER	**10**

SYNCHRONIZED SWIMMING CAP
CH 8: Telescope Towers

MAXIMUM HEALTH	0
SPEED	0
ARMOR	**10**
CRITICAL HIT	**10**
CRITICAL HIT MP	0
ELEMENTAL POWER	0

TIN FOIL HAT
CH 13: The Future of Skylands

MAXIMUM HEALTH	0
SPEED	0
ARMOR	**10**
CRITICAL HIT	0
CRITICAL HIT MP	0
ELEMENTAL POWER	**15**

TRASH CAN LID
CH 10: Secret Sewers of Supreme Stink

MAXIMUM HEALTH	0
SPEED	0
ARMOR	10
CRITICAL HIT	0
CRITICAL HIT MP	0
ELEMENTAL POWER	10

TURTLE SHELL HAT
CH 1: Soda Springs

MAXIMUM HEALTH	0
SPEED	0
ARMOR	7
CRITICAL HIT	0
CRITICAL HIT MP	0
ELEMENTAL POWER	0

VOLCANO HAT
CH 9: Mystic Mill

MAXIMUM HEALTH	0
SPEED	0
ARMOR	0
CRITICAL HIT	15
CRITICAL HIT MP	0
ELEMENTAL POWER	0

WEATHER VANE HAT
Mystery Gate

MAXIMUM HEALTH	?
SPEED	?
ARMOR	?
CRITICAL HIT	?
CRITICAL HIT MP	?
ELEMENTAL POWER	?

WILLIAM TELL HAT
CH 15: Skyhighlands

MAXIMUM HEALTH	0
SPEED	0
ARMOR	0
CRITICAL HIT	25
CRITICAL HIT MP	0
ELEMENTAL POWER	0

Other Hats

CANDLE HAT
Arena: Drain of Sorrows

MAXIMUM HEALTH	0
SPEED	0
ARMOR	0
CRITICAL HIT	0
CRITICAL HIT MP	0
ELEMENTAL POWER	25

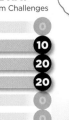

CANDY CANE HAT
Beat all Kaos Doom Challenges

MAXIMUM HEALTH	0
SPEED	10
ARMOR	20
CRITICAL HIT	20
CRITICAL HIT MP	0
ELEMENTAL POWER	0

EGGSHELL HAT
Arena: Phoenix Nest

MAXIMUM HEALTH	0
SPEED	0
ARMOR	25
CRITICAL HIT	0
CRITICAL HIT MP	0
ELEMENTAL POWER	0

FROSTFEST HAT
Portal Master Rank: 40

MAXIMUM HEALTH	0
SPEED	20
ARMOR	0
CRITICAL HIT	0
CRITICAL HIT MP	0
ELEMENTAL POWER	0

MEDIEVAL BARD HAT
Portal Master Rank: 22

MAXIMUM HEALTH	0
SPEED	0
ARMOR	32
CRITICAL HIT	0
CRITICAL HIT MP	0
ELEMENTAL POWER	0

MONGOL HAT
Portal Master Rank: 25

MAXIMUM HEALTH	0
SPEED	0
ARMOR	0
CRITICAL HIT	32
CRITICAL HIT MP	0
ELEMENTAL POWER	0

NIGHT CAP
Arena: Dreamquake

MAXIMUM HEALTH	0
SPEED	0
ARMOR	0
CRITICAL HIT	25
CRITICAL HIT MP	0
ELEMENTAL POWER	0

OLD RUINS HAT
Portal Master Rank: 18

MAXIMUM HEALTH	0
SPEED	8
ARMOR	0
CRITICAL HIT	12
CRITICAL HIT MP	0
ELEMENTAL POWER	0

ORACLE HAT
Portal Master Rank: 34

MAXIMUM HEALTH	0
SPEED	15
ARMOR	0
CRITICAL HIT	0
CRITICAL HIT MP	0
ELEMENTRAL POWER	0

PLANET HAT
Arena: Exhaust Junction

MAXIMUM HEALTH	0
SPEED	10
ARMOR	0
CRITICAL HIT	0
CRITICAL HIT MP	0
ELEMENTAL POWER	0

PYRAMID HAT
Arena: Quicksand Coliseum

MAXIMUM HEALTH	0
SPEED	0
ARMOR	10
CRITICAL HIT	20
CRITICAL HIT MP	0
ELEMENTAL POWER	0

RAVER HAT
Portal Master Rank: 10

MAXIMUM HEALTH	0
SPEED	8
ARMOR	5
CRITICAL HIT	0
CRITICAL HIT MP	0
ELEMENTAL POWER	0

SHEEPWRECKED HAT
Portal Master Rank: 37

Stat	Value
MAXIMUM HEALTH	0
SPEED	0
ARMOR	0
CRITICAL HIT	**37**
CRITICAL HIT MP	0
ELEMENTAL POWER	0

SHIRE HAT
Portal Master Rank: 14

Stat	Value
MAXIMUM HEALTH	0
SPEED	**9**
ARMOR	**5**
CRITICAL HIT	0
CRITICAL HIT MP	0
ELEMENTAL POWER	0

WILIKIN HAT
Portal Master Rank: 30

Stat	Value
MAXIMUM HEALTH	0
SPEED	**8**
ARMOR	0
CRITICAL HIT	**20**
CRITICAL HIT MP	0
ELEMENTAL POWER	0

WIZARD HAT
Arena: Brock's Rumble Clubhouse

Stat	Value
MAXIMUM HEALTH	0
SPEED	**10**
ARMOR	0
CRITICAL HIT	**10**
CRITICAL HIT MP	0
ELEMENTAL POWER	0

WOODEN HAT
Portal Master Rank: 5

Stat	Value
MAXIMUM HEALTH	0
SPEED	0
ARMOR	**5**
CRITICAL HIT	**17**
CRITICAL HIT MP	0
ELEMENTAL POWER	0

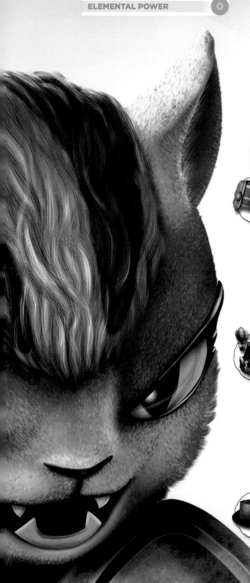

Hats from Auric's Shop at Skylands Academy

COST:
BELLHOP HAT
Complete CH 2

Stat	Value
MAXIMUM HEALTH	0
SPEED	0
ARMOR	0
CRITICAL HIT	0
CRITICAL HIT MP	0
ELEMENTAL POWER	**5**

COST:
CROISSANT HAT
Complete CH 13

Stat	Value
MAXIMUM HEALTH	0
SPEED	0
ARMOR	**15**
CRITICAL HIT	0
CRITICAL HIT MP	0
ELEMENTAL POWER	0

COST:
FLIGHT ATTENDANT HAT
Complete CH 2

Stat	Value
MAXIMUM HEALTH	0
SPEED	0
ARMOR	0
CRITICAL HIT	**5**
CRITICAL HIT MP	0
ELEMENTAL POWER	0

COST:
MINIATURE SKYLANDS HAT
Complete CH 6

Stat	Value
MAXIMUM HEALTH	0
SPEED	**4**
ARMOR	0
CRITICAL HIT	0
CRITICAL HIT MP	0
ELEMENTAL POWER	0

COST:
MOLEKIN HAT
Complete CH 15

Stat	Value
MAXIMUM HEALTH	0
SPEED	0
ARMOR	0
CRITICAL HIT	0
CRITICAL HIT MP	0
ELEMENTAL POWER	**25**

COST:
PALM HAT
Complete CH 6

Stat	Value
MAXIMUM HEALTH	0
SPEED	0
ARMOR	0
CRITICAL HIT	0
CRITICAL HIT MP	0
ELEMENTAL POWER	**10**

COST:
PORK PIE HAT
Complete CH 6

Stat	Value
MAXIMUM HEALTH	0
SPEED	0
ARMOR	0
CRITICAL HIT	**10**
CRITICAL HIT MP	0
ELEMENTAL POWER	0

COST:
RUDE BOY HAT
Complete CH 6

Stat	Value
MAXIMUM HEALTH	0
SPEED	0
ARMOR	**10**
CRITICAL HIT	0
CRITICAL HIT MP	0
ELEMENTAL POWER	0

COST:
SHERPA HAT
Complete CH 13

Stat	Value
MAXIMUM HEALTH	0
SPEED	0
ARMOR	0
CRITICAL HIT	0
CRITICAL HIT MP	0
ELEMENTAL POWER	**15**

	COST: STORM HAT Complete CH 2	
MAXIMUM HEALTH		0
SPEED		**8**
ARMOR		0
CRITICAL HIT		**5**
CRITICAL HIT MP		0
ELEMENTAL POWER		0

	COST: TOUCAN HAT Complete CH 13	
MAXIMUM HEALTH		0
SPEED		**4**
ARMOR		**10**
CRITICAL HIT		0
CRITICAL HIT MP		0
ELEMENTAL POWER		0

	COST: TRIBAL HAT Complete CH 13	
MAXIMUM HEALTH		0
SPEED		0
ARMOR		0
CRITICAL HIT		**15**
CRITICAL HIT MP		0
ELEMENTAL POWER		0

	COST: RAINBOW HAT Complete CH 13	
MAXIMUM HEALTH		0
SPEED		**6**
ARMOR		0
CRITICAL HIT		0
CRITICAL HIT MP		0
ELEMENTAL POWER		0

Trinkets

There are 33 Trinkets to collect. Most are found in the Skylanders Academy, either hidden around the grounds or from Auric's Store in the Main Hall. Other Trinkets come from clearing stages of the Kaos Doom Challenge.

Trinkets From Story Mode

 **BIG BOW OF BOOM**
Skylanders Academy after completing CH 2

 **BILLY BISON**
Skylanders Academy

 **ELEMENTAL DIAMOND**
Skylanders Academy after completing CH 1

 **IRIS' IRIS**
Skylanders Academy after completing CH 2

 **SPYRO'S SHIELD**
Skylanders Academy after completing CH 13

 **STEALTH ELF'S GIFT**
Skylanders Academy in the Grand Library-Mini Only Area

 **WILIKIN WINDMILL**
Skylanders Academy

Other Trinkets

 BATTERSON'S BUBBLE
Portal Master Rank: 4

 CYCLOPS' SPINNER
Portal Master Rank: 38

 DARK WATER DAISY
Portal Master Rank: 20

 ELEMENTAL RADIANT
Portal Master Rank: 33

 KUCKOO KAZOO
Portal Master Rank: 31

 MABU'S MEDALLION
Portal Master Rank: 29

 RAMSES' DRAGON HORN
Portal Master Rank: 16

 RAMSES' RUNE
Portal Master Rank: 12

 SEADOG SEASHELL
Portal Master Rank: 23

 T-BONE'S LUCKY TIE
Portal Master Rank: 26

 TEDDY CYCLOPS
Portal Master Rank: 7

TIME TOWN TICKER
Portal Master Rank: 35

Trinkets from Auric's Shop

 **COST: BLOBBERS' MEDAL OF COURAGE** Complete CH 4

 **COST: BUBBLE BLOWER** Complete CH 2

 COST: ELEMENTAL OPAL Complete CH 9

 **COST: GOO FACTORY GEAR** Complete CH 4

 **COST: LIZARD LILLY** Complete CH 2

 **COST: MEDAL OF GALLANTRY** Complete CH 4

 **COST: MEDAL OF HEROISM** Complete CH 2

 **COST: MEDAL OF METTLE** Complete CH 9

 **COST: MEDAL OF VALIANCE** Complete CH 13

 **COST: PIRATE PINWHEEL** Complete CH 13

 **COST: SNUCKLES' SUNFLOWER** Complete CH 4

 **COST: ULLYSSES UNICLOPS** Complete CH 9

 **COST: VOTE FOR CYCLOPS** Complete CH 2

 **COST: WINGED MEDAL OF BRAVERY** Complete CH 9

Achievements & Trophies

Achievements and Trophies are awarded by the console on which you're playing *Skylanders Trap Team*. Not all consoles award Achievements and Trophies.

ACHIEVEMENT NAME	ACHIEVEMENT DESCRIPTION	XBOX ICON	XBOX POINTS	PS ICON	PS TROPHY
Soda Saver	Complete Chapter 1: Soda Springs		10		Copper
Now YOU Know It All	Complete Chapter 2: Know-It-All Island		10		Copper
Chompy Champ	Complete Chapter 3: Chompy Mountain		10		Copper
Bird Buddy	Complete Chapter 4: The Phoenix Psanctuary		10		Copper
Master of Chefs	Complete Chapter 5: Chef Zeppelin		10		Copper
Squid Seeker	Complete Chapter 6: Rainfish Riviera		10		Copper
Swamp Survivor	Complete Chapter 7: Monster Marsh		10		Copper
Dreamcatcher Catcher	Complete Chapter 8: Telescope Towers		10		Copper
Lumber Liberator	Complete Chapter 9: Mystic Mill		10		Copper
Aroma Avenger	Complete Chapter 10: Secret Sewers of Supreme Stink		10		Copper
Krankcase Kapturer	Complete Chapter 11: Wilikin Workshop		10		Copper
Clock Crusader	Complete Chapter 12: Time Town		10		Copper
Back From the Future	Complete Chapter 13: The Future of Skylands		10		Copper
Rocket Recoverer	Complete Chapter 14: Operation: Troll Rocket Steal		10		Copper
Squadron Star	Complete Chapter 15: Skyhighlands		10		Copper
Desert Dominator	Complete Chapter 16: The Golden Desert		10		Copper
Royal Flusher	Complete Chapter 17: Lair of the Golden Queen		10		Copper
Kaos Komeuppance	Complete Chapter 18: The Utlimate Weapon		10		Copper
Statue Smasher	Destroy 4 stone Chompy heads during Chapter 3: Chompy Mountain		10		Copper

ACHIEVEMENT NAME	ACHIEVEMENT DESCRIPTION	XBOX ICON	XBOX POINTS	PS ICON	PS TROPHY
Preemptive Power	Destroy 1 Dropship in Chapter 4: The Phoenix Psanctuary		10		Copper
Cannon Completest	Destroy 8 Troll Transports during the flying sequence in Chapter 5: Chef Zeppelin		10		Copper
Pipe Down	Destroy 4 stacks of pipes using the crane on Dredger's Yacht during Chapter 6: Rainfish Riviera		10		Copper
No Coins Left Behind	Collect 20 coins while following Marsha through the mist during Chapter 7: Monster Marsh		10		Copper
Ball Sprawler	Knock 12 Golden Balls off the waterfall in the Meditative Pool area in Chapter 8: Telescope Towers		40		Silver
Evilikin Eliminator	Shoot 20 Evilikin Runners during the flying sequence in Chapter 9: Mystic Mill		10		Copper
No Goo For You!	Travel to Splash Station in Chapter 10: Secret Sewers of Supreme Stink without taking any damage from goo		10		Copper
Ride the Rails	Ride the train to the end of the line in Chapter 11: Wilikin Workshop		10		Copper
Da Pinchy Defacer	Destroy 5 Da Pinchy statues in Chapter 12: Time Town		10		Copper
Just to be Safe	Take down every shield unit during the flying sequence in Chapter 13: The Future of Skylands		10		Copper
Exhaust All Possibilities	Complete the arena battle without getting hit by rocket exhaust in Operation: Troll Rocket Steal		10		Copper
Look Ma, No Rockets!	Shoot down 30 Air Pirates without using rockets in Chapter 15: Skyhighlands		40		Silver
Garden Gladiator	Destroy 10 cacti during Chapter 16: The Golden Desert		10		Copper
Highwire Act	Complete all the tile floor puzzles without falling during Chapter 17: Lair of the Golden Queen		10		Copper
Do a Barrel Roll	Collect 9 coins while falling down the Machine Heart in Chapter 18: The Utlimate Weapon		10		Copper
Savior of Skylands IV	Complete Story Mode on any difficulty setting		150		Gold
Dream a Little Nightmare	Complete Story Mode on the Nightmare difficulty setting		150		Gold
Kaos Mode Master	Defeat 100 enemies in Kaos Mode		20		Copper
Star Star	Earn 50 Stars in Kaos Mode		75		Silver
Arena Mogul	Unlock Brock's special arena		10		Copper
Chairman of the Rumble Club	Complete all Arena levels		75		Gold
Not Out of Your Element	Unlock your first Elemental area		10		Copper
Hero Hunter	Capture 10 Villains		30		Copper
Skystones Scavenger	Collect 20 Skystones		20		Copper
All the Way Up!	Level up any Skylander to level 20		30		Silver
Wow, That's Tough!	Achieve Portal Master Rank 5		20		Copper
Road to Redemption	Complete a captured Villain's quest		10		Copper
IMPOSSIBLE!!!	Earn all other Trophies (PS3 Only)	—	—		Platinum

Signature Series Strategy Guide

Written by Howard Grossman and Ken Schmidt

DK/BradyGames, a division of Penguin Group (USA).
800 East 96th Street, 3rd Floor
Indianapolis, IN 46240

ISBN: 978-0-7440-1558-4

Printing Code: The rightmost double-digit number is the year of the book's printing; the rightmost single-digit number is the number of the book's printing. For example, 13-1 shows that the first printing of the book occurred in 2013.

17 16 15 14   4 3 2 1

Printed in the USA.

BradyGAMES Staff

Vice President and Publisher
Mike Degler

Licensing Manager
Christian Sumner

Digital Publishing Manager
Tim Cox

Marketing Manager
Katie Hemlock

Operations Manager
Stacey Beheler

Credits

Development Editor
Jennifer Sims

Book Designer
Tim Amrhein

Production Designer
Areva
Julie Clark

SKYLANDERS TRAP TEAM

BRADYGAMES OFFICIAL STRATEGY GUIDE

FREE Searchable & Sortable eGuide

Go to www.primagames.com/code
and enter this unique code:

4kh4-qzz8-rsb9-a5rc

Meet the Trap Masters

Kaos has blown up the walls of the feared Cloudcracker Prison, freeing the most notorious villains in Skylands. Learn everything you need to know about the all new Trap Masters!

Become the Ultimate Portal Master

- ✳ Save the Skylands with our Complete Story Walkthrough
- ✳ Find every Hat, Legendary Treasure, Villain Stash, and more
- ✳ Study the Abilities, Upgrades, and Strategy for every Skylander and Villain
- ✳ Earn awesome rewards in Kaos Doom Challenge and Arena Mode

That's Not All!

- ✳ Skystones Smash
- ✳ Hats and Trinkets
- ✳ Achievements and Trophies
- ✳ And Much More!

BRADYGAMES

ACTIVISION

www.bradygames.com   www.activision.com